SAME–SEX MARRIAGE

Putting Every Household at Risk

MATHEW D. STAVER

BROADMAN
& HOLMAN
PUBLISHERS

NASHVILLE, TENNESSEE

0-8054-3196-9

Published by Broadman & Holman Publishers
Nashville, Tennessee

Dewey Decimal Classification: 306.84
Subject Heading: MARRIAGE \ HOMOSEXUALITY \
SAME-SEX MARRIAGE

Unless otherwise noted, Scripture quotations are from the Holy Bible,
New International Version, copyright © 1973, 1978, 1984 by
International Bible Society.

1 2 3 4 5 6 7 8   09 08 07 06 05 04

Table of Contents

Acknowledgments

*A*s in the case with any book, many people are responsible for the finished product. This book is no exception. I am blessed to work with wonderful people at Liberty Counsel. They are not only my colaborers who have a passion for this ministry; they are also my dear friends.

I received great feedback and insight on the various drafts of the book from Walter and Nancy Kerr, Rena Lindevaldsen, and Erik Stanley. Annette Stanley's expertise in word processing and her skill in proper citation format for this kind of publication have been invaluable. Candy McGuire has faithfully read and reread the chapters of this book and has made many excellent recommendations to improve clarity of the text.

I also wish to thank the great staff at Broadman & Holman Publishers and LifeWay Christian Resources. They are a great team.

Finally, I wish to thank my wife, Anita. As an attorney herself who works by my side every day, she has provided incredible support and inspiration to this project, in particular, and to the mission of Liberty Counsel. She is a wonderful wife, a respected colleague, and my very best friend.

Introduction

I have written on many topics, but more than most topics, the subject of same-sex marriage has caused me to extend my vision into the future to consider its ramifications. I have come to appreciate more than ever something we take for granted—that marriage is between a man and a woman, and children need a mother and father.

My prayer is that this book moves you to compassion and concern. I hope it helps you to understand better the homosexual psyche and causes you to have genuine concern for gays and lesbians. I want to impress upon you the time of history in which we live. Most of all, I pray that this book inspires you to action and motivates you to become engaged in the most important cultural battle of our lifetime— to advance and defend marriage between one man and one woman.

When I founded Liberty Counsel in 1989, the organization focused its education and public interest litigation ministry in two primary areas: religious liberty and the sanctity of human life. It wasn't until the mid-1990s that Liberty Counsel added a third main category to its mission: namely, the traditional family, which includes marriage between one man and one woman. Since then Liberty Counsel has been actively engaged in advancing and defending the traditional family on many fronts.

I never imagined I would spend so much time dealing with a subject that seems so basic and simple. When gathered with friends and colleagues to discuss same-sex marriage and homosexuality, we are sometimes struck with the thought that the topic of human sexuality is elementary, a discussion in which even children can understand the obvious distinctions between male and female. Yet, despite the obvious, there are those who argue that the notion of male and female is outdated, stereotypic, and should be abandoned. The implications of this reasoning are unsettling and destructive.

Same-sex marriage is nothing less than the abandonment of gender distinctions. You can't have same-sex marriage and continue to believe that gender is relevant.

The union of a man and a woman in what we call marriage has been accepted as foundational in every lasting society.

The purpose of marriage between one man and one woman is self-evident. Traditional marriage is pure common sense. To say that marriage should include people of the same gender denies the obvious. Same-sex marriage is the ultimate rejection of objective reality. The acceptance of same-sex marriage would create an environment in which generally accepted normative rules are cast off and where only the most radical factions of society have their way for a moment—that is, until their actions cause their house of cards to implode for lack of substance and meaning.

Homosexuality is rooted in fractured emotions. Although the causes of homosexuality vary, a common thread in virtually every case is some sort of sexual or emotional brokenness. Homosexuality often sprouts out of deep hurt, and the activity leads to further suffering and pain. Like dominos, one causing another to fall, hurting people hurt people.

Yes, the subject of same-sex marriage can be addressed using common sense and objective reality. The same-sex marriage agenda is profound not only for its cultural implications but also because of the fundamental issues it raises regarding human development and the importance of the traditional family, in which children experience love and are properly taught about the wonder of what God created, namely, male and female.

Today we have a choice to make, and this choice is the most important cultural decision we will ever make in our lifetime. One choice is to remain unconcerned. Keep silent. Do your own thing and ignore the fact that you are living on the fault line of a tectonic plate about to explode that is grinding and rumbling under pressure. You may fool yourself for a moment. You may even be content for a while, but the earthquake will happen. It's just a matter of time.

However, there is another choice, the goal of which is achievable. Whether we like it or not, we are living on a cultural fault line. Yet there is hope for this culture. It is not too late to stop the earthquake. I believe that the same-sex marriage movement moved too fast, the agenda was too aggressive, and the timing premature. Until recently, the majority of people who believe in marriage between one man and one woman have remained silent in this cultural war. But the sleeping giant is beginning to awake. It is time for that giant (you and me and those who believe in traditional marriage) to draw a line in the sand. This battle can be won. It is worth your time to understand the issues and to become involved in the most important issue of our time.

CHAPTER 1
Why Defend Marriage between a Man and a Woman?

*T*he scene was surreal. The thoughts and emotions that raced through my mind are virtually indescribable. Before the hearing in San Francisco, I stood peering out of a large glass window of the courthouse, which is situated on a corner of a major intersection. Diagonal to the courthouse is a park. Viewing the scene from left to right, the first sight you see is young children playing on swings and slides. The scene is peaceful and innocent.

Panning your vision to the right, you see trees scattered throughout a large open public park. As you continue to scan to the right, your vision comes to the paved intersection parallel to the park where large media trucks aimed their satellite dishes at the heavens. Continuing to move your gaze, you cross the street to city hall. Outside on the sidewalk, running from the entrance and snaking around the huge building, were same-sex couples waiting in line to enter the domed structure to obtain a same-sex "marriage license." Other people were holding protest signs, some for and some against same-sex marriage.

All the while I was posed above the scene looking down from the security of the courthouse, about to enter the courtroom to argue that the city of San Francisco and its mayor, Gavin Newsom, ought to be stopped from breaking the law. Looking down the hallway of the courthouse where I stood, media from all over the world packed the corridor. There was no room to pass. Cameras and microphones pointed at me as I made my way through the crowd and into the courtroom, where I argued a simple point of law: the mayor must obey the statewide law that says marriage is between one man and one woman.

The city attorney had participated in some of the ceremonies at city hall. The city argued the mayor is not bound by clear state law that limits marriage to one man and one woman. The city conspired with the most radical elements of the same-sex marriage movement. The state attorney general was apparently aware that these licenses were going to be issued before the first ceremony was conducted, which explained why he remained silent for so long while the mayor literally deputized hundreds of members from homosexual organizations to assist the city in breaking the law.

Back in court I pleaded with the judge to put an end to the madness by issuing an emergency order stopping the mayor and the city from issuing these same-sex "marriage licenses." Following the court hearing, I walked down the hallway to the press conference room. At the podium were scores of microphones. The entire room was filled with cameras and journalists representing every major newspaper in America, along with news sources from Asia and Europe. One reporter asked if the mayor's actions were a setback to those who believe in traditional marriage. "Absolutely not," I said. "The rebellious actions of the mayor have unmasked the radical agenda of the same-sex marriage movement set on dominating the culture. These actions will serve to wake up the sleeping giant of the majority of Americans who believe in marriage between one man and one woman and heretofore have remained silent, but who now will become involved in this cultural war to preserve marriage between one man and one woman."

After the hearing I stayed with our client, Randy Thomasson, who is the founder of Campaign for California Families, while our Senior Litigation Counsel, Rena Lindevaldsen, was escorted by one of our security contingent across the street to city hall where she had to work on the wording of a proposed order. En route, Rena was recognized by a proponent of same-sex marriage who shouted death threats and damned her to hell. As she came out of city hall, two men were exchanging vows at the entrance near the sidewalk. A mother was walking by, holding the hand of her small child. Stopping to observe the event, the mother exclaimed, "How sweet." What kind of message did she just teach her young boy?

Rena and I were escorted by three large security guards to a heavily tinted Suburban and whisked off to the airport. There we discussed litigation strategy while we waited to board our plane. A male America West attendant announced the boarding process of another flight, and over the intercom system for all to hear, he pointed out a woman standing in line to board while he made sexually provocative observations about the woman's breasts. Rena and I thought we must have misunderstood what he said, but then he asked for her seat assignment and stated that he wanted to follow her on board so that he could perform a lap dance on her. We really did hear him right the first time. This is San Francisco, the scene of this cultural war.

Shortly after Rena approached the attendant and told him that his comments were offensive (for which he did not apologize), we boarded the red-eye flight back to Orlando. This was the second trip to San Francisco with a return red-eye flight in one week. On the plane Rena and I exchanged thoughts and drew out strategy on our legal pad. We thought through every angle like we were studying for a final exam. After several hours of plotting legal strategy, we sat back in our seats in an attempt to rest for a couple of hours. Soon it was morning, and we landed at 8:30 in Orlando.

It was good to be home, but there are many more battles to fight. The court eventually stopped Mayor Newsom and the city from breaking the law. Reflecting on the scene, I can't get my mind off those children in the park. They were laughing, running, and having a good time—pure innocence in motion, playing on the edge of a fault line, unaware of what was taking place just a few hundred feet away. We must draw a line in the sand to protect the children.

The debate over same-sex marriage is a debate over marriage itself. Some people view marriage from personal experience, and for some that experience may have been painful. With respect to divorce, your perspective on marriage may vary from the vantage point of being a child of divorce, a divorcee, or one who has happily remarried. However, many have a positive experience of marriage and family. Some feminists believe marriage is the symbol of a patriarchal, male-dominated society. Same-sex advocates sometimes describe marriage as a weakened, stereotypic institution that divides society by sex, but they still desire some form of "marriage" that recognizes their same-gender unions.

Depending on your perspective, several questions frequently arise over the same-sex marriage debate. The most common questions are: "What is marriage for, and why shouldn't two people who love each other be allowed to marry?" "How will same-sex marriage hurt my marriage, and how will it hurt the institution of marriage?" "Will same-sex marriage have any adverse impact on children or the lives of individuals?" "Is equal protection violated by prohibiting same-sex marriage?" "With all the discussion of amending the United States Constitution to preserve marriage between one man and one woman, shouldn't marriage be left to the individual states?" "Why should the state be involved in marriage at all?" "Wouldn't it be best for the state to get out of the marriage business and to leave the matter to churches or private secular ceremonies?"

All of these questions are legitimate, and all go to the heart of marriage itself. We now turn to address some of these questions in this chapter and the rest of this book.

What Is Marriage For?

The same-sex marriage movement has crystallized the difference between two distinct views of marriage. The recent view, advocated by same-sex proponents, can be summed up as follows: "Marriage is an essentially private, intimate, emotional relationship created by two people for their own personal reasons to enhance their own personal well-being. Marriage is created by the couple, for the couple."[1] Under this view the human arrangement is merely a private, and, perhaps in some cases a sexually intimate, relationship that deserves a license by the government in order to obtain certain legally recognized benefits. This view of marriage believes that it is discriminatory to favor one kind of personal relationship (between a man and a woman) over other kinds of relationships (between people of the same sex). Marriage expert and author Maggie Gallagher notes, "This view of marriage as primarily an emotional good created by the private couple leads to calls (and in countries outside the United States to judicial rulings and legislation) to abolish any distinction between cohabitation and marriage, between what some call formal and informal unions."[2] Those who advocate this private view believe marriage is "just one lifestyle choice among many."[3]

The historic view of marriage does not consider the institution to be merely a private relationship but rather a public good. Gallagher describes this view of marriage as follows:

> What every known human society calls marriage shares certain basic, recognizable features, including most especially the privileges accorded to the reproductive couple in order to protect both the interests of children and the interests of the society.
>
> Marriage is everywhere the word we use to describe a publicly acknowledged and supported sexual union between a man and woman which creates rights and obligations between the couple and any children the union may produce. Marriage as a public tie obligates not only the fathers, but the fathers' kin to recognize the children of this union. In every society, marriage is the sexual union where childbearing and raising is not only tolerated but applauded and encouraged. Marriage is the way in which every society attempts to channel the erotic energies of men and women into a relatively narrow but highly fruitful channel—to give every child the father his or her heart desires. Above all—normal marriage is normative. Marriage is not primarily a way of expressing approval for [an] infinite variety of human affectional or sexual ties; it consists, by definition, of isolating and preferring certain types of unions over others. By socially defining and supporting a particular type of sexual union, the

society defines for its young what the preferred relationship is and what purposes it serves.[4]

Understanding marriage as a public good is fundamentally different from viewing it as merely a private relationship. As Gallagher further explains:

> Marriage is the fundamental, cross-cultural institution for bridging the male and female divide so that children have loving, committed mothers and fathers. Marriage is inherently normative: it is about holding out a certain kind of relationship as a social ideal, especially when there are children involved. Marriage is not simply an artifact of law; neither is it a mere delivery mechanism for a set of legal benefits that might as well be shared more broadly. Laws of marriage do not create marriage, but in societies ruled by law, they help trace the boundaries and sustain the public meanings of marriage.
>
> In other words, while individuals freely choose to enter marriage, society upholds the marriage option, formalizes its definition, and surrounds it with norms and reinforcements, so we can raise boys and girls who aspire to become the kind of men and women who can make successful marriages. Without this shared, public aspect, perpetuated generation after generation, marriage becomes what its critics say it is: a mere contract, a vessel with no particular content, one of a menu of sexual lifestyles, of no fundamental importance to anyone outside a given relationship.
>
> The marriage idea is that children need mothers and fathers, that societies need babies, and that adults have an obligation to shape their sexual behavior so as to give their children stable families in which to grow up.[5]

In a culture where almost one out of every two marriages ends in divorce and where adoption and artificial insemination are alternatives to traditional male-female procreation, one may ask whether the essence of marriage has already been undermined. After all, some argue that the birth control pill separated sex from procreation, and thus procreation from marriage. While it is true there are many strains placed on marriage and some exceptions to procreation, the fact remains that artificial insemination is rare, and adoption is available in virtually every case only because traditional procreation between a man and a woman produced a child. The fact is, some who follow marriage trends see signs of a "new marriage movement" in America.[6] Divorce rates have begun to decline, and the rate of illegitimacy has appeared to level off after doubling every decade from 1960 to 1990. Teen pregnancy and sexual activity are down, the number of stay-at-home moms is increasing, and a "new generation of children of divorce appears on the brink of making a commitment to lifelong marriage. In 1977, 55 percent of American teenagers thought a divorce should be harder to get; in 2001 75 percent did."[7]

The problem with endorsing gay marriage is not that it would allow a handful of people to choose alternative family norms, but that it would require society at large to gut marriage of its central presumptions about family in order to accommodate a few adults' desires.

The debate over same-sex marriage, then, is not some sideline discussion. It *is* the marriage debate. Either we win—or we lose the central meaning of marriage. The great threat unisex marriage poses to marriage as a social institution is not some distant or nearby slippery slope, it is an abyss at our feet. If we cannot explain why unisex marriage is, in itself, a disaster, we have already lost the marriage ideal.

Same-sex marriage would enshrine in law a public judgment that the public desire of adults for families of choice outweighs the need of children for mothers and fathers. It would give sanction and approval to the creation of a motherless or fatherless family as a deliberately chosen "good." It would mean the law was neutral as to whether children had mothers and fathers. Motherless and fatherless families would be deemed just fine.[8]

Marriage passes the torch from one generation to the next. While we do not impose fertility tests on those desiring to be married, "every marriage between a man and a woman is capable of giving any child they create or adopt a mother and a father. Every marriage between a man and a woman discourages either from creating fatherless children outside the marriage vow."[9] "Successful societies support and prefer marriage not only because children need mothers and fathers, but also because societies need babies. It is a truism frequently forgotten by large complex societies: only societies that reproduce survive."[10]

While America has not experienced depopulation due to its high immigration rate, "every western, industrialized nation has had sub-replacement birth rates."[11] For example, by the year 2050, "Italy's population is projected to decline by more than a quarter. The political, economic, and cultural implications of European depopulation are likely to be profound."[12] In 2003, the United Nations released *The World Population Prospects: The 2002 Revision*,[13] which stated: "For the first time, the United Nations Population Division projects that future fertility levels in the majority of developing countries will likely fall below 2.1 children per woman, the level needed to ensure the long-term replacement of the population, at some point in the twenty-first century. By 2050, the medium variant of the *2002 Revision* projects that 3 out of every 4 countries in the less developed regions will be experiencing below replacement fertility."[14]

Marriage is serious business. It is not merely a private, personal relationship isolated from its impact on society. Since children are involved in the average marriage, whether by traditional male-female procreation, adoption, or artificial insemination, the government has the right, indeed the duty, to regulate marriage in order to prefer the highest aspired ideal—a relationship between a man and a woman where children are welcomed and nourished.

Will Same-Sex Marriage Hurt Children?

When considering the impact same-sex marriage would have on children, three different points of reference must be examined. These include studies of children raised by same-sex couples, studies of children raised by a single parent, and the mental and physical health risks associated with same-sex activity. Chapter 3 will address this subject in more detail.

The pro-homosexual book entitled *Different Mothers: Sons and Daughters of Lesbians Talk about Their Lives* reveals some interesting insight into children raised in homosexual households. The editor, Louise Rafkin, notes, "Their lives, both their emotional lives and public lives, are affected by our lifestyles."[15] A few of the descriptions are worth noting. The first story comes from a twenty-five-year-old named Kyneret Hope: "I experienced [lesbian] separatism as a constant level of anger and negativity. . . . That was part of the lifestyle I knew, there was always a downside: men were called mutants, straight women were considered disowned sisters who wasted women-energy on men, and other lesbians were sometimes accused of being government spies sent to infiltrate and undermine the community. Anyone who was not like us was evil, and I had to be careful not to cross over to the enemy's camp."[16]

Michael, a twenty-seven-year-old male, described his experience:

Lesbians should not fill their children with their own fears and hatreds. I say this after considering the causes of needless pain in my past, and my troubles understanding the present. . . . I do recall wishing our mothers were more attentive to us than each other. We kids would get together and have sex, males or females, in any combinations—unbeknownst to our parents, but ironically, I don't think any of us knew what our mothers' lesbianism really meant. . . . Until I was sixteen or so, I was sexually abused by many straight men, "friends" of my mothers', whom I was occasionally left with. I wondered what was going on in this planet? The end result of all this abuse is that today I don't trust people. . . . Lesbians who hate or fear men take this out on boy children. I suspect the same thing might happen with gay fathers and girl children.[17]

Twenty-year-old Kathlean Hill reported her experience: "I just remember thinking that all lesbians felt the same way my mother felt about everything. If that were true, then all lesbians would talk about men as crude, destructive, dishonest, sleazy creatures that were really not supposed to exist. They were a mistake. . . . Terre called my sister and me 'baby dykes,' making us wear the small hand-crafted lesbian signs she had made for us by a local lesbian jeweler. Both my sister, Maureen, and I have always been extremely resentful of that. It always seems so unfair to label a child's sexuality so young."[18]

Twenty-one-year-old Carey Conley describes her frustration, stating, "I was angry that I was not part of a 'normal' family and could not live with a 'normal' mother. I wondered what I did to deserve this. Why did my biological mother let a lesbian mother adopt me?"[19] Finally, twenty-three-year-old Adam Levy speaks of his sexual promiscuity, declaring that he has "no rules about sexual behavior" because "when his mom broke the big rule—the one that says only men and women get married—I began to question other rules which had designs on my life."[20]

Children need mothers and fathers. Children who are raised outside of intact marriages where there is a mother and a father "are at greater risk for a large number of serious personal and social problems, even after controlling for race, income, and family background."[21] Numerous studies show that children do not fare well when they lack fathers, or have the so-called absent father syndrome.[22] Moreover, children do not do well when they lack mothers.[23]

Will Same-Sex Marriage Hurt People?

Homosexuality is a destructive lifestyle both physically and emotionally. Same-sex marriage cannot be viewed in isolation from homosexual activity and its consequences on those who engage in such practices, and especially on children raised in such an environment.[24]

Paula Ettelbrick, the former legal director of the Lambda Legal Defense and Education Fund (a pro-homosexual public interest law firm), commented, "Being queer is more than setting up house, sleeping with a person of the same gender, and seeking state approval for doing so. . . . Being queer means pushing the parameters of sex, sexuality, and family, and in the process transforming the very fabric of society."[25] Homosexual activist and writer Michelangelo Signorile states that homosexuals have a different notion of monogamy than do heterosexuals. "For these men the term 'monogamy' simply doesn't necessarily mean sexual exclusivity. . . . The term 'open relationship' has for a great many gay men come to have one specific definition: a relationship in which the partners have sex on the outside often, put away the resentment and jealousy, and discuss their outside sex with each other, or share sex partners."[26] Signorile also reveals why he wants same-sex marriage in these words: "A middle ground might be to fight for same-sex marriage and its benefits and then, once granted, redefine the institution of marriage completely, to demand the right to marry not as a way of adhering to society's moral codes but rather to debunk a myth and radically alter an archaic institution."[27] The homosexual activist further declares his intention: "It is also a chance to wholly transform the definition of family in American culture. It is the final tool with which to dismantle all sodomy statutes, get education about homosexuality and AIDS into public schools, and, in short, usher in a sea of change in how society views and treats us."[28] Tom Stoddard, another same-sex proponent, notes that "enlarging the concept [of marriage] to embrace same-sex couples would necessarily transform it into something new. . . . Extending the right to marry to gay people—that is, abolishing the traditional gender requirements of marriage—can be one of the means, perhaps the principal one, through which the institution divests itself of the sexist trappings of the past."[29]

One study of male homosexuality found that few homosexual relationships last longer than two years, with many men reporting hundreds of lifetime partners.[30] In a study of male homosexuality in *Western Sexuality: Practice and Precept in Past and Present Times*, the author found that most male homosexual relationships last no more than two years.[31] Other studies have confirmed these findings that male homosexual relationships last only between two and three years.[32] Even a biased, pro-homosexual propaganda national survey, conducted in part by the Partner Task Force for Gay and Lesbian Couples and its cocreator, who refers to himself only by the name of "Demian," found that female unions last only 4.9 years, and that 9 percent of female unions had nonmonogamy agreements.[33]

A study of 156 males in homosexual relationships found them to last between one and thirty-seven years, but these relationships were sexually promiscuous. "Only seven couples have a totally exclusive sexual relationship, and these men all have been together for less than five years. Stated another way, all couples with a relationship lasting more than five years have incorporated some provision for out-side sexual activity in their relationships."[34] "[O]utside sexual activity was the rule for male couples and the exception for heterosexuals."[35]

Numerous studies reveal the high rate of sexual promiscuity, particularly among males. A comprehensive study published by A. P. Bell and M. S. Weinberg showed that 43 percent of white male homosexuals had sex with five hundred or more part-ners, and 28 percent had one thousand or more sex partners.[36] Other studies report similar findings.[37] In contrast, between 75 and 81 percent of husbands and between 77 and 85 percent of wives have remained faithful to their marital vows.[38]

"Same-gender sexual orientation is significantly associated with each of the suicidality measures," according to one study.[39] Additionally, "gay, lesbian, and bisexual young people are at increased risk of mental health problems, with these associations being particularly evident for measures of suicidal behavior and multi-ple disorder[s]."[40] A New Zealand study singled out major depression, anxiety disorder, conduct disorder, nicotine dependence, and other substance abuse as areas in which young people who identified themselves as homosexual were at greater risk.[41] Another commentary on the research noted that "homosexual people are at a substantially higher risk for some forms of emotional problems, including suicidality, major depression, and anxiety disorder."[42] Lest you think that the increased health problems are related to the social stigma of homosexuality, a study in the Netherlands, where same-sex marriage is legal, reported the following: "Psychiatric disorders were more prevalent among homosexually active people compared with heterosexually active people," and further noted that "people with same-sex sexual behavior are at greater risk for psychiatric disorders."[43]

On average, mental illness is more prevalent in same-sex households than in heterosexual households. A national survey of lesbians, published in the *Journal of Consulting and Clinical Psychology*, found that 75 percent of the nearly two thousand respondents have pursued psychological counseling of some kind, and many have obtained long-term treatment for depression.[44]

Domestic violence is also statistically higher in same-sex as compared to heterosexual households. One study found that 31 percent of lesbians surveyed reported having experienced one or more incidents of physical abuse in their relationships,[45] and another study found that slightly more than one-half of the lesbians reported having been abused by their female partner.[46] In the book *Men Who Beat the Men Who Love Them: Battered Gay Men and Domestic Violence,* research found that the incidence of domestic violence among gay men was nearly double that of the heterosexual population.[47] One victimization study of 2,881 homosexuals "demonstrates that intimate partner abuse among urban MSM [men who have sex with men] is a very serious public health problem."[48] In contrast, married women in traditional families experience the lowest rate of violence compared with women in other types of relationships.[49]

The *Archives of General Psychiatry* published a study of twins that showed homosexuals with same-sex partners were at greater risk for overall mental health problems and 6.5 times more likely than their heterosexual twins to have attempted suicide.[50] Homosexuals are three times more likely than heterosexuals to suffer from mood disorders, five times more likely to suffer from bipolar disorders (manic depression), and twice as likely to suffer from major depression, neuroses, eating disorders, and phobias.[51] Again, these mental health problems cannot be blamed upon social stigma, as a report published in the *Harvard Mental Health Letter* noted that in the Netherlands, a country especially open to homosexuality, homosexuals still exhibited a much higher incidence of mental health problems.[52]

Same-sex activity also increases disease and decreases life expectancy. Statistics from the Centers for Disease Control show that homosexuals continue to be the highest at-risk group for HIV/AIDS.[53] A study published in the *International Journal of Epidemiology* found that the life expectancy for Canadian gay and bisexual men has been reduced to the life expectancy experienced by all men in the year 1871.[54] In addition to a significant increase in AIDS infection, male homosexuals have a 37-fold increase in anal cancer, a 4-fold increase in Hodgkins Disease, a 2.7-fold increase in cancer of the testicles, and a 2.5-fold increase in lip cancer.[55] Other increased risks include sexually transmitted diseases such as the human papilloma virus; cervical cancer in women; Hepatitis A, B, and C; gonorrhea; syphilis; gay bowel syndrome; Kaposi's sarcoma; and anal cancer.[56]

If society were to sanction same-sex marriage, a higher percentage of children and adults would be adversely affected emotionally and physically. Hurting people hurt people. No wonder marriage between one man and one woman is a public good rather than merely an individual private relationship.

How Will Same-Sex Marriage Hurt the Institution of Marriage?

Stanley Kurtz, who holds a Ph.D. from Harvard University in anthropology, and who is a research fellow at Stanford University's Hoover Institution, has written an insightful article regarding the impact of same-sex marriage in the Netherlands and the Scandinavian countries (Norway, Denmark, and Sweden).[57] In 1998 the Netherlands adopted a system of marriage-like registered partnerships open to both same-sex and opposite-sex couples, and then in 2001, the Netherlands legalized same-sex marriage. About a decade before the adoption of registered partnerships in the 1990s, the Netherlands began to legally equalize marriage and cohabitation. Kurtz notes that since the Dutch parliamentary proposals for gay marriage and/or registered partnerships were introduced and debated in 1996, and continuing through and beyond the legalization of same-sex marriage in 2001, "the out-of-wedlock birth rate in the Netherlands has been increasing at double its previous speed."[58] Kurtz notes that in 1996, a campaign for same-sex marriage went into high gear, and about that time the unusually low Dutch out-of-wedlock birthrate began to rise at a rate of about 2 percent per year, in contrast to its earlier average increase of 1 percent per year. However, the number of heterosexual couples entering into registered partnerships in the 1990s is simply too small to account for the increased out-of-wedlock birthrate. Since 2001, when same-sex marriage was legalized, the illegitimate birthrate has continued to increase at the rate of 2 percent per year. Kurtz notes that same-sex marriage "increased the cultural separation of marriage from parenthood," and now the out-of-wedlock birthrate has climbed to 29 percent.[59]

In Scandinavia the picture is even worse. "Marriage is slowly dying in Scandinavia. A majority of children in Sweden and Norway are born out of wedlock. Sixty percent of first-born children in Denmark have unmarried parents."[60] Although the Scandinavian countries of Norway, Denmark, and Sweden do not have full-blown same-sex marriage, they do have registered partnerships, which are the equivalent of a Vermont-style civil union for same-sex couples. These laws were passed in the late 1980s and the early 1990s, while Scandinavian marriage was already in decline. At the time many Scandinavians were having children out of wedlock, although it was still typical for parents to marry sometime before the birth of the second child. Kurtz points out that marital decline in Scandinavia is the product of a confluence of several factors, including contraception, abortion, women in the workplace, cultural individualism, secularism, and the welfare state. Significantly, "Scandinavian law tends to treat marriage and cohabitation alike."[61] Between 1990 and 2000, Norway's out-of-wedlock birthrate rose from 39 to 50 percent, while Sweden's rose from 47 to 55 percent.[62] Kurtz made the following observation:

> [The research] suggests that gay marriage is both an effect and a cause of the increasing separation between marriage and parenthood. As rising out-of-wedlock birth rates disassociate heterosexual marriage from parenting, gay marriage becomes conceivable. If marriage is only about a relationship between two people, and is not intrinsically connected to parenthood, why shouldn't same-sex couples be allowed to marry? It follows that once marriage is redefined to accommodate same-sex couples, that change cannot help but lock in and reinforce the very cultural separation between marriage and parenthood that makes gay marriage conceivable to begin with.[63]

Kurtz reiterates that "gay marriage is both an effect and a reinforcing cause of the separation of marriage and parenthood."[64] Gay marriage split the Norwegian Lutheran Church, and some liberal clerics who called for same-sex marriage gained visibility. While the church was weakened by the split, the secular social scientists, who argue that marriage and cohabitation should be treated equally, gained prominence. Kurtz describes the impact of the gay marriage debate: "Norway's gay marriage debate, which ran most intensely from 1991 through 1993, was a culture-shifting event. And once enacted, gay marriage had a decidedly unconservative impact on Norway's cultural contests, weakening marriage's defenders, and placing a weapon in the hands of those who sought to replace marriage with cohabitation. . . . Particularly in Norway—once relatively conservative—gay marriage has undermined marriage's institutional standing for everyone."[65]

Interestingly, despite the push for gay marriage, the number of gay marriage-like partnerships remains small. By the year 2000, only 2,372 couples had registered after nine years of the Danish law, 674 after four years of the Norwegian law, and 749 after four years of the Swedish law.[66] This has led some to observe that the goal of same-sex marriage in the Scandinavian countries "was not marriage but social approval for homosexuality" and that "the low numbers of registered gay couples may be understood as a collective protest against the expectations (presumably, monogamy) embodied in marriage."[67]

Kurtz gives this sobering observation of the several stages a country goes through leading up to same-sex marriage and the dissolution of marriage itself:

> In stage one, cohabitation is seen as a deviant or avantgarde practice, and the vast majority of the population produces children within marriage. Italy is in this first stage. In the second stage, cohabitation serves as a testing period before marriage, and is generally a childless phase. Bracketing the problem of underclass single parenthood, America is largely at this second stage. In stage three, cohabitation becomes increasingly acceptable, and parenting is no longer automatically associated with marriage. Norway was at this third stage, but with recent demographic and legal changes has entered stage four. In the fourth stage (Sweden and Denmark), marriage and cohabitation become practically indistinguishable, with many, perhaps even most, children born and raised outside of marriage. . . . These stages may vary in duration, yet once a country has reached a stage, return to an earlier phase is unlikely. . . . Yet once a stage has been reached, earlier phases coexist.[68]

The influential American Law Institute has proposed a series of legal reforms ("Principles of Family Dissolution") designed to equalize marriage and cohabitation. The adoption of these legal reforms would be a giant step toward the Scandinavian system. If same-sex marriage were legalized, marriage and parenthood would be further separated, and the equalization of marriage and cohabitation would be virtually certain.

Kurtz also points out that a disturbing trend is occurring in Scandinavia, namely a tendency of Scandinavians to marry only after giving birth to the second child. Same-sex marriage separates parenthood from marriage because it institutionalizes the idea that cohabitation is equal with marriage. What's happening in Scandinavia suggests that "parents might simply stop getting married altogether, no matter how many children they have."[69] The Scandinavian marriage institution is often the bellwether for family reform throughout the world, first beginning in Europe and then moving across the globe.

Kurtz warns about having a patchwork of marriage in America. He says that we simply can't have same-sex marriage in one state and not another. With American mobility and the media, the "cultural effects would be national."[70] He warns against testing gay marriage in some states, debunking the idea that America can experiment with same-sex marriage. He warns that same-sex marriage would be neither containable nor revocable. "By the time we see the effects of gay marriage in America, it will be too late to do anything about it. Yet we needn't wait that long. In effect, Scandinavia has run our experiment for us. The results are in."[71]

Why Shouldn't Two People Who Love Each Other Be Allowed to Marry?

Some people may ask, "Why not same-sex marriage?" The question misunderstands the importance of marriage. The better question might be, Why same-sex marriage? Two people, or for that matter multiple people, can cohabitate with one another, and among them create individual contractual obligations, execute wills and trusts, and list one another as beneficiaries, and thus receive most of the legal equivalents of marriage.

Marriage between one man and one woman is a public good that is best for society, and particularly its children and future generations. Legalizing same-sex marriage would equalize same-sex relations with marriage and parenthood. In doing so, marriage and parenthood would be severed, and the structure of children raised with a mom and a dad would suffer. It is one thing to tolerate personal relationships that are different from ours, but it is another thing for society to elevate such a relationship to a preferred status, and that's what same-sex marriage would do. The implications would be profound.

To sanction same-sex marriage would be to say that there is no relevance to gender and thus result in the abolition of gender. Indeed, many same-sex and transsexual proponents advocate the abolition of gender, stating that the concept of male and female is an outdated, stereotypic model that needs to be abolished.[72]

We have never supported every conceivable combination of human relationships through law and policy. To the contrary, marriage has always been a national policy between one man and one woman. Utah's battle over polygamy is instructive for our purposes. In 1862, the United States Congress passed the Morril Act, which prohibited polygamy in the territories, disincorporated the Mormon Church, and restricted the church's ownership of property.[73] In *Reynolds v. United States*,[74] the U.S. Supreme Court upheld the Morril Act, stating that polygamy has always been "odious" among the Northern and Western nations of Europe, and from "the earliest history of England polygamy has been treated as an offense against society."[75] The court noted, "It is within the legitimate scope of the power of every civil government to determine whether polygamy or monogamy shall be the law of social life under its dominion."[76]

In 1882, Congress passed the Edmunds Act, which prohibited polygamists from holding political office and disqualified them from serving on juries.[77] Then in 1887, Congress passed the Edmunds-Tucker Bill, which required, among other things, wives of polygamous relationships to testify against their husbands. On October 6, 1890, the Mormon church officially approved a Manifesto that required the church to no longer sanction polygamous marriages.[78]

As a condition to be admitted to the Union, Congress required the inclusion of anti-polygamy provisions in the constitutions of Arizona, New Mexico, Oklahoma, and Utah.[79] For Arizona, New Mexico, and Utah, the Enabling Acts permitting these states to be admitted to the Union required that the antipolygamy provisions be "irrevocable," and that in order to change their laws to allow polygamy, each state would have to persuade the entire country to change the marriage laws.[80] Idaho adopted the constitutional provision on its own, and the fifty-first Congress, which admitted Idaho into the Union, found its constitution to be "republican in form and . . . in conformity with the Constitution of the United States."[81] To this day Arizona, Idaho, New Mexico, Oklahoma, and Utah state in their constitutions that polygamy is "forever prohibited."[82] The national ban on polygamy, or better, the national policy of marriage between one man and one woman, is enforced in many ways. A juror who has a conscientious belief that polygamy is right may be challenged for cause in a trial for polygamy,[83] and anyone who practices polygamy is ineligible to immigrate to the United States.[84]

If same-sex marriage were sanctioned, it would be virtually impossible to ban polygamy. Among "the likeliest effects of gay marriage is to take us down a slippery slope to legalize polygamy and 'polyamory' (group marriage)."[85] When Tom Green was put on trial for polygamy in Utah in 2001, several articles and editorials appeared in various newspapers supporting the practice of polygamy (*The Village Voice, Washington Times, Chicago Tribune,* and *The New York Times*).[86] Although the ACLU initially tried to minimize the idea of the slippery slope between gay marriage and polygamy, the ACLU itself defended Tom Green during his trial and declared its support for the repeal of all "laws prohibiting or penalizing the practice of plural marriage," and Steven Clark, the director for the Utah ACLU stated, "Talking to Utah polygamists is like talking to gays and lesbians who really want the right to live their lives."[87]

Polygamy typically involves one man with multiple wives, whereas polyamory involves a variety of human relationships. "Unlike classic polygamy, which features one man and several women, polyamory comprises of the bewildering variety of sexual combinations. There are triads of one woman and two men; heterosexual group marriages; groups in which some or all members are bisexual; lesbian groups, and so forth."[88]

If you think that polyamory is far-fetched, then do a simple word search for polyamory on the Internet, or consider the movement's authoritative guide written by Deborah Anapol, entitled *Polyamory: The New Love without Limits*. After the Federal Defense of Marriage Act was passed in 1996, an article appeared in *Loving More*, the flagship magazine of the polyamory movement, calling for polyamorists to base their movement on the gay rights model. Indeed, Paula Ettelbrick, former legal director for Lambda Legal Defense and Education Fund, supports same-sex marriage and state-sanctioned polyamory. Ettelbrick teaches law at the University of Michigan, New York University, Barnard, and Columbia.[89] A number of other law professors similarly promote polyamory, including Nancy Polikoff at American University, Martha Fineman at Cornell University, Martha Ertman at the University of Utah, Judith Stacey, the Barbara Streisand professor of contemporary gender studies at the University of Southern California, and David Chambers at the University of Michigan.[90]

In Canada, where several courts ruled in favor of same-sex marriage, the move to abolish traditional marriage and establish polyamory has already been set in motion. In December 2001, the Law Commission on Canada, established by the Canadian parliament to serve the parliament and the Justice Ministry, issued a report entitled *Beyond Conjugality*. This report directed judges to consider whether the individuals before them are "functionally interdependent," regardless of their actual marital status. The report also recommended the creation of a legal structure permitting people to register their personal relationships with the government and the legalization of same-sex marriage. All this occurred even before the Canadian courts ruled in favor of same-sex marriage.[91]

"Once we say that gay couples have a right to have their commitments recognized by the state, it becomes next to impossible to deny the same right to polygamous, or even cohabiting relatives and friends. And once everyone's relationship is recognized, marriage is gone, and only a system of flexible relationship contracts is left."[92]

Will Same-Sex Marriage Hurt My Marriage?

A frequently asked question is, "How will same-sex marriage hurt my marriage?" As it relates to the relationship between my wife and me, it will not directly hurt *my* marriage, but it will hurt the culture, and that is what I am concerned about. The love between my wife and me is secure, and same-sex marriage will not disturb our relationship. However, same-sex marriage will cataclysmically disturb the culture, will hurt people, and in particular, children. Again, while marriage has a private aspect, it is a public institution that impacts the entire society. We cannot isolate marriage inside the four walls of a home. Our attitude and public policies toward marriage will affect the culture, and in my opinion, same-sex marriage will damage the culture.

Do you really want your children to open up the pages of the *Washington Post* or your local newspaper, turn to the kids' section, and read an article entitled "Defining Marriage," which tells your child how "normal" it is for two people of the same sex to be married? That is what the *Washington Post* did in an article published just for kids.[93] Or do you want your child to come home and tell you that at school the teacher read to the class a story from the book *The King and the King*? The book talks about a prince who was in love with a citizen of the kingdom, but there was a problem—the citizen was of the same sex as the prince. The law barred same-sex marriage, so when the prince became the king, he legalized same-sex marriage and married the citizen, and the two were joined as kings. This incident actually occurred in an elementary school in Wilmington, North Carolina.[94] Legalizing same-sex marriage would make these events common, every-day occurrences.

Is Equal Protection Violated by Prohibiting Same-Sex Marriage?

Some people think of equal protection in a cavalier manner, erroneously believing that any restriction on marriage violates equal protection. Such reasoning is wrong and has never been part of state or federal jurisprudence. The Supreme Court has noted that "[u]nless a classification trammels fundamental personal rights or is drawn upon an inherently suspect distinction such as race, religion or alienage, our decisions presume the constitutionality of the statutory discriminations and require only that the classification challenged be rationally related to a legitimate state interest."[95] Not all distinctions are impermissible. Even distinctions based upon race, religion, or alienage may be permissible in certain circumstances.

Preserving marriage between one man and one woman does not violate equal protection any more than gender-specific restrooms. Marriage has never been open to any and every one. As already noted, the Supreme Court has approved banning polygamous marriages, and most states ban incestuous marriages and place age restrictions on marriage. These restrictions have never been thought to violate equal protection.

Some argue that same-sex marriage proponents want marriage for its benefits. If benefits is the issue, then instead of deconstructing marriage itself, advocates of same-sex marriage should focus on the specific benefit desired. For example, if homosexual couples desire to secure Social Security dependent benefits, then they should lobby to change the law regarding Social Security rather than create a new form of marriage. Marriage is more than benefits. Marriage is a universal human institution. Marriage predated America, as it did every civilized society. Thus, before there was any law regarding marriage, marriage existed. Marriage will exist if the Social Security system disappears. Marriage is not merely a set of benefits. The laws and benefits associated with marriage are not marriage but are designed to support the institution because it is so fundamental to our society and future existence. Laws that promote marriage between one man and one woman to the exclusion of any other are supported by compelling governmental interests in the preservation of society and the public good.[96]

Should Marriage Be Left to the States?

Although for different reasons, same-sex marriage opponents and some states' rights advocates oppose amending the United States Constitution to protect marriage between one man and one woman. I am an advocate of states' rights, but I strongly support amending our Constitution to protect traditional marriage. The Constitution is unlike a statute and should not be amended for light or transient reasons. However, I support amending the Constitution because marriage between one man and one woman is, and always has been, a federal matter, and the act of amending the Constitution is an exercise in states' rights.

The discussion earlier regarding polygamy highlights American history regarding our national concern over marriage. Preserving traditional marriage was of such paramount importance that a number of the states were not admitted to the Union without first banning polygamy. The United States Supreme Court ruled that the federal government had authority to prosecute polygamy under the Mann Act.[97] While states have been permitted to regulate the edges of marriage, such as the ceremonies, dissolution, support, custody, and visitation, the states have never been allowed to modify its very essence—the legal union of one man and one woman.

Marriage will be national one way or another. Either the courts will dictate marriage policy or the people will. If a federal constitutional amendment is not adopted, the courts will no doubt alter traditional marriage policy. Four of the seven state court justices in Massachusetts incredibly concocted a right to same-sex marriage in that state's constitution.[98] The constitution of Massachusetts was drafted by none other than John Adams, our first vice president and second president of the United States, who himself was a devout Christian. Acknowledging that neither the history of the constitution nor the state statutes envisioned same-sex marriage, four of the justices nevertheless imposed their own will upon the entire state. The citizens of Massachusetts were, therefore, left with no other choice but to overturn this radical decision by a state constitutional amendment.

On September 21, 1996, Congress passed the Federal Defense of Marriage Act.[99] This law declared that no state or territory is required to recognize a same-sex marriage sanctioned by another state or territory. While this law is designed to ensure that the sovereignty of a state is not overridden by another state's same-sex marriage law, there is no guarantee that this law will be upheld by the courts. Considering the judicial activism of the Massachusetts Supreme Judicial Court, we dare not trust the courts to hold sacred the institution of marriage. Considering the mobility and the impact that marriage has on transactions between the states, we would find ourselves embroiled in endless litigation for years over whether one state should accept a same-sex marriage sanctioned by a sister state.

Marriage is not something with which we should experiment, and it is certainly not amenable to have same-sex marriage in some states but not in others. Whether imposed judicially or otherwise, marriage, in whatever form, will be and always has been national.

The only way for the people in America to have a voice in marriage is to exercise their right under the Constitution to enshrine marriage once and for all between one man and one woman. To do so requires two-thirds of the U.S. House and Senate to pass an amendment, and then three-quarters of the states (38) must ratify the amendment through their state legislatures. The required number of states has already gone on record since 1996 declaring support for traditional marriage by specifically enacting legislation protecting marriage between one man and one woman and expressly banning same-sex marriage. During this time a number of states amended their state constitutions. These amendments can still be challenged in the courts. Thus, it is only by the passage of a federal marriage amendment that the states may protect the will of the people. Marriage is clearly too important to be left to the whim of a few judges. It has been and must continue to be national, and it must always be between one man and one woman.

Why Doesn't the State Get Out of Licensing Marriage?

Some argue that the states should have nothing to do with marriage, and thus should not license marriage. In this way marriages could consist of either private religious or secular ceremonial services but with no state sanction. While this argument has some surface appeal, it fundamentally misunderstands the importance of marriage and its impact on society. The state has always been empowered to regulate in order to protect the public health and welfare of its citizens. Thus, we have laws protecting our personal security and property rights. Although consensual, we have laws regarding prostitution, gambling, and private drug use. The reason society has chosen to regulate these areas of our lives is because these private acts have public consequences. The same is true with marriage. Marriage is not merely a personal, private act. Children are part of marriage, and as such, the greater society is affected. It is neither wise nor desirable to deregulate marriage because, in so doing, our society would suffer. No, marriage is a public good, and it is precisely one of the areas in which the government should and must continue to regulate in order to protect the public good.

"Marriage is not merely a private taste or a private relation; it is an important public good. As marriage weakens, the costs are borne not only by individual children or families but by all of us taxpayers, citizens, and neighbors. We all incur the costs of higher crime, welfare, education and health-care expenditures, and in reduced security for our own marriage investments. Simply as a matter of public health alone, to take just one public consequence of marriage's decline, a new campaign to reduce marriage failure is as important as the campaign to reduce smoking."[100]

Society is affected by marriage, and would be damaged by same-sex marriage. Listen to the story of Jackii Edwardsm who summarized her experience of being raised by a lesbian mother: "We constantly wonder if we will eventually become gay. There is humiliation when other kids see our parents kissing a same-sex lover in front of us. Trust me, it's hard on the children, no matter how much they love their gay parent. The homosexual community may never admit it, but the damage stemming from their actions can be profound."[101]

Sanctioning same-sex marriage would have a profound destabilizing effect on the health, welfare, education, and morals of the country. We should not play Russian roulette with marriage. We must draw a line in the sand and preserve marriage once and for all between one man and one woman.

CHAPTER 2
Setting Boundaries Saves Lives

Anyone who has been around children knows they like to test their boundaries. Whether taking a bath, brushing their teeth, or going to bed on time, children will test the patience of their parents. Kids test their boundaries in order to expand them. While at times these boundaries might seem like negative enforcement barriers, they actually provide security, safety, and a sense of well-being.

A policy preserving traditional marriage between one man and one woman and prohibiting same-sex marriage is a boundary that literally saves lives and preserves the culture. Alan Chambers, who was once involved in the homosexual lifestyle and who now dedicates his life to help those trying to escape its grasp, stated it best when he wrote:

One of the reasons I oppose same-sex marriage.

I remember being a lonely 18-year-old searching for Mr. Right. I remember the ache to have a man hold me, protect me, love me and devote his life to me. I remember thinking that I would do anything to fill that insatiable need. I did everything short of praying for my knight in shining armor to show up on my doorstep. I was certain that the missing piece of my life's puzzle was going to be found in the man of my dreams.

Nearly 14 years later, I am happy, content and satisfied emotionally, physically, spiritually, sexually and relationally. Indeed, my needs were met by a man who has filled my life with the greatest security, intimacy and love imaginable. The man I met, however, was Jesus Christ. Because of Christ my needs were met, my life was changed and this month I celebrated my 6th wedding anniversary with my wife, Leslie.

Had same-sex marriage been legal in 1990, I am certain that I would have tested that option. I met men whom I wanted to "marry." Yet, as

I look back as a mature adult, I realize that I wasn't searching for a man as much as I was searching for an answer, a drug if you will, to numb the pain and make me feel better about who I was. The law kept me from making one, if not many, huge mistakes. And while honoring and pre-serving the sanctity of heterosexual marriage is the bedrock of my opposi-tion to redefining marriage to suit a few, I believe a positive by-product of keeping same-sex marriage illegal is that it will save tens of thousands of hurting young people like me from the biggest mistake of their lives: look-ing for a man to meet a need that only God can meet.

I encourage you to take a stand for today's gay youth by opposing same-sex marriage; they may not thank you today, but protecting them now provides them with a better chance of being around to thank you later.[1]

As Alan poignantly describes, had he been permitted to enter into a same-sex marriage, he probably would have "married one of his sexual partners." If the gov-ernment places its stamp of approval on homosexual relationships by legalizing same-sex marriage, the once illegal practice will be elevated to a preferred status, equivalent to marriage between a man and a woman. For most people, if some-thing is legal, it is also moral. If marriage laws define no difference between oppo-site-sex and same-sex unions, then there will be no boundaries around virtually any manifestation of human sexuality.

The testimonies posted on the Exodus International Web site have a consistent theme.[2] These individuals who sought homosexual relationships in order to satisfy inner needs felt pain, emptiness, and often a feeling of worthlessness. Through var-ious circumstances the testimonies unanimously show how each one had their needs met by Jesus Christ. Perhaps a friend called and invited them to church, or long-time friends walked with them in the valley of their homosexual struggles. Wrapping these individuals in the web of a legally binding same-sex marriage, topped off with property disputes and custody considerations, means they would encounter a more difficult time freeing themselves from a destructive lifestyle.

Common sense and millennia of human history state the obvious—the natural order of the human species is that human sexuality and procreation occur between opposite-sex rather than same-sex couples. If we remain silent or indifferent on set-ting the boundaries of marriage, then we are complicit in approving the ruin of many precious lives. Neutrality or indifference is not an option. While some will not appreciate our position prohibiting same-sex marriage and while some may become downright offended, it is our right—indeed, it is our duty—to draw the boundaries around marriage between one man and one woman.

Children Need a Father and a Mother

Male Gender Identity

The most obvious boundaries of human sexuality are also the most visible. We live in a world demarcated by two genders, male and female. There is no third or intermediate category. Sex is binary. A healthy developing boy needs to affirm and embrace his maleness.

Some boys have more difficulty embracing their maleness than girls do their femaleness, and this may be why male homosexuals far outnumber female lesbians.[3] Homosexuality in boys often stems from gender nonconformity. This nonconformity in boys results in two, seemingly opposite, reactions. First, in the early stages, the boy shuns his maleness. Second, as this disassociation with males progresses, the boy ultimately idolizes the male and longs to have his inner self filled with the maleness he lacks and thus becomes attracted to males. "Childhood gender nonconformity turns out to be a very strong predictor of adult sexual preference among . . . males."[4] Speaking of this gender nonconformity, an organization that works with males desiring to leave the homosexual lifestyle describes the following:

Somehow, even as boys or young teenagers, we felt like we were never "man enough." We felt like we didn't live up to the masculine ideal. We saw ourselves as too fat or too skinny, too short or too awkward, not athletic enough or tough or strong or good-looking enough—or whatever other qualities we admired in other males but judged to be lacking in ourselves. It was more than low self-esteem; it was low gender esteem—a deficiency in our core sense of gender upon which our whole self image is built. Other males just seemed naturally masculine, but masculinity never came naturally to us. We aspired to it but were mystified by how to achieve it. Among other males, we felt different and lonely.

Feeling deficient as males, we pined to be accepted and affirmed by others, especially those whose masculinity we admired most. We began to idolize the qualities in other males we judged to be lacking in ourselves. Idolizing them widened a gulf we imagined between ourselves and the so-called "real men," the Adonis gods of our fantasies. In idolizing them, we increased our sense of our own masculine deficiency. It also de-humanized the men we idolized, putting them on a pedestal that deified them and made them unapproachable.

At the same time we idolized certain male traits or maleness generally, many of us came to fear other boys and men. Born with unusually sensitive and gentle personalities, we found it easy for many of us to feel different from and rejected by our more rough-and-tumble peers growing up. We came to fear their taunts and felt like we could never belong. Many of us feared the sports field and felt like we could never compete. Many of us felt rejected by our fathers and feared that we could never measure up or would never really matter to them.[5]

Dr. Joseph Nicolosi, who specializes in counseling gays and lesbians, stated, "I have never met a single homosexual man who said he had a close, loving, and respectful relationship with his father."[6] One author has gone so far as to say that there is "not a single even moderately well-controlled study that we have been able to locate in which male homosexuals refer to father positively or affectionately. On the contrary, they consistently regard him as an antagonist."[7]

Maintaining the boundaries of gender, as traditional marriage certainly does, is important for both genders but particularly for boys. "Girls can continue to develop in their feminine identification through the relationship with their mothers. On the other hand, a boy has an additional developmental task—to disidentify from his mother and identify with his father."[8]

Clinical professor of psychiatry at UCLA Ralph R. Greenson described this developmental process:

> The male child, in order to maintain a healthy sense of maleness, must replace the primary object of his identification, the mother, and must identify instead with his father. I believe it is the difficulties inherent in this additional step of development, from which girls are exempt, which are responsible for certain special problems in the man's gender identity, his sense of belonging to the male sex. . . . The male child's ability to disidentify will determine the success or failure of his later identification with his father.[9]

A study of male homosexuality in the *Archives of Sexual Behavior* noted that Sigmund Freud (1916) described the mothers of homosexuals as excessively loving and their fathers as retiring or absent. The article also noted that Stekel (1930) reported the characteristics of strong, dominant mothers and weak fathers. Then in 1936, researchers Terman and Miles found mothers of homosexuals to be especially demonstrative, affectionate, and emotional while the fathers were "typically unsympathetic, autocratic, or frequently away from home."[10]

Dr. Nicolosi speaks of a classic triadic relationship found in most homosexual males.

> Repeatedly, researchers have found the classic triadic (three-way) relationship in the family backgrounds of homosexual men. In this situation, the mother often has a poor or limited relationship with her husband, so she shifts her emotional needs to her son. The father is usually

nonexpressive and detached and often is critical as well. So in the triadic family pattern we have the detached father, the over involved mother, and the temperamentally sensitive, emotionally attuned boy who fills in for the father where the father falls short.[11]

Researchers headed by Irvin Bieber published a study that is still considered a landmark in the field regarding the development of homosexuality in males. Beiber wrote: "The 'classical' homosexual triangular pattern is one where the mother is CBI [close-binding-intimate] with the son and is dominant and minimizing toward her husband who is a detached father, particularly a hostile-detached one. With more statistical analysis, the chances appear to be high that any son exposed to this parental combination will become homosexual or develop severe homo-sexual problems."[12] Other studies of male homosexuals suggest that the father need not be *hostile* toward the son, but rather merely *indifferent.*[13] For boys, proper role models of a father and mother are critical to the development of their maleness. A study of homosexual male adults reported by Ray Evans found that the mothers of homosexuals:

> more often were considered puritanical, cold toward men, insisted on being the center of the son's attention, made him her confidant, were "seductive" toward him, allied him against the father, openly preferred him to the father, interfered with his heterosexual activities during ado-lescence, discouraged masculine attitudes and encouraged feminine ones. The fathers of the homosexuals were retrospectively considered as less likely to encourage masculine attitudes and activities, and (the studies' subjects) spent little time with their fathers, were more often aware of hat-ing him and afraid he might physically harm them, less often were the father's favorite, felt less accepted by him, and in turn less frequently accepted or respected by the father. . . . The results strongly suggested poor parental relationships during childhood for the homosexual men, at least as seen in retrospect.[14]

Psychologist Evelyn Hooker notes that the study by Evans is important because it partially confirms Bieber's assumption regarding the causal relationship between parental relations in early childhood and adult homosexuality.[15] Other studies have confirmed the finding of Bieber that male homosexuality is often associated with poor parental relations.[16] "In summary, then, it would seem that the family pattern involving a combination of a dominating, overly intimate mother *plus* a detached, hostile or weak father is beyond doubt related to the development of male homo-sexuality."[17] While homosexuality is multifaceted, it is most certainly a develop-mental problem that is almost always associated with poor family relations, particularly between father and son.[18]

From birth to approximately eighteen months, boys receive their foundational security primarily from their mothers. "Ideally, an infant's first year or two of life is spent developing a deep, secure bond of love with the mother that leads to a healthy sense of personal identity."[19] David Blankenhorn notes that for the boy, the mother's love is an "unquestioned source of comfort and the foundation of human attachment." He comments, "If mothers are likely to devote special attention to their children's present physical and emotional needs, fathers are likely to devote special attention to their character traits necessary for the future, especially qualities such as independence, self-reliance, and the willingness to test the limits and take risks."[20] Sociologist David Popenoe noted that "fathers tend to stress competition, challenge, initiative, risk taking and independence. Mothers in their care-taking roles, in contrast, stress emotional security and personal safety."[21] Popenoe continues, "While mothers provide an important flexibility and sympathy in their discipline, fathers provide ultimate predictability and consistency. Both dimensions are critical for an efficient, balanced, and human child-rearing regime."[22]

Beginning at the age of approximately eighteen months and continuing to roughly the age of five, the boy needs verbal and physical affirmation of his maleness. At around eighteen months the boy is able to begin to see the differences between male and female. At this time the father becomes more significant, and the boy tries to reach out to him and form a closer bond with the father. Once the boy's gender identity is formed, he can develop gender stability.[23] Bonding with the father is critical during these formative years. Of course, a boy raised in a dysfunctional or nonfunctional family is not doomed to grow up homosexual, but such a family structure may predispose the young boy to homosexual considerations. It is typically during this phase of the boy's development that he emphasizes his gender identity and strongly differentiates between boys and girls. Thus, "the normally developing boy spurns the company of little girls."[24] Unlike mothers who tend to be nurturing and protective of their children, fathers are more apt to engage in rough-and-tumble play with their sons, and this activity encourages the male identity.[25]

There are many ways that a boy may resist associating with a masculine identity. Dr. Richard Fitzgibbons describes a so-called "sports wound," by which he means that a boy who is not athletic can be teased by his peers, and such teasing can negatively affect the boy's self-image, his relationships with peers, his gender identity, and his body image. He notes that a boy's negative view of his masculinity and his loneliness can lead him to crave the masculinity of his male peers.[26] Sometimes fathers can agitate a boy's masculinity when the boy fails to conform to the image that the father demands, whether it is in sports or in any other masculine characteristic.

If the boy is rejected by his peers and if his father demeans the boy's self-image, ignores him, or does little to affirm the boy's masculinity, the boy can end up rejecting his maleness while at the same time craving it. An organization that reaches out to males desiring to leave homosexuality explains:

> Our fear and hurt at feeling rejected by the male world often led us to disassociate ourselves from the masculine—the very thing we desired most. These feelings also led us to prejudice as some of us began consciously or subconsciously to deride men as inferior. . . . Often we succumbed to the common psychological phenomenon of being most critical of what we most envied. Or most feared. . . .
>
> In our own experience, and from the experience of many gay men we have known, it seems very rare for a man who struggles with homosexuality to feel that he was sufficiently loved, affirmed and mentored by his father growing up, or that he identified with his father as a male role model. In fact, oftentimes the father-son relationship is marked by either actual or perceived abandonment, extended absence, hostility or disinterest (a form of abandonment).[27]

The boundaries of male and female are critically important for the development of boys to men. To boys, and to girls, gender is important. The dichotomy between sexes is critical. That boundary is maintained by insisting on what is obvious, that marriage must remain between one man and one woman.

The typical homosexual male failed to properly assimilate his masculine identity. This occurs in one of several ways as already noted, including, but not necessarily limited to, some type of emotional detachment or even rejection by the father, rejection by his masculine peers, or sexual domination by another male.[28] The result is still the same: the boy rejects his masculinity while, at the same time, he craves that which he rejects.[29] Although lesbianism among females may have similar causes, the causes are more varied.

Female Gender Identity

While this book is not designed to address the causes of homosexuality or lesbianism, the point of the immediate discussion is that the gender of the two sexes is important; and binary sex sets a clear, definable boundary. That boundary would be blurred, indeed obliterated, by same-sex marriage. The delicate balance of boys accepting their masculinity and girls their femininity would be clearly upset by same-sex marriage. The very notion of same-sex marriage suggests that gender is irrelevant, but gender is indeed relevant; it is essential.

Commenting on lesbianism and how it may differ from male homosexuality, Dr. Nicolosi writes:

> Male homosexuality tends to follow a relatively predictable developmental pattern, . . . but lesbianism is less predictable and more likely to

alternate, during the woman's lifetime, with periods of heterosexuality. Many lesbians believe their sexuality is a choice they made as an outgrowth of their feminist political interests. Still, I believe the most common pathway to lesbianism is a life situation that creates a deeply ambivalent attitude toward femininity, conveying the internal message "its not safe or desirable to be a woman."[30]

Psychoanalyst Elaine Siegel says that her lesbian patients typically experienced a severe arrest in ego development.[31] The mother may sometimes act generally immature, be emotionally fragile and even aloof from the needs of her daughter, and thus the daughter may reject the femininity of the mother. A narcissistic (self-absorbed) mother may interfere with her daughter's separation and individuation and propel her in the direction of lesbianism, but severe hurt by a male may also communicate the same message of insecurity and vulnerability. Psychiatrist Richard Fitzgibbons states the following:

> A number of women who become enthralled in same-sex relationships had fathers who were emotionally insensitive, alcoholic, or abusive. Such women, as a result of painful childhood and teenage experiences, have good reason to fear being vulnerable to men. . . .

> Women who have been sexually abused or raped as children or adolescents may find it difficult or almost impossible to trust men. They may, therefore, turn to a woman for affection and to fulfill their sexual desires.[32]

In order to promote a healthy self-esteem and identification with her feminine identity, "there should be a warm mother-daughter intimacy along with a father who does not promote identification of the daughter with himself. Indeed, a healthy relationship with Mom provides the most important foundation for the incorporation of femininity and heterosexuality."[33] Sometimes a healthy identification between the mother and daughter may face a traumatic interruption. Such interruptions may include severe depression in the mother which causes the father to take over the child rearing, in which case the mother may be withdrawn and the father becomes the object of strength and stability.[34] "In terms of psychosocial transmission, the message to the daughters seemed to be that being female was unsafe. The mothers had a great deal of difficulty in instilling in their daughters a sense of pride and confidence about being female."[35]

"Women who become lesbians have usually decided, on an unconscious level, that being female is either undesirable or unsafe."[36] Sometimes the girl might experience early sexual molestation, or she might perceive her mother as a negative or weak feminine object she wants to avoid, or perhaps she may have experienced some rejection from a male. One study of lesbianism noted: "The girls had difficulty in forming an emotional connection to their mothers. In some instances, it seemed to us that either a girl failed to identify with her mother, or disidentified from her mother because she perceived her mother as weak, incompetent or help-less. In fact, many of the mothers devalued their own efficacy and regarded the female gender role with disdain."[37]

A girl's relationship with her mother and an unhealthy interaction with her father are certainly factors leading to lesbianism. Sexual abuse may also play a crit-ical role. "In women, abuse can lead to a deep fear and even hatred of men if the perpetrator is a male. Men are no longer 'safe.' The woman's deep need to connect with another individual leads her right into close relationships with other women, often women who have been wounded in similar ways. This sets the stage for les-bian bonding to occur."[38]

Psychotherapist and former lesbian Andria Sigler-Smalz describes the emotional deficits often found in lesbian relationships:

Female relationships lean toward social exclusivity rather than inclu-sivity, and it is not unusual for a lesbian couple to increasingly reduce con-tact with family members and previous friends. This gradual withdrawal serves to insure control, and protects against separateness and perceived threats to their fragile bond.

The propelling drive in the lesbian relationship is the woman's same-sex emotional and nurturing deficits, and these deficits are generally not sexualized to the same degree as seen in male sexuality. For the female homosexual, "emotional attraction" plays a more critical role than does sexual attraction. . . .

While lesbian partnerships generally are of longer duration than male relationships, they tend to be fraught with emotional intensity and held together by the "glue" of jealousy, over-possessiveness and various manip-ulative behaviors.

During the course of the relationship, the "highs" are very high, and the times of conflict, extreme. Excessive time together, frequent telephon-ing, disproportionate card or gift-giving, hastily moving in together or merging finances, are some of the ways separateness is defended against. In such relationships, we see the counterfeit of healthy attachment—that is, emotional dependency and over-enmeshment. . . . There is often a des-perate quality to the emotional attraction in women that struggle with lesbianism.[39]

If the mother has a history of severe and chronic sexual abuse by a father, step-father, or a close relative or if she experienced domestic violence, causing her to feel unsafe with males, she can transmit these feelings to her daughter. "The girl who has been unable to make a satisfactory identification with a same-sex love object (the mother) will harbor repressed rage against the very thing she loves because, on the one hand, she desires it but, on the other hand, she has been hurt by it."[40]

Same-Sex Attractions: Rejecting, Idolizing, and Longing to Fill Emotional Deficits

Whether it is male homosexuality or female lesbianism, one common feature between the two is rejecting, idolizing, and longing to fill the emotional deficit of the same sex.

Homosexuality represents not an *indifference to* gender but a *deficit* in gender. Deficit-based behavior comes from a heightened sensitivity to what one feels one lacks, and it is characterized by compulsivity and drivenness—but a person will persist in the behavior despite social disadvantage and grave medical risk. Deficit-based behaviors often have a quality of caricature, seen vividly in "leather" bars, where men are dressed up as soldiers and policemen, wearing studded belts and carrying instruments of torture. Such exaggerated behavior actually represents a heightened awareness in pursuit of the internally deficient gender—that is, maleness—but in caricatured ways.[41]

Similar to the caricatures fantasized by male homosexuals of the strong, powerful "macho men," some lesbians may engage in sadomasochism.[42] One lesbian psychotherapist stated the following:

I can't remember the exact moment when I started to notice that many of our lesbian publications, erotic anthologies, conferences and books were referring to sado-masochism in an approving or erotically positive way.

Suddenly, it seemed, s/m has become mainstreamed, even celebrated, particularly among younger lesbians. Whips, chains, and master-slave role-plays don't seem to shock us as they once did. . . .

Instead of challenging s/m, so many lesbians are now embracing it as glamorous and hip, a way to be "sex positive" and "in-your-face queer."[43]

Not all lesbians engage in sadomasochism. However, one thing in common between homosexuality and lesbianism is, at some point, an emotional rejection is followed by an emotional attachment to the same sex.

Social Peer Pressure and the Influence of the Media

Environmental causes for homosexual practices may also include peer pressure, adolescent rebellion and the desire to be different or noticed. Homosexual activity appears to be increasing among adolescent females. While the causes of this experimentation may have similar sources of rejection or a desire to feel important or loved, many young people, who would otherwise not experiment with homosexuality, are doing so because it is trendy or the "in" thing to do.

When Britney Spears and Christina Aguilera kissed Madonna during the MTV Music Video Awards in 2003, the stunt may have been designed to shock the audience, but it is also a symptom of a trend. A newspaper article described the following scene:

"Kiss! Kiss! Kiss!"

A group of teenagers is gathered at a party. Music is playing; smuggled booze is flowing. Two girls grin sheepishly at each other as a crowd goads them on.

Finally, the teens relent, rewarding their audience with some mouth-on-mouth action.

It is not an unusual scene, according to South Florida high school students who say the newest trend for teen girls isn't wearing the latest designer jeans or driving a cool car, but declaring themselves to be bisexual.

"Some do it for attention. Some do it because guys like it. And some do it just because they can. It's definitely a fad," says Stranahan High student Christy Shalley, president of the Fort Lauderdale school's Gay Straight Alliance.

Jessie Gilliam, Program Manager for Youth Resource—a national website created by and for gay, lesbian and bisexual young people—says the trend is known as "bisexual chic," or in many cases, "faux bisexual." It usually starts with some hand-holding or grinding on the dance floor, then progresses from there.

"It's a countrywide thing," she says.[44]

Homosexual advocates take advantage of the growing-up process where young people question their values and identity, including their sexual identity. David Sternberg, quoted by the newspaper article described in the above story, then a senior at Spanish River High in Boca Raton, Florida, said, "Nobody's parents know" what their children are doing in school, and he stated that "if they think they know, they really don't know."[45] He added that some girls may truly be questioning their sexuality but others just want to be perceived as "hot." "Girls go for the whole mystery thing. And guys usually think it's attractive. It's a turn-on. It's more of a teasing thing. At parties, girls randomly kiss, and guys are like, 'Oh! That's awesome!'"[46] he said.

One girl of Wilton Manors, Florida, stated that she first experimented with girls because of the way guys reacted. The seventeen-year-old girl said, "I liked the attention," adding that though she has had a boyfriend for two years, she occasionally kisses girls in front of him. Then she stated, "He likes it. It's fun."[47]

The trend of adolescents experimenting with bisexuality was also reported in the *Washington Post*. In an article entitled "Part Way Gay?" a typical Friday night scene was described as follows:

> You can see this new trend on Friday nights outside Union Station, sweethearts from high schools around the Washington area, some locking lips, others hanging out in their tight blue jeans and puffy winter parkas, talking on their cell phones.
>
> You can see them in the hallways of high schools like South Lake and Reston, Magruder and Rockville or Coolidge in the District. In 2002 at Coolidge, a teacher got so fed up with girls nuzzling each other in class and in other public places that he threatened to send any he saw to the principal's office.[48]

Fed by pro-homosexual lyrics or stage shows of pop artists, MTV, or prime-time television, young people are experimenting with homosexuality because some consider it faddish. The *Washington Post* article described girls at a private school in North Washington charging boys ten dollars to watch them kiss. Chandra Harris, a junior at High Road Upper School in Beldsville, started going out with girls when she was fourteen following a breakup with her boyfriend. "At first I thought that going out with a girl was nasty," she said. "Then I went to a club and did a big flip-flop. I have been off and on with girls and guys since then."[49]

Another girl, a junior at Anacostia High, described her first love as a guy who was in the marines stationed in North Carolina. She dated this guy for two years, but she also began dating a female high school basketball player. She said, "Whoever likes me, I like them."[50] The casual nature of some young people regarding sexual boundaries is shocking.

Chloe Root, a sophomore at Brown University, stated that she first had a crush on a girl at age twelve but continued to date guys until her senior year of high school in Ann Arbor, Michigan. Then she "fell in love" with a girl, and she has been dating her ever since. "If something happened to my relationship with Julie, I could see myself with a boy again,"[51] Root said. "There are some days I notice I am thinking girls are pretty and other days I am thinking there are a lot of good-looking guys at this school."[52]

The *Washington Post* article also described a man named David Shapiro, head of the Edmund Burke School, a private, college-preparatory program in northwest Washington. In 2002 the school had a "diversity" day in which students and teachers stood together in a circle. In one of the exercises, participants were asked to move inside the circle if they defined themselves as gay or lesbian. One female teacher stepped forward but no students. The leader then asked for those who described themselves as bisexual to enter the circle. Of the approximate sixty students, fifteen stepped forward—eleven girls and four boys.[53]

This trend toward sexual experimentation and bisexuality is urged on by beer commercials where guys fantasize about two female friends fighting in a fountain. Another driving force is Internet pornography. When young boys or men access Internet pornography to view women, they encounter group orgies or female-on-female sexual encounters. The same is true for females viewing Internet pornography. They encounter male and female homosexual activity. Viewing opposite-sex homosexuality may tend to break down sexual mores, leaving the viewer with a more accepting attitude of homosexuality or bisexuality.

Binary Sex Is Normative

Although some advocates of same-sex marriage argue that homosexuals are "born that way," the current research suggests otherwise. Chapter 6 will address this subject in more detail. However, even if there were genetic tendencies that might predispose a person to be more susceptible to same-sex attractions, there is no question (even among the most ardent pro-homosexual researchers) that homosexuality is primarily influenced by developmental and environmental factors. Irrespective of its cause, the bigger question is, "What is normative?" Consider obesity. While some researchers suggest a genetic predisposition to obesity, the same research also suggests that not all people with these alleged genetic predispositions become obese.[54] Even if researchers could agree upon a genetic predisposition to obesity, that conclusion would not equate to obesity becoming normative. By observing the natural and average weight of males and females, society delineates standards for obesity. Even more so with homosexuality than body mass index, there are clearly established boundaries between male and female. Sex is male and female. It is binary. Speaking of the interrelation between genetic predisposition and obesity, Dr. Nicolosi writes:

> Our genes provide only one influence—a predisposition, in some people to gain weight. There is also a family influence ("Did Mom put Coca-cola instead of milk in your baby bottle?"), cultural influence ("Did your extended family celebrate get-togethers with marathons of fried sausage and pastas?"), situational stressors ("Are you under a lot of pressure at work, causing you to drink beer and snack in front of the TV all night?"), and, of course, your own choice to exercise self-control ("Did you choose to diet, or do you simply give in to the comfort and pleasure of eating?").[55]

Like obesity, some people might have a genetic predisposition to developing alcoholism. The mere fact that one has a genetic predisposition toward alcoholism or obesity does not mean that a person will become obese or an alcoholic, nor does it mean that obesity and alcoholism are normative. The same is true of homosexuality. Irrespective of whether there are genetic predisposing factors, the clear and indisputable norm for human sexuality is visible and observable, and it is male and female. Same-sex marriage would blur this distinction by making normative that which is abnormal. Treating as normal that which is clearly abnormal by removing the boundaries of human sexuality would broaden the emotional injuries and increase the number of people who reject, and then come to idolize, members of their own sex.

Whether one believes in a genetic or environmental cause is irrelevant. What is relevant is that a boundary is established irrespective of the origin of homosexuality. It makes no difference to the victim of a motor vehicle accident whether the driver of the other car was drunk as a result of casual drinking or consumed too much alcohol because of an alcoholic disease. For the victim and for the drunk driver, the results are the same, irrespective of the reason the driver was drunk. The same is true for same-sex unions.

Human Behavior Needs Gender Boundaries

One of the reasons the so-called "bisexual chic" trend is particularly harmful to adolescent females lies partly in the difference between the interpersonal relationships of girls and boys. Adolescent girls tend to share their feelings more than boys, and thus they also tend to develop closer relationships with members of the same sex than do boys. In the past, developing such a close relationship has been considered nothing more than just that, a close relationship. However, in light of homosexual advocacy groups, like the Gay, Lesbian and Straight Education Network (GLSEN) or Parents and Friends of Lesbians and Gays (PFLAG), urging adolescents to experiment early and often with same-sex relationships, some might confuse typical friendship with lesbianism. Adolescent girls may easily become confused about their sexuality. That's why we need boundaries.

Human behavior needs established boundaries. It is simple common sense. A football game would be chaotic if there were no sidelines, end zones, goalposts, or rules. While these rules and boundaries may seem confining, they are actually liberating. They allow the game to proceed. Any sport without boundaries and rules would eventually become boring and pointless.

While no one wants to pay a speeding fine, traffic laws make transportation possible. Consider how chaotic an intersection becomes when a traffic light fails. If there were no lines dividing a two-lane highway, or no rules stating on which side you must drive, then taking a trip would become a fearful, even deadly, adventure.

As soon as you bring a pet dog into a new home, the dog inspects every room in the house. If the dog is outside, the boundaries of the yard are carefully inspected and marked. Knowing that there is a boundary and a territory within the dog's control gives security and meaning to the animal.

Accepting same-sex marriage requires the rejection of gender. Same-sex marriage essentially says that gender doesn't matter, that children fare just as well when raised in a single-gender household as with a mom and a dad. Of course, this is not true. Children need a mother and father. They need boundaries, especially between male and female. Healthy children accept their gender but are not sexually aroused by it.

Laws banning same-sex marriage are necessary not only to preserve traditional marriage between a man and a woman but also to preserve the lives of those who are tangled in the web of improper sexual relations. If, as a society, we accept same-sex marriage or other same-sex unions, we become personally responsible for the pain and misery of many innocent people because we have fostered a system of law that encourages them to follow a path of confusion, emptiness, and pain. We must set boundaries on human sexuality. That boundary is clearly demarcated between male and female.

CHAPTER 3

Our Children at Risk

S ame-sex marriage advocates realize the importance of changing the culture by molding the minds of children. In a pro-homosexual article entitled "Future Shock," Patricia Warren exclaims, "Whoever captures the kids owns the future."[1]

Legally sanctioning same-sex marriage would have far-reaching social, moral, economic, and political ramifications. Certainly public education would be affected. Curriculum addressing human sexuality and family will by necessity redefine *family* to include anyone who associates with another in a "loving" relationship. Books like *Heather Has Two Mommies*[2] and *Daddy's Roommate*[3] would become standard textbooks. These two books have already been used to teach first-grade students in some public schools.[4]

Exploiting the Youth

One high school in Framingham, Massachusetts, pushed the envelope in a class designed to promote "tolerance" for sexual preferences. This class involved a "role reversal" exercise in which the students were given a handout that asked the following questions: "Is it possible that you are heterosexual because you fear the same sex? If you have never slept with someone of the same sex, how do you know you wouldn't prefer that? Is it possible you merely need a good gay experience?"[5]

Recognizing the importance of capturing the minds of children, homosexual groups have developed strategies to teach youth that exploration of one's "sexual identity" is healthy and normal. For example, Outright Vermont explains in a 2000 report that its "target population" is youth between ages fourteen and twenty-two and provides highlights of its *government-funded* activities conducted for public school students. These included: (1) "Safe Sex Parties," which provided "fun exploration of sexuality & safe sex activities including demonstrations, guided practice & skill evaluation for barrier use"; (2) social events, where "barriers & other safe sex supplies were available at the door & in the bathroom"; (3) "weekend retreats" where "all retreat participants practiced & were evaluated on their barrier use skills & were given a variety of barriers to take home; and (4) training in proper needle-cleaning techniques for those using hormones to alter gender characteristics.[6]

GLSEN (Gay, Lesbian, and Straight Education Network) has a guide designed for use in public schools to eradicate "institutionalized heterosexism." In determining whether "institutional heterosexism" exists, the authors ask such questions as: "Are gender-specific bathrooms and locker rooms the only option in your school?", "Do proms, homecoming and athletic events have exclusive votes for 'kings' and 'queens'?"[7]

PFLAG (Parents and Friends of Lesbians and Gays) created a brochure entitled, "Be Yourself: Questions and Answers for Gay, Lesbian, Bisexual and Transgender Youth,"[8] which contains recommended reading that encourages exploration of one's "sexual identity" at an early age. For example, some of the recommended material states, "My first experience was with a much older man. . . . When I was fifteen, he must have been twenty-nine, thirty. . . . I seduced him. . . . It was a wild night."[9] One source declares, "My sexuality is as fluid, infinite, undefinable, and ever-changing as the north-flowing river. . . . Sexuality is not black or white . . . it is gray."[10] Another book for children states, "I had been having sex with a man since I was fourteen."[11] The same recommended source declares "For gay liberation to have any value for youth, people must be reminded, preferably in fifth- or sixth-grade sex education classes, that gay is not only good, but probably a part of most sexual make-ups."[12]

PFLAG also explains that "being GLBT [gay, lesbian, bisexual or transsexual] is as much a human variation as being left-handed. . . . One or two sexual experiences with someone of the same sex may not mean you're gay. . . . GLBT people have some sexual experiences with the opposite gender. . . . Your school years are a time of figuring out what works for you, and crushes and experimentation are often part of that."[13]

In order to illustrate that PFLAG and GLSEN are not merely promoting tolerance but are instead promoting a radical sexual revolution for youth, a brief description of some of the recommended reading resources listed by one or both of these organizations is summarized below:

- A graphic description of two ten-year-old boys engaged in homosexual sex described as a child recollection of Malcolm Boyd, an Episcopal priest.[14]
- Describing a pedophilia encounter between a fifteen-year-old and a twenty-nine-year-old.[15]
- Describing a homosexual encounter between two cousins, ages twelve and sixteen.[16]

- A story about three seventeen-year-old boys exploring their homosexual attractions. This book contains frequent themes about the boys viewing sexually explicit magazines and movies as well as graphic depictions of male homosexual arousal and also features a scene in which one of the teen boys has anal intercourse with a twenty-nine-year-old man he met via the Internet.[17] In this story, the boy's mother is an officer in the local PFLAG chapter.
- Describing a fifteen-year-old girl recounting that she came out to her family at age eleven and to her entire elementary class at age twelve.[18]
- Describing a sexual encounter with a transsexual.[19]
- A graphic description of a thirteen-year-old meeting a man on a bus who lures him to a restroom where they engage in sex.[20]
- Describing a boy raised by two homosexual males who experienced anal intercourse at age fifteen with a man, age thirty.[21]
- Relating a story of an eighteen-year-old boy who began to be molested at the age of ten by his mother's boyfriend, who eventually became the boy's stepfather, in which the boy states, "That wasn't my first sexual experience, so I'm not scarred by it or anything."[22]
- Describing the experiences of young boys having sex with adults.[23]

Some of the quotes from the reading sources recommended by GLSEN and/or PFLAG include the following:

- "Young people are just as capable of exploring their sexual identity as adults."[24]
- "I've been doing drag for about ten years, on and off . . . my fantasies were all about whipping. I started reading up on S/M [sadomasochism], and it was making me interested in sex for the first time. . . . I realized that, for what I was doing, I could be getting good money."[25]
- "I first began to come out when I was 11. In terms of my family, I was fortunate because my parents have always been accepting of my sexual identity. . . . So at the age of 12 I came out to my entire elementary school, which included grades K–8."[26]
- "Although it's common to feel more strongly attracted to one sex or the other, many people feel at least some amount of attraction for both sexes. . . . Our sexual behaviors are seldom absolute."[27]
- "Sexuality is not black or white . . . it is gray."[28]
- "I identify as bisexual, and have since I was about six or seven. . . . I sort of experimented when I was young."[29]
- "I was in sixth grade and attending a Catholic school in San Francisco when I came out to a small group of people."[30]

- "Each of us should have the freedom to explore our sexual orientation and find our own unique expression of lesbian, bisexual, gay, straight, or any combination of these."[31]
- "I think the first time I actually thought about being bi or questioned my sexuality was when, under the influence, I kissed a girl. I would have been thirteen. . . . I was really heavy into drugs and stuff like that."[32]
- "The Bible says very little about homosexuality. Amidst the hundreds of thousands of other teachings, responsibilities, laws and prohibitions, there are only a handful of statements that might possibly apply to sex between a man—and none that address lesbian sexuality."[33] [This statement is incorrect, as the book of Romans addresses women who "exchanged their natural relations for unnatural ones."][34]

The books recommended by GLSEN and PFLAG for minors illustrate that the homosexual movement is radical; it is out of step with the mainstream. Many other sordid and grotesque details could have been listed above from the "recommended" reading lists of these organizations. Verbatim descriptions have, for the most part, been eliminated due to their graphic nature and sexually explicit language. These groups, and those like them, prey on children and pretend to promote tolerance, when in reality, their efforts will destroy a generation and radically alter the culture.[35] Understand this: GLSEN and PFLAG are not considered radical groups within the homosexual community. They are mainstream to the movement.

Not content indoctrinating our youth with the message that homosexual activity is as healthy and normal as heterosexual conduct, that such sex should have no constraints or boundaries, and that anyone who speaks against homosexuality is "intolerant,"[36] same-sex advocates are also bent on challenging traditional notions of family and morality through legislative and judicial means.

Children Raised by Homosexual Parents Face Adverse Consquences

The same-sex marriage movement seeks to advance its agenda by adopting or parenting children.[37] Homosexuals often point to the overcrowded foster care system to support their arguments in favor of legalizing same-sex adoption.[38] However, the solution to the foster care problem is not same-sex adoption. Moving children from foster care to same-sex couples may appear to solve one problem, but, in fact, it creates an even greater problem. States should not place children in harm's way. Make no mistake, *the hand that rocks the cradle rules the world.*

Children raised by homosexuals are more likely to engage in same-sex sexual relationships, and thus open themselves up for increased physical and mental health problems as well as social challenges. When considering the best interest of children, disease and life expectancy should also be considered. It is not in the best interest of children to place them in homes where they are more likely to become orphans or be tugged apart by frequent custody battles or placed in the midst of rotating sexual partners. The adopted child of the first homosexual adoptive parents in New Jersey[39] was orphaned at age five, when both homosexual parents died of disease.

Although statistics cannot characterize every situation, as there are exceptions to most rules, due to equal protection concerns, an adoption policy must either open the door to all homosexual adoptions or to none. In other words, if adoption were open to homosexuals, then it must be open to both male and female homosexuals, and if open to homosexuals, it must be open to bisexuals and transsexuals. The legislature may not pick and chose between male and female homosexual parents, nor may such a policy favor only AIDS-infected or hard-to-place children. Adoption is all or nothing. Either homosexuals may adopt or they may not. There are many reasons adoption should not be open to those engaged in homosexual activity.

A mountain of research has concluded that children raised in single-sex households (ones that lack either a mother or a father) "are at greater risk for a large number of serious personal and social problems, even after controlling for race, income and family background."[40] If, after eliminating income as a factor, the research shows that children raised in single-sex households fare poorly compared to their counterparts raised by a mother and a father, then doubling the sex (male-male or female-female) will logically fare no better, especially when considering the developmental stages that children experience.

Psychological Health

As early as fourteen months of age and between ages eighteen and thirty-six months, a young boy learns to establish his physical and gender identity, and if the father is absent, the result can be traumatic.[41] A study of seven hundred junior high school students showed significantly less persistent symptoms of depression in households with a mother and a father as compared to a single-parent household.[42] The absent father syndrome has been found to increase the likelihood of drug addiction and depression.[43] A Swedish study found that children raised in single-parent families were 56 percent more likely to develop signs of mental illness than children raised in an intact married home with a mother and father.[44]

Children raised in single-sex households are at greater risk of suicide than children living with their natural parents.[45] Although the increased risk of suicide may or may not be traceable solely to single-sex parenting, it is certainly related to divorce,[46] and most children living in same-sex households have experienced the divorce of their natural parents. Thus, the psychological trauma is even greater because these children have to cope with both divorce and changing gender roles.[47]

On average, mental illness is more prevalent in the homosexual community. A national survey of lesbians, published in the *Journal of Consulting and Clinical Psychology*, found that 75 percent of the nearly two thousand respondents pursued psychological counseling of some kind, and many had obtained long-term treatment for depression.[48] These findings were confirmed by studying twins, where the researchers concluded that the homosexual twins were 6.5 times more likely than their heterosexual twins to have attempted suicide.[49] Other research, published in the *Archives of General Psychiatry* under the title "Same-Sex Sexual Behavior and Psychiatric Disorders," found that homosexuals are three times more likely than heterosexuals to suffer from mood disorders, five times more likely to suffer from bipolar disorders (manic depression), and twice as likely to suffer from major depression, neuroses, eating disorders, and phobias.[50] Research has confirmed that even in gay-friendly countries, such as the Netherlands where same-sex marriage is legal, homosexuality poses a substantially increased risk of mental illness.[51]

Social Development

A critical analysis of the studies relied upon by some homosexual advocacy groups reveals serious flaws in the research methodology, leading other social scientists to dismiss the data as scientifically unfounded. A review of the homosexual parenting studies conducted by Robert Lerner, Ph.D. and Althea K. Nagai, Ph.D. found "that the methods used in these studies are so flawed that the studies prove nothing."[52] A detailed chart containing their findings is included in their book.[53] The extensive survey indicates that every one of the studies reviewed fails in at least one of ten tests for scientific accuracy. Some of the common problems include: (1) failure to use a testable hypothesis, or an attempt to prove a negative hypothesis;[54] (2) lack of control methods (including not controlling variables like income and education and no comparison to heterosexual households);[55] (3) no references to the measures used to establish the validity of the studies;[56] (4) absence of representative samples including self-selected sample groups;[57] and (5) failure to show that the results are not a function of chance factors.[58]

Professors Judith Stacey and Timothy Biblarz, at the University of Southern California, examined twenty-one studies on parenting by homosexuals and found serious problems with both the methodology and the conclusions of the studies.[59] The authors found that "there are no studies of child development based on random, representative samples of [same-sex] families."[60] An older study examining the then-existing research on gay parenting similarly questioned the validity of the research. The author notes that the studies involved small, self-selected samples.[61]

"Research findings to date are not definitive, however, because most of the studies are based on small samples of convenience, retrospective data, or self-report instruments subject to social desirability biases."[62]

A commentary on the research by openly lesbian Charlotte Patterson of the University of Virginia reveals "deeply flawed quantitative studies using nonprobability samples," meaning the study participants were not randomly selected.[63] The subjects in Dr. Patterson's study were self-selected, raising the problem that "when either or both the study and comparison groups know the purpose of the study and have a large stake in the substantive outcome, one almost inevitably introduces very serious sample selection biases into a study. The participants have every incentive to paint themselves in the best possible light."[64] In addition, Dr. Patterson's study relied on a small sample of ninety-five people.[65] Patterson herself admits that the studies present "methodological challenges," and raise serious questions "with regard to sampling issues, statistical power, and other technical matters," that they lack "control groups," involve "relatively small samples," and the "assessment procedures" are inadequate.[66]

In an unsuccessful challenge to Florida's adoption statute, Dr. Patterson testified on behalf of the homosexual plaintiffs. In dismissing the case, the court described Dr. Patterson's testimony as "questionable."[67] The court further noted:

> Dr. Patterson's impartiality also came into question when prior to trial, she refused to turn over to her own attorneys copies of documentation utilized by her in her studies. This court ordered her to do so (both sides having stipulated to the Order), yet she unilaterally refused despite the continued efforts on the part of her attorneys to have her do so. Both sides stipulated that Dr. Patterson's conduct was a clear violation of this court's order. Her attorneys requested that sanctions be limited to the exclusion of her personal studies at trial and this court agreed to do so.[68]

Another example involves the study by Dr. Melanie Kirkpatrick. Both samples in this study were recruited through advertisements in feminist publications, which "is likely to minimize rather than maximize differences between homosexual and heterosexual respondents."[69]

The study by Drs. Tasker and Golombok begins with a hypothesis that there is no difference between homosexual and heterosexual parents, a hypothesis that is impossible to confirm.[70] In addition, the study did not take into consideration significant differences in extraneous variables present in the homosexual and heterosexual control groups.[71]

Although David K. Flaks employed a comparison group matched with the homosexual parents, the matching was imprecise.[72] In the study the homosexual group was on average older and more educated than the heterosexual group, the homosexual mothers was less likely to work outside of the home, and the homo-sexual parents and their partners were likely to make more money.[73] The existing studies on same-sex parenting present an impossible task of "mak[ing] large scale generalizations . . . that would be applicable to all children."[74] Researchers have uni-versally concluded that the gay parenting studies are flawed for numerous reasons.[75]

The avalanche of criticism against gay parenting studies has led many same-sex proponents to abandon arguments that there is no difference between children raised in same-sex households compared to those raised in heterosexual house-holds.[76] Kate Kendall of the National Center for Lesbian Rights stated, "There's only one response to a study that children raised by lesbian and gay parents may be somewhat more likely to reject notions of rigid sexual orientation—that response has to be elation."[77] The significance of these differences can be a matter of opin-ion, but the existence of differences is an increasingly well-accepted fact.[78]

An Australian sociologist compared one hundred and seventy-four elementary school children living in three different types of households consisting of 58 chil-dren of heterosexual cohabitating couples, 58 children of heterosexual married cou-ples, and 58 children of homosexual couples, of which 47 were lesbian and 11 gay men, all of which included at least one of their biological parents.[79] All these chil-dren were being raised by couples, not single parents. The study found that the children of married couples fared best, and the children of homosexual couples did worst in nine out of thirteen categories, which included language, mathematics, sports, sociability, attitude regarding school and learning, parent-school relation-ship, sex identity relating to gender roles, school-related support (referring to par-ents helping with homework), and parental aspirations for the children's education and career goals. Three of the areas in which children of homosexuals scored higher included social studies, personal autonomy of the child, and household tasks.[80] The report noted that there were no significant differences regarding control and pun-ishment of the children. "Overall, the study has shown that children of married cou-ples are more likely to do well in school, in academic and social terms, than children of cohabitating heterosexual and homosexual couples. . . . Married couples seem to offer the best environment for a child's social and educational development."[81]

Children of homosexual parents also show increased promiscuity generally and are therefore at greater risk for teen pregnancy, sexually transmitted diseases, and AIDS. Despite their personal bias favoring same-sex parenting and fervent attacks on those who disagree, professors Stacey and Biblarz acknowledged that "recent stud-ies indicate a higher proportion of children of lesbigay parents are themselves apt to engage in homosexual activity."[82] A "significantly greater proportion of young adult children raised by lesbian than heterosexual mothers . . . reported having had a homo-erotic relationship (6 of the 25 young adults raised by lesbian mothers—24 percent compared with 0 of the 20 raised by heterosexual mothers). . . . Relative to their counterparts with heterosexual parents, the adolescent and young adult girls raised by lesbian mothers appear to have been more sexually adventurous and less chaste. . . . Children raised by lesbian co-parents should and do seem to grow up more open to homoerotic relationships."[83] Other studies confirm that "children raised by homosexuals were found to have greater parental encouragement for cross-gender behavior [and] greater amounts of cross-dressing and cross-gender play/role behavior."[84] "Children (especially girls) raised by lesbians appear to depart from traditional gender-based norms, while children raised by heterosexual mothers appear to conform to them."[85]

Although the best information available indicates that approximately 1.4 percent of the female population consider themselves to be homosexual or bisexual, and about 2.8 percent of the male population identify themselves in this way,[86] one study found that 12 percent of children of lesbians became active lesbians themselves, a rate almost seven times the base rate of lesbianism in the entire adult female population.[87] Another study found that 9 percent of the adult sons of homosexual fathers grew up to practice homosexuality, a rate that is three times higher than the average male population.[88] Another study found that none of the children in the heterosexual families experienced a lesbian or gay relationship; in contrast, of the children raised in homosexual families, 29 percent of the daughters and 13 percent of the sons reported having at least one same-sex relationship.[89] An article published in the *Archives of Sexual Behavior* reviewing the existing studies concluded that "children raised by homosexuals were found to have greater parental encouragement for cross-gender behavior [and] greater amounts of cross-dressing and cross-gender play/role behavior."[90] Numerous studies on single-sex parenting reveal that adolescents raised without both their mother and father are more sexually promiscuous.[91]

Another study found a significant increase in the risk of incest among children raised by homosexual parents. "A disproportionate percentage—29 percent of the adult children of homosexual parents had been specifically subjected to sexual molestation by that homosexual parent, compared to only 0.6 percent of the adult children of heterosexual parents having reported sexual relations with their parent. . . . Having a homosexual parent(s) appears to increase the risk of incest with a parent by a factor of about 50."[92]

Other Life Factors

Children who engage in homosexuality (as children or adults) will experience the same physical health complications and mortality rates as those who currently practice homosexuality. Additionally, mortality rates of the parents, combined with the short duration of homosexual relationships, particularly among males, will complicate the children's lives in several ways. Most children in same-sex households are already the product of divorce, which exponentially increases the risk of suicide. Children who are raised by homosexual parents, whether or not the product of divorce, are more likely than children raised by heterosexual parents to lose one of their same-sex parents before they reach adulthood by reason of disease or termination of the relationship.

Children raised in single-sex households experience an increase in infant mortality by about 50 percent.[93] Even adjusting for age, race, education, and poverty, infant mortality among singe-sex parents is significantly increased. This is evidenced by many factors and is confirmed by a high infant mortality rate in countries such as Sweden, where there is a nationalized health care system that provides strong support for single parents.[94] Children raised in single-sex households commit more crime and have higher delinquency rates.[95] Living in a home with a nonbiological parent "has turned out to be the most powerful predictor of severe child abuse yet."[96] One researcher found that a preschooler living with a nonbiological father was forty times more likely to be sexually abused than one living with two biological parents.[97] "Children of divorced or unwed parents have lower grades and other measures of academic achievement, are more likely to be held back and less likely to finish high school."[98]

The same-sex marriage movement is dangerous to the best interests and well-being of our children and grandchildren. Homosexual advocacy groups are aggressively targeting children and youth. If same-sex marriage were legalized, more children would be caught in the crosshairs of what amounts to a sexualized political revolution.

In one study of lesbian couples with children, the authors reported, "Even individuals who believe that same-sex relationships are a legitimate choice for adults may feel that children will suffer from being raised in such families."[99]

Someone might say, "I'm personally opposed to same-sex marriage, but I don't see how allowing two people of the same sex to marry will affect me." Can you really continue to ignore what is happening to our children? Will you go about your daily routine overlooking the harm inflicted on children by those who want to abolish any and all sexual restraints? In this information age, you have no excuse for ignorance.

Take a few moments and look closely into the eyes of a five-year-old child. Pause your thoughts for at least thirty seconds. Is it honestly appropriate to encourage children to experiment with their "sexual identity" at such a tender age? You may not think same-sex marriage will affect you, but you are wrong. It will affect you, and most importantly, it will affect the children. We have no right to experiment with their destiny.

CHAPTER 4
From Desensitization to Conversion

*M*arshall Kirk and Hunter Madsen articulated an elaborate strategy for achieving acceptance of homosexuality and ultimately of entirely transforming marriage and the traditional family. Being homosexual themselves, Kirk and Madsen wrote a book entitled *After the Ball*, which has become a "guiding manifesto" for "pragmatic gay activism." Both are Harvard trained. Kirk is a researcher in neuropsychiatry, a logician, and a poet who writes full-time from his home in Cambridge, Massachusetts; Madsen, who calls San Francisco his home, received his doctorate in politics and is an expert in public persuasion and social marketing. The book they coauthored touts itself as "laying the groundwork for the next stage of the gay revolution."[1]

In order to achieve acceptability of gays and lesbians, Kirk and Madsen declare what has become obvious to anyone who has encountered the same-sex movement, namely, for the gay agenda to achieve success, homosexuals need to be portrayed as "victims," and those who oppose them must be vilified. "In any campaign to win over the public, gays must be portrayed as victims in need of protection so that straights will be inclined by reflex to adopt the role of protector."[2] Ads should feature gays as "wholesome and admirable."[3] "It makes no difference that the ads are lies; not to us, because we're using them to ethically good effect."[4] The media must be used to "desensitize straights to gays and gayness."[5]

The objective of vilifying those who oppose homosexuality is to make them look "so nasty that the average American will want to dissociate themselves from them."[6] "We also intend, by this tactic, to make the very expression of homohatred so discreditable that even Intransigents [sic] will eventually be silenced in public—much as rabid racists and anti-Semites are today. The best way to make homohatred look bad is to vilify those who victimize gays."[7] Those who oppose homosexuality, they say, should be compared to the "Klansmen demanding that gays be slaughtered or castrated," "hysterical backwoods preachers, drooling with hate to a degree that looks both comical and deranged," "menacing punks, thugs, and convicts that speak coolly about the 'fags' they have bashed or would like to bash," and to "Nazis."[8] Kirk and Madsen go on to say that "gays can undermine the moral authority of homo-hating churches over less fervent adherents by portraying such institutions as anti-quated backwaters, badly out of step with the times and with the latest findings of psychology."[9]

Kirk and Madsen set forth a media propaganda campaign that is designed to fol-low three stages, which they call desensitization, jamming, and conversion. The the-ory behind the desensitization phase is that "novelties cease to be novel if they just stick around long enough; they also cease to activate alerting mechanisms."[10] This phase of the campaign is designed "to desensitize straights to gays and gayness, inun-date them in a continuous flood of gay-related advertising, presented in the least offensive fashion possible. If straights can't shut off the shower, they may at least even-tually get used to being wet."[11]

The next phase in the quest to move from desensitization to conversion involves jamming. "As the name implies, Jamming involves the insertion into the engine of a pre-existing, incompatible emotional response, gridlocking its mechanisms as thoroughly as though one had sprinkled fine sand into the workings of an old-fashioned pocket watch."[12] Jamming uses a psychological process known as associa-tive conditioning (when two feelings are juxtaposed—one good and one bad or indifferent—in order to transfer the one feeling over and in place of the other) and direct emotional modeling (the tendency to feel what you perceive others are feel-ing). The goal here is to make those who oppose homosexuality feel shame, and thus the same-sex marriage movement will link repugnant images to those who oppose the agenda. These images include being labeled a bigot, being filled with hate, and being perceived with respect to homosexuality like the Klu Klux Klan is to African-Americans.[13]

The "desensitization" and "jamming" phases are part of a strategy leading up to what Kirk and Madsen call "conversion."

> By Conversion, we actually mean something far more profoundly threatening to the American Way of Life, without which no truly sweep-ing social change can occur. We mean conversion of the average American's emotions, mind, and will, through a planned psychological attack, in the form of propaganda fed to the nation via the media. We mean "subverting" the mechanism of prejudice to our own ends—using

the very processes that made Americans hate us to turn their hatred into warm regard—whether they like it or not.[14]

The authors' objective is to portray an image of homosexuals as normal, but they do not intend permanently to disassociate themselves from the more bizarre elements of the homosexual community:

Our ultimate objective is to expand straight tolerance so much that even gays who look unconventional can feel safe and accepted. But like it or not, by the very nature of the psychological mechanism, desensitization works gradually or not at all. For the moment, therefore, unconventional-looking gays are encouraged to live their lives as usual, but out of the lime-light. Drag queens must understand that the gay stereotype is already heavily skewed in their direction, and that more balance should be achieved by leaning in the opposite direction for a while. In time, as hos-tilities subside and stereotypes weaken, we see no reason why more and more diversity should not be introduced into the projected image. This would be healthy for society as well as for gays.[15]

The homosexual propaganda campaign begins with an attempt to fool the gen-eral public into thinking that there is no difference between heterosexuals and homosexuals, and then once accepted, to push for expanded protection for an assortment of sexual paraphilias. "First, you get your foot in the door, by being as *similar* as possible; then, and only then—when your one little difference is finally accepted—can you start dragging in your other peculiarities, one by one. You ham-mer in the wedge narrow end first. As the saying goes, Allow the camel's nose beneath your tent, and his whole body will soon follow."[16]

Although written in 1987 as a satirical piece to mock religious foes of homo-sexuality, the *Homosexual Manifesto*[17] is at the same time shocking in its assertions while revealing in its similarities to the political agenda advanced today by same-sex marriage advocates.[18]

We shall sodomize your sons, emblems of your feeble masculinity, of your shallow dreams and vulgar lies. We shall seduce them in your schools . . . in your seminaries, in your youth groups, in your movie the-ater bathrooms . . . in your houses of Congress, wherever men are with men together. . . . All laws banning homosexual activity will be revoked. Instead, legislation shall be passed which engenders love between men. . . . There will be no compromises. We are not middle-class weaklings. . . . Those who oppose us will be exiled. . . . The family unit, which only dampens imagination and curbs free will, must be eliminated. . . . All churches who condemn us will be closed.[19]

The media propaganda campaign is not the only assault being waged by the same-sex marriage movement. Legal and legislative battles include (1) lowering the age of consent to permit sex between adults and minors, (2) silencing opposition to the homosexual agenda through the passage of hate crimes laws, diversity training programs, gay tolerance codes, and mandatory counseling, (3) passing "sexual orientation," "gender identity" or "gender expression laws," (4) passing domestic partnership laws and forcing employers that contract with government entities to enact such laws no matter where the employer is located, (5) invalidating laws prohibiting adoption by same-sex couples, (6) passing laws allowing transsexuals to change their sex designated on their birth certificates, (7) abolishing gender and thus making the sex of male and female irrelevant, and (8) challenging state and federal laws which ban same-sex marriage.[20]

It takes no stretch of the imagination to envision the consequences stemming from extending legally protected rights to engage in any private consensual same-sex activity. Incremental extension of rights and benefits to those engaged in homosexual conduct lead to results that are far-reaching and disastrous.

In 1999, the Vermont Supreme Court declared that same-sex couples were entitled to the same benefits and protections as married couples and mandated that the legislature enact laws to provide those benefits and protections.[21] Some of the reasons relied upon by the court included that (1) "Sexual Orientation is among the categories specifically protected against hate-motivated crimes in Vermont," thus belying the fact that the state frowns upon same-sex unions,[22] (2) Vermont had enacted statewide legislation prohibiting discrimination on the basis of sexual orientation, and (3) Vermont had removed barriers to adoption by same-sex couples by extending legal rights and protections to couples who dissolve their "domestic relationship."[23] The incremental steps that the state of Vermont took over the years led the Vermont Supreme Court to conclude that the state had abandoned its longstanding disapproval of same-sex unions, and, therefore, that there was no reason to exclude homosexuals from marriage or marriage-like benefits.

An address given by Kees Waaldjik, a professor who wrote the Netherland's same-sex-marriage bill, also demonstrates how incremental steps led to the Dutch same-sex marriage law and ultimately mandated full acceptance of same-sex marriage.[24]

> Legislative recognition of homosexuality starts with decriminalization, followed or sometimes accompanied by the setting of an equal age of consent, after which anti-discrimination legislation can be introduced, before the process is finished with legislation recognizing same-sex partnership and parenting.

The "law of standard sequences" implies . . . that . . . each step seems to operate as a stimulating factor for the next step. For example, once a legislature has enacted that it is wrong to treat someone differently because of his or her homosexual orientation, it becomes all the more suspect that the same legislature is preserving rules of family law that do precisely that.[25]

He then goes on to explain the "extremely gradual and almost perversely nuanced (but highly successful) process of legislative recognition of same-sex partnership in the Netherlands."

Since the 1970s and 1980s Dutch cohabiting couples have increasingly been given similar legal rights and duties as married couples. One after the other changes were introduced in rent law, in social security and income tax, in the rules on immigration, state pensions, and death duties, and in many other fields. And in none of these fields any distinction was made between heterosexual and homosexual cohabitation. There was never a "law on same-sex cohabitation." All recognition was given in the context of a more general overhaul of the rules of a specific field. Simultaneously cohabitation contracts and partner testaments became common, and were fully recognized by the courts. This evolution was more or less completed when it was made illegal for any employer and for any provider of goods or services, to distinguish between married and unmarried couples. . . .

In the 1970's fostering became a possibility for gay and lesbian and other unmarried couples. Having a homosexual orientation or relationship stopped being a bar to keeping (access to) your children after a divorce. And the newer form of de facto parenting by same-sex couples, artificial insemination by women in lesbian relationships, was never banned in the Netherlands. . . . On 1 January 1998 legislation came into force making joint authority [over children] also available to same-sex couples.

So what to mankind, and to all its representatives at this conference, may seem a giant step—the opening up of the institution of marriage to same-sex couples—will, for the Dutch, only be another small change.[26]

Waaldjik's paper reveals that changes in the law tend to happen at a slow, incremental pace. Legalizing same-sex marriage would "radically alter" and permanently abolish the marriage institution.[27] The outspoken homosexual activist, Michelangelo Signorile, acknowledged that the goal of the homosexual movement is to "fight for same-sex marriage and its benefits and then, once granted, redefin[e] the institution of marriage completely, to demand the right to marry not as a way of adhering to society's moral codes but rather to debunk America and radically alter an archaic institution."[28] Don't think for one moment that the same-sex marriage movement will be content with huddling under the "marriage" umbrella. Once the same-sex marriage barrier is broken, a wide range of sexual paraphilia rights are sure to follow, including, but not limited to, pedophilia (sex with children). If you think I'm exaggerating, one such advocate admits that the "ultimate goal" is "not just equal rights for 'lesbians and gay men,' but also freedom of sexual expression for young people and children."[29]

A gay man's life is almost always promiscuous, and as such, risky and downright dangerous. Although setting forth the following as a critique of this lifestyle, Kirk and Madsen accurately describe how this comes about:

> When one is young and inexperienced, the tamest, most vanilla-flavored gay sex—mere cuddling and mutual masturbation—is more than enough to do the trick; it's new and forbidden, "dirty," and exciting. As one gains experience, vanilla sex with one partner becomes familiar, tame, and boring, and loses its capacity to arouse. At first, the increasingly jaded gay man seeks novelty in partners, rather than practices, and becomes massively promiscuous; eventually, all bodies become boring, and only new practices will thrill. Two major avenues diverge in this yellow wood, two nerves upon which to press: that of raunch, and that of aggression.[30]

Kirk and Madsen then go on to describe grotesque kinds of sex, including fetishes and sadomasochism. They also write about their experiences with "restroom sex" while at Harvard, and to their credit, argue that such sexual urges ought to be controlled, not because they are necessarily wrong, but because such antics won't be viewed well by the greater heterosexual populace, and that is, after all, their target audience.

Later in their book Kirk and Madsen engage in a discussion about finding "Mr. Right." "Who is he, this unattainable Platonic ideal, this golem stalking our love lives? And why do we continue to yearn for him after he disappoints us time and time again? Are we mad?"[31] The "preponderance of gay men . . . [will] spend the next twenty years wandering from bar to bar, humming, 'Someday My Prince Will Come.'"[32] Unable to find "Mr. Right," the gay man, "bowing to the inevitable," settles for an "open relationship" which allows him to temporarily find a partner while the two mutually agree to have other sex partners.[33] A "restless gay man is more apt to be led astray by a cute face in the subway or supermarket. Two gay men are double trouble."[34] Former practicing homosexual William Aaron explains why homosexual men do not practice monogamy. He writes: "In the gay life, fidelity is almost impossible. Since part of the compulsion of homosexuality seems to be a need on the part of the homophile to 'absorb' masculinity from his sexual partners, he must be constantly on the lookout for [new partners]. Consequently the most successful homophile 'marriages' are those where there is an arrangement between the two to have affairs on the side while maintaining the semblance of permanence in their living arrangements."[35]

In order to understand the goal of the homosexual agenda of moving from merely being tolerated by heterosexuals to dominating them, you have to understand the general psyche of the movement. A good friend of mine, who grew up thinking he was gay and enmeshed himself into the gay lifestyle, anonymous sex and all, but who did find "Mr. Right" (Jesus Christ) and is now happily married to a woman, revealed to me a perceptive insight that is relevant here.

I described to him an event where I spoke at a public meeting about a proposed "sexual orientation" ordinance. After the homosexuals won that first round of public meetings by a narrow vote, I approached some leaders of the gay organizations and held out my hand as a gesture to shake their hands. No one from the group would shake my hand, and instead, after the media had left, they began raising their voices and calling me names.

Unable to speak rationally with them, I held out my hand in one last attempt, but no one would take it. One person asked, "Why do you want to shake my hand," to which I responded, "Because I want to let you know that I don't hate you. I don't agree with your actions, but I respect you as a person."

No luck. No one would shake my hand. I told my friend, "When the media is present, these gay activists present a pleasant public persona and make us look like villains, ascribing to our motives and actions invectives that are simply not true, making us look like bigots. But when the media is not around, these same people do exactly what they wrongfully accuse us of doing, and they act so childish. Why is that?"

He answered, "Because they are emotionally arrested. They are fourteen-year-olds with a forty-year-old's bank account." Don't get me wrong. This statement is not meant to demean, to belittle, or to create a strawman argument so I can easily knock down the opponent. This statement is merely meant to be descriptive, and in reality, the more you understand the homosexual psyche, the more you will come to realize the truth of this statement.

As this book points out elsewhere, homosexuality is caused primarily by developmental and environmental factors. The emotional development of most gays and lesbians has been prematurely arrested, almost frozen in time, as it were, at the adolescent development stage. Although what we typically deal with in this arena is adults, they are emotional adolescents in an adult body. The combination can be lethal. Armed with more wisdom and financial resources than an adolescent but filled with the conflicting and premature emotions of an adolescent, the resulting expression can, at times, appear rational and at other times wildly insane.

As with any adolescent, they have an urge to rebel, to throw tantrums, to be self-ish, and to seek revenge. They need self-esteem, desire approval, and congregate in cliques. And when you cross their path at the wrong time, when you challenge their actions, or more particularly their essence, be careful because you will experience their rage. In their mind they are right and the world is wrong, outdated, and out of step with the times.

To those of us who believe that homosexuality is wrong, unnatural, and that a person can choose to leave the gay lifestyle, and to those of us who believe in marriage between one man and one woman, the homosexual movement first holds out the olive branch of "tolerance," but the real goal is to convert you and then dominate the opposition. Total repression of any opposing voice, vilification of any person who stands in their way, absolute dominance of the culture—these are the goals of the homosexual movement, part of which are being advanced by the same-sex marriage agenda.

The same-sex marriage movement is radical at its very core and will surely desta-bilize society. While the cameras are rolling and the journalists are writing, the face of the same-sex marriage movement may present itself as tolerant, even mainstream, but the agenda is intolerant and radical. If the camel's nose ever gets underneath the tent, the tent is history. The camel is coming, but it's not too late to prevent the creature from bringing down the house.

CHAPTER 5
Silencing the Opposition

*T*he homosexual and same-sex marriage agenda poses one of the biggest threats to religious liberty and freedom of speech. Although you'll hear rhetoric about tolerance and equal rights, the movement is anything but tolerant.

Consider for a moment the case of Cheryl Clark and Elsey McLeod in Denver, Colorado. Shortly after the two entered into a lesbian relationship, Ms. Clark adopted a child from China. Ms. McLeod was not part of the adoption and did not pay the adoption expenses. Ms. Clark finalized the adoption, and then sometime later she became a Christian. She then felt convicted that the lesbian relationship between her and Ms. McLeod was wrong, so she took her child and went her separate way. Months later Ms. McLeod filed suit, claiming that she, who has no legal parental rights over the child, should be awarded custody and visitation. She also complained about the fact that Ms. Clark attended a church that believed in marriage between one man and one woman. In the lobby of Ms. Clark's church was a literature rack containing, among other items, literature from Focus on the Family and Promise Keepers.

The trial judge, John W. Coughlin, ruled that (1) Ms. McLeod, who legally has no parental rights over the child, should be awarded parental and visitation rights, and most importantly, (2) *Ms. Clark, the child's mother, must not "expose" her minor child to any "religious teachings or upbringing" that "may" be considered "homophobic."* Under this court order, Ms. Clark would be in contempt of court if (1) she were reading chapter 1 of the book of Romans with her daughter, (2) she and her daughter attended church and the pastor preached on marriage between one man and one woman or on homosexuality, (3) the pro-family literature remained in the church's literature rack, (4) she and her daughter were riding in the car listening to a Christian radio program addressing the subject of traditional marriage or homosexuality, or (5) she sent her child to a Christian church or Sunday school where the topic of marriage or homosexuality was discussed.[1] This case is a harbinger of things to come if the same-sex marriage movement is not defeated.

Consider another case involving Linda Kantaras. The scene begins with Margo Kantaras born indisputably as a woman in Ohio. Long after reaching adulthood, Margo watches a program on MTV regarding transsexuals undergoing sex-change surgery. Margo then moves to Texas and enrolls for sex-change surgery at the Rosenberg Clinic. She begins taking testosterone hormones for a year and then undergoes a total mastectomy and hysterectomy. Margo continues to retain her female vagina, and she does not have surgery to implant artificial male genitalia. Margo then changes her name to "Michael" and moves to Florida. Margo/Michael meets Linda, who is pregnant with a child from a broken relationship. Margo/Michael befriends Linda, and although Linda knows that Margo/Michael is a transsexual, that she retains her female genitalia and lacks male genitalia, the two become friends, and eventually they travel to Seminole County, Florida, where Margo/Michael fills out a marriage application form stating she is "male." The two then become "married." A second child is born to Linda by artificial insemination, the donor being Margo/Michael's brother.

Margo/Michael refuses to allow Linda to attend church, so Linda secretly begins attending a Bible study with a friend at a local fast-food restaurant. One day Linda accepts Jesus as her Lord and Savior and becomes a Christian. Within a day or two, Linda is convicted that the relationship she is in with Margo/Michael is wrong. Linda tells Margo/Michael, and soon Margo/Michael files for "divorce" and seeks custody of Linda's two children.

The National Center for Lesbian Rights, headquartered in San Francisco, takes up Margo/Michael's case and flies in "experts" in transsexualism who testify during a three-week trial that was broadcast on Court TV. These so-called "experts" testify that "gender" is primarily in your mind, not in your biology or physiology.

Trial judge Gerard O'Brien issues a nine-hundred-plus-page opinion, in which he block quotes huge sections from various law review articles and several international cases. Judge O'Brien rules that the notion of gender as binary (male and female) is an "outdated 19th century" concept, and that sex or gender is primarily a state of mind. Thus, the essence of his ruling is that a person who is one sex but thinks or wants to be another sex should legally be considered so, and thus Florida's law banning same-sex marriage was not violated. The judge ruled that although Margo/Michael was born female with XX chromosomes, she became "harmonized" by undergoing plastic surgery to match her body and mind, and thus, for purposes of marriage, she should be considered "male."

Margo/Michael is "harmonized," the judge said, but Linda is not. The judge noted that Linda's Christian beliefs have caused her to reject lesbianism and transsexualism as normative, and thus these beliefs would drive a wedge between Linda's own children and Margo/Michael. Despite the fact that Linda is a fit parent, is the biological mother of both children, and the uncontradicted testimony declared that Linda's children want to be with her, Judge O'Brien removed them from their mom and gave custody to the transsexual, Margo/Michael. All this happened despite the testimony that when asked by Linda's son why Margo/Michael did not have a male sex organ, Margo/Michael would tell the young boy that "it falls off" when you reach the mid-thirties![2]

The two cases of Cheryl Clark and Linda Kantaras are merely portents of what's to come if we cross the gender divide and legalize same-sex marriage. Indeed, if this were to happen, these cases would become routine and no longer seem bizarre. We would incur even more severe encroachments on parental rights and individual liberty.

In order to advance the same-sex marriage movement, homosexual advocacy groups are calling for the passage of local and federal laws adding "sexual orientation" to the list of hate crimes. If "sexual orientation" hate crime laws are adopted, the impact of these laws could prove disastrous for people of faith and those who oppose homosexuality as normative. Every state has laws that prohibit conspiracy to commit crimes. It is conceivable that preaching or teaching against homosexual conduct could be prosecuted as conspiracy to commit a hate crime. For instance, a minister could preach a sermon that urges those listening to "actively oppose the promotion or acceptance of the homosexual lifestyle in the community." An individual who hears this message and applies it in a way prohibited by the hate crimes law could be prosecuted under such a law, and the minister could also be prosecuted for conspiracy.

The possibility for prosecution is likely in states with expansive definitions of conspiracy where the law only requires "agreement" to pursue an objective that may be lawful (i.e., opposition to the homosexual lifestyle) in an unlawful manner and that the crime committed was a natural and foreseeable consequence of the agreement. As long as a jury could find that there was an agreement to oppose the homosexual lifestyle and that the crime (unlawful means of pursuing the objective) was a natural and foreseeable consequence of the sermon, the minister could be convicted.

You should also be aware that some crimes covered by hate crimes laws do not involve physical contact with the alleged victim. Some crimes involve mere "intimidation," or a "threat" or "force of threat" to commit a crime. An alleged victim could claim that he was "intimidated" or "threatened" in regard to his person or property, and could further claim that since he was homosexual, that this "intimidation" or "threat" was because of his "sexual orientation," and thus the prosecutor could enhance the crime by applying the hate crimes law. It should be clearly understood that hate crimes laws cover more than what the average person considers to be a violent physical crime.

As an example of how prosecution for "hate speech" or hate crimes could come about, consider the fact that many homosexual activists accuse Christian conservatives of causing the death of Matthew Shepard, an openly gay college student who was beaten to death in Wyoming. During the *Today Show* on October 12, 1998, shortly after the death of Matthew Shepard, reporter Katie Couric stated:

> Some gay-rights activists have said that some conservative Christian political organizations, like the Christian Coalition, the Family Research Council and Focus on the Family, are contributing to this anti-homosexual atmosphere by having an ad campaign saying, "If you're a homosexual, you can change your orientation." That prompts people to say, "If I meet someone who's homosexual, I'm going to take action and try and convince them or try to harm them." Do you believe that such groups are contributing to this climate?[3]

To his credit, Wyoming Governor Jim Geringer, who was asked the question, stated in reply that he would not "trade one type of stereotype or hate for another" and that listeners shouldn't "categorize people unfairly."[4]

As a further example by a governmental body in this country, the consolidated City and County of San Francisco sent a letter of condemnation to several conservative Christian organizations denouncing their "role" in the death of Matthew Shepard. Several pro-family groups sought to place advertisements in the San Francisco media regarding the "Love Won Out" campaign. This advertising campaign was designed to run full-page newspaper ads that were not condemnatory or critical; rather, the ads stated that change is possible for those who desire to leave homosexuality. The city condemned the ads and urged the media not to run them. The city then issued the following letter:

> I am writing at the direction of the Board of Supervisors concerning hate crimes which was [sic] discussed at their meeting of October 13, 1998. Supervisor Leslie Katz denounces your hateful rhetoric against gays, lesbians and transgendered people. What happened to Matthew Shepard is in part due to *the message being espoused* by your groups that gays and lesbians are not worthy of the most basic equal rights and treatments. It is not an exaggeration to say that *there is a direct correlation between these acts of discrimination, such as when gays and lesbians are called sinful and when major religious organizations say they can change if they tried, and the horrible crimes committed against gays and lesbians.*[5]

Here we have a governmental body stating there is a "direct correlation" between the speech of conservative Christian organizations and hate crimes committed against homosexuals. This surely could form the basis for a prosecution related to conspiracy. Indeed, based on the opinion of the San Francisco governing authorities, conspiracy is not even required. The letter states there is a "direct correlation" between speech and hate crimes.

The City and County of San Francisco followed up this letter with a resolution condemning the Christian organizations for wanting to place ads with the local media. Again, these proposed ads, which were carefully crafted to offer Christian love in a noncondemning way, were cited by the city as hate speech that leads to hate crimes.[6] The city's resolution stated:

WHEREAS, A coalition of religious political conservative organizations have introduced a nationwide television advertisement campaign to encourage gays and lesbians to change their sexual orientation; and,

WHEREAS, This coalition includes the Family Research Council, the Concerned Women for America, and the Center for Reclaiming America; and,

WHEREAS, The aforementioned organizations promote an agenda which denies basic equal rights for gays and lesbians and routinely state their opposition to toleration of gay and lesbian citizens; and,

WHEREAS, The radical religious political conservative coalition previously introduced a printed advertisement campaign which a prominent San Francisco newspaper chose to accept and publish; and,

WHEREAS, The vast majority of medical, psychological, and sociological evidence supports the conclusion that sexual orientation cannot be changed; and,

WHEREAS, Advertising campaigns which insinuate sexual orientation can be changed by conversion therapy or other means are erroneous and full of lies; and,

WHEREAS, *Advertising campaigns which insinuate a gay or lesbian orientation is immoral and undesirable create an atmosphere which validates oppression of gays and lesbians and encourages maltreatment of gays and lesbians;* and,

WHEREAS, *There is a marked increase in anti-gay violence which coincides with defamatory and erroneous campaigns against gays and lesbians;* and,

WHEREAS, *An unfortunate, extreme result of these anti-gay campaigns is violence and even death;* now, therefore, be it

RESOLVED, That the Board of Supervisors of the City and County of San Francisco urges local television stations not to broadcast advertising campaigns aimed at "converting" homosexuals.[7]

At the time the above resolution was passed by San Francisco in 1998, Gavin Newsom served on the Board of Supervisors, and he voted in favor of the resolution. In December 2003, Newsom became the mayor of San Francisco. On January 20, 2004, Mayor Newsom attended President George W. Bush's State of the Union address as the guest of Democratic House Minority Leader Nancy Pelosi. During the president's remarks he spoke about marriage between one man and one woman. Two weeks later Newsom called a meeting with his staff to begin the process of issuing so-called same-sex "marriage licenses." His chief of staff, an openly gay man, called upon the National Center for Lesbian Rights for legal assistance. A meeting was soon convened that included the mayor's key staffers, the National Center for Lesbian Rights, the ACLU, and Equality California, a group that lobbies for same-sex marriage.

Once the plan was conceived to illegally change the marriage application forms, the city officials notified other government officials of their scheme, including the city attorney's office, two homosexual members of the city Board of Supervisors, Congresswoman Nancy Pelosi, Senator Dianne Feinstein, Democratic Committee Chairman Terry McAuliffe, and even California's Democratic attorney general, Bill Lockyer. On February 10, 2004, Mayor Newsom issued a press release stating his intentions. His staff selected two elderly women to receive the first "licenses," and then in a private ceremony on February 12 (a national holiday celebrating Lincoln's birthday), the mayor presided over the ceremony, and over four thousand such "licenses" were issued to same-sex couples.[8]

Mayor Newsom kept City Hall open on the weekend and two scheduled holidays (February 12, Lincoln's birthday; 14, Saturday; 15, Sunday; and 16, Presidents Day), and deputized hundreds of same-sex marriage activists to assist in processing these illegal licenses. These licenses were illegal because marriage law is a statewide policy which cannot be altered or amended by local government. The mayor had no more authority to issue same-sex marriage licenses than he had to declare war against a foreign nation. In performing these illegal acts, the mayor and his cohorts violated ten California civil laws, one criminal law, and two sections of the California constitution. Although the mayor recognized these laws banned same-sex marriage, he publicly refused to obey them.[9]

If government officials go so far as to issue a resolution labeling as hate speech any message that says homosexuality is wrong or is a choice, that such speech has a direct correlation to violent crime, and if they are willing to violate civil and criminal laws in order to push their same-sex marriage agenda, what do you think will happen to you if same-sex marriage becomes legal? If same-sex marriage proponents have their sexually immoral ideas enshrined in law, then people of faith and those who support the traditional family will have their speech deemed "hate speech" and their activities criminalized.

Homosexual organizations and governmental leaders who contend that speech against homosexuality is "hate speech" or causes hate crimes against homosexuals will use the force of law to crush their opposition. If you still believe that the same-sex marriage movement merely calls for tolerance, just look at the actions of Mayor Newsom. Well, you might say, "These events occurred in San Francisco, and that city is more liberal than most." I'll grant you that point, but on the issue of homosexuality, San Francisco is only more liberal than some parts of the country because it began the progression down the homosexual rights road in the 1970s, whereas other parts of the country didn't begin considering this issue until the 1980s or 1990s. San Francisco is thus a picture of the future. Moreover, ushering in same-sex marriage would be to morality and personal liberty what compounding interest is to investments. For a while, it may appear that the interest on the principle increases at glacial speed, but there is a point where the compounding factor takes off like a rocket. What took San Francisco thirty years to achieve would be accomplished in a few years if same-sex marriage were legalized. There are other cities that already come close to San Francisco in terms of creating a liberal environment for homosexuality.

I have encountered two sides of the homosexual agenda throughout this country. The public persona side presents the face of tolerance and equal rights. However, when the cameras are turned off and the reporters have hurriedly left to write their stories, these same people who smiled and spoke of tolerance have shouted epithets at me, written vile and false statements, and will do anything to vilify and demonize anyone who is opposed to homosexuality.

In reference to the above-mentioned San Francisco resolution, some of the pro-family groups filed suit against the city. A federal court ruled that the city of San Francisco had a "duty" to urge private media sources to refuse placement of the advertisements from Christian organizations, ads that merely advocated homosexuals can change their sexual preferences.[10] Doing its duty? Can you imagine if a city issued a resolution condemning homosexual behavior? Do you think a court would rule that the city was merely doing its duty? I think not. If there ever was a wolf in sheep's clothing, it is same-sex marriage. While it might appear gentle from the outside, once it undresses and reveals its true identity, the beast is ready to devour its opposition.

In other countries people of faith have faced prosecution for merely expressing opposition to homosexuality. No physical crime was necessary. Just pure speech that said homosexuality is wrong formed the basis of prosecution and fines. In order to consider the impact of legalizing same-sex marriage, we must consider what is occurring throughout the world. Some countries have progressed down the homosexual rights path farther than the United States. What's happening elsewhere is a road map of things to come if we sanction same-sex marriage in this country.

Antidiscrimination ordinances in other countries have been a source of increasing difficulties for religious organizations and clergy. For instance, Canada has a broad antidiscrimination provision in its Charter of Rights and Freedoms.[11] This provision has been interpreted to prohibit discrimination on the basis of "sexual orientation." The implications of this interpretation are troubling for religious organizations and clergy. Dr. Laura Schlessinger, the widely publicized talk show host, was rebuked by Canada's Broadcast Standards Council for her speech on homosexuality.[12] The Council stated that Dr. Laura's views on homosexuality required Canadian broadcasters who carry her show to make an announcement about the Council's ruling before the show is aired.

Dr. Jerry Falwell's *Old-Time Gospel Hour* program, which has aired in Canada for more than thirty years, must be edited to exclude any negative mention of homosexuality. The same program Dr. Falwell airs in the United States may not air in Canada because of the antidiscrimination provisions in that country. Other Christian broadcasters, such as Dr. James Dobson, also must edit their broadcasts of comments that might be deemed critical of homosexuality.[13]

A complaint was filed in Canada regarding an ad run in the Saskatoon *Star Phoenix* that displayed Bible verses against homosexuality.[14] The ad featured a drawing of two men holding hands with a diagonal line through a circle superimposed over the figure. Next to this image were several Scripture citations. The Saskatchewan Human Rights Commission forced the person who placed the ad and the newspaper that ran it to pay fines to each one of the three complainants and also required them to pay an additional $4,500 for the government's expert witnesses.[15] The Commission wrote in its order, "It is obvious that certain of the Biblical quotations suggest more dire consequences and there can be no question that the advertisement can be objectively seen as exposing homosexuals to hatred or ridicule."[16]

Similarly, a complaint was filed against Mayor Dianne Haskett of London, Ontario, who refused to declare Gay Pride Week. The Ontario Human Rights Commission found the mayor in violation of Canada's Human Rights Act and fined the city $10,000. Three weeks later Haskett won her contested mayoral election by a landslide.[17]

In other countries the same result is occurring. A broadcaster in the United Kingdom airing a program known as the "God Channel" was fined £20,000 (approximately $35,000 US at the time) for an ad that described homosexuality as an abomination.[18] The Independent Television Commission in the United Kingdom ruled that the ad violated several provisions of the advertising code because of its negative reference to homosexuality and fined the broadcaster.[19]

In a widely publicized incident, homosexuals filed a complaint in a Dutch court against Pope John Paul II for his statement that "homosexual acts are contrary to the laws of nature." The complaint was later dropped after the Dutch court ruled that the Pope's status as a leader of the Roman Catholic Church and the Vatican state afforded him immunity from prosecution.[20] However, antidiscrimination laws were the basis for the complaint against the Pope, and even though the Pope was immune because of his status, a priest would not enjoy the same immunity.

Sexual orientation antidiscrimination laws have a definite impact on freedom of speech and religion. Incrementalism leads down the road to antidiscrimination laws that elevate sexual behavior to a protected legal status. Further elevating sexual behavior by opening the door to same-sex marriage would exponentially expand homosexual rights and shrink the rights of those who believe in gender, in traditional marriage, and who oppose deviant sexual behavior.[21]

The movement to redefine the family through the vehicle of same-sex marriage is without question one of the most urgent social and moral crises facing America and the world. If same-sex marriage is recognized, then 95 percent of the homosexual agenda will have been achieved. It will be just a matter of time before that agenda infiltrates and undermines every part of the culture, from the classroom to the courtroom, from Congress to city hall, from private affairs to business, from the family to our fundamental freedoms. Certainly there is no constitutional, historical, or logical basis for same-sex marriage. There is no cultural mandate. The weight of history does not come down on the side of same-sex marriage. The vast majority of Americans oppose same-sex marriage. One may then ask with the dumbfounded look of Detective Colombo: "With history, social mores, political, and judicial precedent opposed to same-sex marriage, how can we seriously consider the possibility that same-sex marriage will be legalized?" The answer lies in Edmond Burke's oft-quoted truism: "All that is necessary for evil to triumph is for good men to do nothing."[22]

Speak now, or forever hold your peace.

CHAPTER 6

Reinventing History: Sexual Preference Is Not a Civil Right

The traditional family has never faced as great a threat as it does today from same-sex marriage. The goal of the homosexual agenda is to bury the traditional family and, in its place, create a new culture symbolized by same-sex marriage. Extending legal protection to sexual preferences and recognizing same-sex marriage will not simply alter American culture and traditional marriage, it will destroy the culture and the sacred institution. The battle over civil rights for women and people of color is far different than the quest to elevate sexual behavior to a preferred and protected status. Recognizing a legal union between two people of the same sex will precipitate a cultural meltdown.

Elevating personal sexual preferences to a civil right on the one hand, or accepting same-sex marriage on the other hand, has nothing to do with tolerance. The words *tolerance* and *homophobia* are terms used to silence critics of homosexuality. Make no mistake. The radical homosexual agenda is anything but tolerant. Tolerance is not the goal of the homosexual movement, nor is it the goal of same-sex marriage. The homosexual movement is seeking to use the vehicle of marriage to force homosexuality on an unwilling population. The movement will destroy anything in its path that resists.[1]

Historical Revisionism of Homosexual Culture

Homosexuality experienced a rapid historical revision during the twentieth century, and it continues to advance into the twenty-first century. This revisionism is symbolically illustrated by the emergence of the Metropolitan Community Church

("MCC"), which was founded in 1968.[2] Catering to gays and lesbians, the denomination's Web site declares that Scripture does not condemn homosexuality, and that homosexual relationships should be *celebrated and affirmed*![3] The MCC Web site states that the real sin that occurred in Sodom and Gomorrah was not homosexuality but the failure of its citizens to feed the poor.[4] Despite modern-day attempts to rewrite history and alter historical theology, history and the biblical text remain the same.[5] Every lasting culture throughout recorded history has channeled sex into heterosexual marriage.[6]

American law derived its principles from the common law of England.[7] Sir William Blackstone (1723–1780) was a professor of common law at Oxford University. His four-volume publication known as the *Commentaries on the Laws of England* was the authoritative textbook for the development of American law, and these commentaries were "the manual of almost every student of law in the United States" during the early years of this country.[8] It has been well understood that "common law was grounded on the law of God."[9] Blackstone commented upon divine revelation and the law of nature, also known as natural law. "Upon these two foundations, the law of nature and the law of revelation, depend all human law; that is to say, no human law should be suffered to contradict these."[10] James Wilson, Associate Justice of the first United States Supreme Court and signer of both the Declaration of Independence and the United States Constitution, observed: "Human law must rest its authority ultimately upon the authority of that law which is divine. . . . Far from being rivals or enemies, religion and law are twin sisters, friends, and mutual assistants. Indeed, these two sciences run into each other."[11]

The Declaration of Independence speaks of both the natural law (which forms the foundation of the English and American common law) and revealed law when referring to "the Laws of Nature and of Nature's God."[12]

Homosexuality is repudiated in the common law because it violates the natural and revealed law. In the sixth-century encyclopedic collection of Roman law known as *Corpus Juris Civilivis*, under the sponsorship of Emperor Justinian, the following statement is made: "Sodomy is high treason against the King of heaven."[13]

In the Middle Ages, St. Thomas Aquinas, a disciple of natural-law theory, called homosexuality "contrary to right reason" and "contrary to the natural order."[14] The earliest English secular legislation on the subject dates to 1533 BC, when Parliament under Henry VIII classified "buggery" (a euphemism for same-sex activity, bestiality, and anal intercourse) as a felony.[15] Blackstone referred to homosexuality as "the infamous crime against nature,"[16] a phrase used interchangeably in common law for sodomy.

"[Sodomy] was made a felony by an English statute so early that is was a common-law offense in this Country, and statutes expressly making it a felony were widely adopted."[17] *Black's Law Dictionary* states that sodomy "is often defined in statutes and judicial decisions as meaning 'the crime against nature,' . . . or as carnal copulation, against the order of nature."[18] Proscriptions against "'homosexuality' have ancient roots."[19] "Sodomy was a criminal offense at common law and was forbidden by the laws of the original thirteen states when they ratified the Bill of Rights. . . . In fact, until 1961, all fifty states outlawed sodomy."[20]

Until the latter part of the twentieth century, American culture and policy confined sex to marriage.[21] Then along came Alfred C. Kinsey, who in 1948 published the now discredited book known as *Sexual Behavior in the Human Male*.[22] Kinsey's so-called research sought to overthrow traditional notions of sex and sexuality and erroneously stated that 10 percent of the American population is homosexual. This figure has since been discredited, and a more reliable analysis suggests that the figure is closer to between 1 and 2.5 percent.[23] Despite the fact that Kinsey's research has now been proven to be fraudulent and that he even made up many of his findings[24] in order to justify his own appetite for homosexual sex,[25] some homosexual advocates still use Kinsey's statistics.

Up until 1973, the American Psychiatric Association (APA) classified homosexuality as a psychiatric disorder.[26] In 1970 gay activists attended the APA's annual convention in San Francisco where they interrupted a presentation by a leading psychiatrist, Irvin Bieber, and thereby created pandemonium. The following year Dr. Kent Robinson convened a panel at the APA convention, which included activists from the homosexual community. On May 3, 1971, homosexual activists stormed the convention, seized the microphone, and delivered a diatribe against the psychiatric profession stating, "You may take this as a declaration of war against you."[27] Two years later in 1973, under continued pressure from homosexual activists, the APA's Nomenclature Committee declassified homosexuality as a mental disorder.[28] "Shortly thereafter, the term 'sexual preference' began to give way to 'sexual orientation' in homosexual publications and then in the psychiatric and psychological literature."[29]

Springing from the psychological literature, "sexual orientation" is often taken to mean "homosexuality." Given that its inclusion in policies is the singular work of the homosexual pressure groups, that is a reasonable deduction. However, the two words constitute an umbrella term for numerous sexual behaviors, including paraphillias, which are sexual disorders. According to the Therapeutic Manual of the American Psychiatric Association, there are at least twenty distinctive sexual variations of "sexual orientation," and perhaps many more.[30]

Riding the crest of the sexual revolution wave of the 1970s, homosexual activists pushed for legal recognition. They began their quest by using the term *sexual orientation* to establish the idea that homosexuality was genetic and thus beyond personal choice. Having been successful gaining acceptance, the homosexual movement is now beginning to move away from the term *orientation* back to the term *preference,* or to newer terms such as *gender fluidity* or *gender expression* in order to pave the way for every conceivable form of sexual expression. In the meantime, the movement argued that sexual behavior should be protected as a civil right, and thus homosexual activists began borrowing the terminology used during the Civil Rights era.

History of the 1964 Civil Rights Act— An Overview of Historically Protected Categories

In order to gain power, the homosexual movement has sought to ride the civil rights train. Using words like *civil rights, discrimination,* and *tolerance,* the homosexual and same-sex marriage movement has successfully fooled many to believe their cause is just and that sexual behavior should be permitted to climb the platform atop the civil rights pedestal. However, a person's sexual preference is not a civil right and has nothing in common with the civil rights movement of the twentieth century.

The federal law known as the Civil Rights Act of 1964 (Act) was part of a landmark legislative attempt to remedy discrimination on account of "race, color, religion, sex, or national origin." Title II[31] of the Act prohibits discrimination or segregation in places of public accommodation. Titles III[32] and IV[33] ban discrimination in public facilities and in public education. Title VI[34] prohibits discrimination against recipients of federally assisted programs. Title VII[35] addresses discrimination in the workplace. This employment discrimination provision applies to any employer with fifteen or more employees for each working day in each of the twenty or more calendar weeks in the current or preceding calendar year.[36]

The Civil Rights Act of 1964 laid the foundation for future civil rights laws that were later adopted by the several states, including local governmental subdivisions such as municipalities. An understanding of the historical background and reasons for the Civil Rights Act of 1964 is important when considering adding any new class of persons to a protected civil rights category.

The Historical Background of the Civil Rights Act of 1964

The two driving forces behind the Civil Rights Act of 1964 arose primarily out of discrimination against African-Americans and secondarily out of discrimination against women.

The Thirteenth, Fourteenth, and Fifteenth Amendments

On December 6, 1865, the Thirteenth Amendment to the United States Constitution was ratified by the states.[37] The Thirteenth Amendment abolished slavery and involuntary servitude. This amendment authorized Congress to enforce its provisions by appropriate legislation.

The Fourteenth Amendment was ratified on July 9, 1868.[38] This amendment affords the right of citizenship to any person born or naturalized in the United States and subject to the jurisdiction thereof and also prohibits states from abridging the privileges or immunities of citizens of the United States and from depriving any person of life, liberty, or property without due process of law and further from denying any person within its jurisdiction the equal protection of the laws. The amendment authorized Congress to enforce its provisions.

On February 3, 1870, the Fifteenth Amendment was ratified by the states.[39] This amendment states that the right to vote shall not be denied by the United States or any state "on account of race, color, or previous condition of servitude." Congress is authorized to enforce these provisions. The amendment was intended to grant the right to vote to people of color. The Fifteenth Amendment did not address the women's suffrage movement.

The Women's Suffrage Movement

The Women's Suffrage Movement was symbolized by Susan B. Anthony. In 1872 she was arrested and fined $100 for casting a vote in the presidential election. Women ultimately won the right to vote on August 18, 1920, when the Nineteenth Amendment was ratified and added to the United States Constitution.[40] The Nineteenth Amendment declares that the right of citizens of the United States to vote "shall not be denied or abridged by the United States or by any State on account of sex."

The "Separate but Equal" Doctrine

In the now infamous case of *Plessy v. Ferguson*,[41] handed down on May 18, 1896, the United States Supreme Court developed the so-called "separate but equal" doctrine. Mr. Plessy was described as a citizen of the United States and a resident of the state of Louisiana of mixed descent, in the proportion of seven-eighths Caucasian and one-eighth African. His outward complexion was apparently more white than black. On June 7, 1892, Mr. Plessy paid for a first-class ticket on the East Louisiana Railway from New Orleans to Covington, in the same state, and thereafter boarded the passenger train and sat in a vacant seat on a coach where Caucasian passengers were allowed to sit. The conductor of the train required Mr. Plessy to vacate the coach and to occupy another seat, solely because he was not of the white race. When he refused, he was forcibly ejected and later imprisoned. The Supreme Court ruled that segregation of this sort was permissible under the so-called "separate but equal" doctrine.

The Era of Desegregation

On May 17, 1954, the United States Supreme Court, in the now famous case of *Brown v. Board of Education of Topeka, Kansas*,[42] overruled the "separate but equal" doctrine enunciated in *Plessy v. Ferguson*. The court in *Brown* ruled that to separate black children from others of similar age and qualifications solely because of their race was unconstitutional.

Rampant Discrimination Continues

Despite four constitutional amendments and a favorable Supreme Court decision, rampant discrimination against African-Americans and women continued. Segregation continued in the form of separate drinking fountains, separate restrooms, and the inability of African-Americans to use public transportation, public parks and facilities, restaurants, and hotels. Educational opportunities were sharply limited. As late as 1963, only twelve thousand of the approximately three million African-Americans in the south attended integrated schools.

In February 1960, African-American students demonstrated at a department store lunch counter in Greensboro, North Carolina, by conducting a sit-in protest that spread to more than one hundred communities. In January 1961, two black students enrolled at the University of Georgia at Athens, marking the first desegregation of public education in Georgia. However, during the fall of 1962, James Meredith attempted to enroll at the University of Mississippi in Oxford. The event generated extreme hostility to the point that 2 men were killed and 375 injured as the state attempted to resist Meredith's admission.

In 1963, President John F. Kennedy warned that he would summon federal marshals against Governor George Wallace if Alabama did not eliminate segregation in public facilities. These events formed the background for the historic 1964 civil rights legislation.

The Civil Rights Act of 1964 Becomes Law

The debate over the Civil Rights Act of 1964 began in 1963 and culminated a year later with the passage of the Act. The House of Representatives first took action on passing the historic legislation. The House held seventy days of public hearings, listened to 275 witnesses, and published 5,792 pages of legislative testimony. The Senate then took up the measure and spent a total of eighty-three days debating the legislation, compiling almost 3,000 pages in the Congressional

Record. On July 2, 1964, President Lyndon Baines Johnson signed the Civil Rights Act of 1964 into law.

As noted above, the Act prohibits discrimination against individuals on account of "race, color, religion, sex, or national origin." All five categories have at one time or another been the subject of no less than five constitutional amendments.[43]

Unifying Characteristics of Protected Classes within the Civil Rights Act of 1964

All five categories, including the category of religion, have several things in common. First, each category has a long history of documented, widespread discrimination. Second, each category of persons has suffered economic disadvantage as a direct result of the discrimination. Finally, each category has immutable characteristics. As will be discussed later, the category of religion contains an immutable characteristic to the extent that the drafters of the First Amendment to the United States Constitution held that a person's right to believe and exercise his or her religion is an inalienable right.

History of Long-Standing, Widespread Discrimination

No one can seriously argue that African-Americans did not suffer rampant, widespread discrimination. Blacks were forced to use separate drinking fountains and restrooms. Rosa Parks symbolized the discrimination blacks experienced in public transportation. African-Americans were prohibited from staying in motels or from patronizing restaurants. African-Americans and other people of color were prohibited from voting until the states ratified the Fifteenth Amendment to the United States Constitution on February 3, 1870.

Women faced a similar history to that experienced by African-Americans and other people of color. Women were prohibited from voting until the Nineteenth Amendment to the Constitution was ratified on August 18, 1920. Like black Americans, women were also excluded from the job markets and from places of political influence. Those of Korean, Japanese, Jewish, and German descent also faced discrimination following World Wars I and II.

People of faith similarly faced discrimination. In the early founding of America, certain minority religions were excluded from the political process. As late as the Revolutionary War, there were established churches in at least eight of the thirteen colonies and established religions in at least four of the other five.[44] In addition to minority Protestant religions, Roman Catholics also faced discrimination that resulted in economic disadvantage. In order to combat the rising influence of Roman Catholic schools, Senator James Blaine introduced a proposed constitutional amendment in 1875 that would have eliminated any indirect funding for

Roman Catholic education. The proposed amendment failed for lack of two-thirds majority vote in the Senate,[45] but several states passed similar amendments to their respective state constitutions, and these provisions are enforced to this day.[46]

Despite the passage of the First Amendment, some states continued to prohibit clergy from holding elected political positions. As late as the 1970s, the state of Tennessee had a law that disallowed clergy from holding political office. The last vestige of such a law was struck down by the United States Supreme Court in 1978.[47] In the home state of Thomas Jefferson, the Commonwealth of Virginia continued to discriminate against churches until 2002, when Liberty Counsel successfully challenged Virginia law that banned churches from (1) incorporating, and (2) owning more than fifteen acres of property. In 2002, Thomas Road Baptist Church became the first church in Virginia since the Revolutionary War to incorporate and the first church to own and manage real and personal property on the same terms and conditions as other secular persons or organizations.[48]

Economic Disadvantage

The widespread discrimination against blacks and women undeniably resulted in direct economic disadvantage. People of color and women were excluded from the economic marketplace. This discrimination also resulted in economic disadvantage against people because of national origin. Blacks and other people of color experienced severe economic disadvantage as a direct result of blatant employment discrimination. The Act served as a catalyst to help remedy this economic discrimination.[49]

Women, like people of color, also have experienced economic disadvantage as a result of long-standing discrimination. The Act was designed to prevent rampant discrimination against women and increase their economic status.[50] People of faith have also encountered long-standing economic discrimination, some of which persists today. The disestablishment movement beginning in the late-1700s resulted in the confiscation of church property, and the vestiges of this economic discrimination against churches continue to be enforced in some states respecting incorporation and the ownership and management of real or personal property.[51]

Immutable Characteristics

Race, color, sex, and national origin share the common bond of having immutable characteristics. Referring to categories such as race and sex, the Supreme Court described these protected classes as "discreet and insular minorities."[52] More than once the Supreme Court has stated that "sex, like race and national origin, is an immutable characteristic determined solely by the accident of birth."[53] An immutable characteristic serves to identify the protected class.

A person's race, color, sex, and national origin are unchangeable characteristics. One cannot transition from one category to another. A person is either born African-American or Caucasian, male or female. There's no such thing as an ex-African-American. The ancestry of a person is fixed at birth. History has indicated that, based on these immutable characteristics, the class of persons within these categories has faced discrimination resulting in economic hardship.

Religion is the sole category within the Civil Rights Act that does not share the exact pattern of an immutable *physical* characteristic as do the other four categories. However, the characteristic of immutability in terms of religion is rooted in the First Amendment, and indeed, predates that Amendment. The drafters of the First Amendment considered the freedom to believe in God and the free exercise of religion to be an inviolable right which may not be alienated by any sovereign government. The First Amendment affords special protection to religion in part because of the history of religious oppression, and this special protection was codified in the Act.

Sexual Preference and Same-Sex Marriage Should Not Be Elevated to a Preferred Status

An objective assessment should be made when considering adding any class of persons to a protected civil rights category, particularly when the consideration is marriage. Same-sex marriage is not a civil rights issue. No culture, particularly America, has ever elevated each and every imaginable cohabitation arrangement to a preferred status. The typical paradigm has been male-female, not male-male or female-female. Common sense and human history underscore why that is so.

The Evidence Does Not Support a History of Long-Standing, Widespread Discrimination Based on Sexual Behavior

A public hearing regarding "sexual orientation" that occurred in Orlando, Florida, is typical of similar debates throughout the country. On April 16, 2002, the Orlando Human Relations Board heard public comment regarding a petition from a private group of homosexual activists to add "sexual orientation" to the city code. The hearing was widely publicized. Homosexual organizations rallied members of the community to be present at the April 16 meeting.[54] Of fifty-one speakers, only three presented potentially legitimate claims of employment discrimination. Two of the people voluntarily quit their jobs, and both were running successful businesses. The third person was fully reinstated in his job, and in reality, this person denied being homosexual.

No legitimate claims of discrimination were presented by any one of the speakers regarding public accommodation. At a subsequent meeting of the Orlando

Human Relations Board conducted on June 20, 2002, board member Hernan Castro, who made a motion to add "sexual orientation" to the city code, stated twice that he heard no evidence or testimony regarding discrimination in the area of public accommodation.[55]

In a three-part series published in the *Orlando Sentinel* in preparation for the April 16 meeting, the newspaper, which also supported the amendment, reported that there are "no dependable statistics on discrimination against gays and lesbians."[56] Yet there were clearly dependable statistics regarding discrimination against people of color and women during the debates that gave birth to the Civil Rights Act of 1964. Evidence of discrimination was not anecdotal or hearsay. The lack of real evidence of long-standing, widespread discrimination based on "sexual orientation" leads to the logical conclusion—a law or policy granting special rights, especially the right to marry, is both improvident and unnecessary.

Sexual Preference Has Not Resulted in Economic Disadvantage

Instead of economic discrimination, the homosexual household enjoys an economic advantage over the average household. An article appearing in the *Orlando Sentinel* noted that gays "generally have a higher discretionary income because most don't have children."[57]

In 1991, *The Wall Street Journal* published information from the Simmons Market Research Bureau and the United States Census data using figures from 1988 revealing that the average homosexual household had higher annual income and spent more money on entertainment than the national average.[58]

A 2001 census of 6,351 self-identified homosexuals reported that 22 percent of gays and 20 percent of lesbians had an income of between $70,000 and $100,000, while 29 percent of gays and 16 percent of lesbians had incomes in excess of $100,000.[59]

There are two competing tensions when studying the economics of gays and lesbians. Those who market the homosexual community stress their economic achievements, while those who argue for a protected class status downplay the economic findings.[60] A foremost advocate of the notion that homosexuals earn no more than heterosexuals is M. V. Lee Badgett, a professor of economics at the University of Massachusetts and the director of the Institute for Gay and Lesbian Strategic Studies, which is associated with the National Gay and Lesbian Task Force.[61] However, the studies do show that male same-sex couples have significantly higher incomes than married couples.[62] Even Badgett admitted that the "census results show that male same-sex couples have household incomes 24 percent higher than married couples."[63] Badgett also had to admit that "the average woman with a female partner earns more than the average heterosexual woman does."[64] One thing is certain: homosexual couples have higher discretionary income and more dispos-able time due to the lack of children.[65]

"In contrast to studies of antidiscrimination laws for women and ethnic minorities, we have produced no evidence that employment protections for sexual orientation directly increase average earnings for members of same-sex house-holds."[66] In addition to the studies on income, other studies have shown that "twice as many college-educated men identify themselves as homosexual as men with high school educations, . . . for women the trend is even more striking. Women with college educations are eight times more likely to identify themselves as lesbians as are women with a high school education."[67]

The economic and political power of the homosexual community illustrates the antithesis of discrimination.

Sexual Preference Does Not Include Immutable Characteristics

On the matter of whether a person's sexual preference meets the immutability requirement, one need not debate whether homosexuality is genetic or environ-mental. The typical definition of "sexual orientation" includes the status of being, or the *perception* of being heterosexual, homosexual, bisexual, transsexual, or even the most recent label, "questioning youth."[68] The definition itself includes the entire spectrum of human sexuality. Homosexual groups are now lobbying to amend laws to include such terms as "gender identity" and "gender expression." Including the entire spectrum of human sexuality by definition cannot be an immutable characteristic.

One does not look at another's brown skin and question whether the person is "transitioning" from Caucasian to African-American or vice versa. A Caucasian may not claim discrimination on the basis of race under the assumption that the employer "perceived" that the employee was African-American. A male may not claim dis-crimination on the basis that the employer assumed he was female. The moving target of human sexuality can never qualify as an "immutable characteristic."

As General Colin Powell pointed out: "Skin color is a benign-behavioral char-acteristic. Sexual orientation is perhaps the most profound of human behavioral characteristics. Comparison of the two is a convenient but invalid argument."[69] Homosexuals have attempted to point to certain "genetic" studies touting the idea that homosexuality is a genetically inherited characteristic. However, many of these studies are fraught with methodological flaws and have not been replicated by rep-utable scientists.[70] In contrast to these flawed methodological studies, which will be discussed below, more than seventy years of therapeutic counseling and case studies suggest homosexuality is a gender identification issue that is environmentally influ-enced.[71] Homosexuals can change their behavior.[72] There are numerous examples of changed sexual behavior documented in many studies, including the landmark research of Masters and Johnson.[73]

Homosexuals often point to a study performed by Simon LeVay who attempted to trace homosexuality to brain structure based upon research on forty-one post-mortem brain samples.[74] LeVay reported that a particular part of the brain structure known as INAH3 was larger in the brains of heterosexual men than in the brains of homosexual men. However, LeVay's study is flawed.[75] LeVay defined homosexuality as "sexual orientation," which he described as "the direction of sexual feelings or behavior toward members of one's own or the opposite sex."[76] LeVay included bisexuality with homosexuality. His definition failed "to require homosexual behavior and does not define which behaviors constitute homosexuality."[77] There is "still no universally accepted definition of homosexuality among clinicians and behavioral scientists."[78]

As Professor Lynn Wardle noted:

> Does merely thinking about having sexual relations with a person of the same sex make one homosexual, or is sexual behavior also required? If feeling is definitive, what level, amount, and intensity of feeling is required? If behavior is necessary, what kind of behavior is deemed defining? Is an isolated incident of sexual experimentation definitive? If not, what frequency is required? How recently must the activity have occurred? What if the subject engaged in both homosexual and heterosexual contact—would he or she be defined as homosexual or heterosexual? What about "changers"—for example, a man who was a practicing heterosexual for 15 years, but 2 months ago abandoned heterosexual for homosexual relations? . . . . No scientific study wishing to be taken seriously can avoid such fundamental definitional issues, but many of the high-profile biological-determinism studies gloss over them.[79]

LeVay gathered his information on the past history of his subjects from hospital records. If the records did not indicate the subject's past sexual history, he classified them as heterosexual since most males are heterosexual.[80] Relying only on past records is itself a significant flaw. Two of the patients' records indicated they had AIDS but did not engage in homosexual activity. LeVay therefore classified both of these subjects as heterosexual.[81]

All of the individuals classified as homosexual had died of AIDS. It is therefore a distinct possibility that the smaller brain size was either due to AIDS or resulted from the medication the subject had taken for the disease.[82] There was no data showing the size of the brain before and after medication or before and after contracting AIDS. The brains were not compared with the subject's parents or siblings. Moreover, no serious consideration was given to the question of whether brain size causes homosexuality or whether the brain size was a consequence of the subject's sexual behavior.[83]

LeVay's study was never repeated by another researcher. More importantly, LeVay himself admitted he had not proven that homosexuality is caused by genetics. LeVay candidly acknowledged: "It's important to stress what I didn't find. I did not prove that homosexuality is genetic, or find a genetic cause for being gay. I didn't show that gay men are born that way, the most common mistake people make in interpreting my work."[84]

Not long after LeVay published his study, geneticist Dean Hammer with the National Cancer Institute claimed to have found a gene that he said formed the basis of male homosexuality.[85] What the media did not report is that two other researchers attempted to reproduce the results of Hammer's study by using a larger and more extensive study of their own, but their findings could not replicate Hammer's conclusions.[86] When Hammer was confronted about whether he had found a so-called gay gene, he responded, "Absolutely not. From twin studies, we already know that half or more of the variability in sexual orientation is not inherited."[87] Hammer went on to state, "The best recent study suggests that female sexual identification is more a matter of environment than heredity."[88]

Another study compared male identical twins, fraternal twins, nontwin brothers, and adopted brothers.[89] This study reported a coordinance rate among homosexuality for identical twins at 52 percent, for fraternal twins at 22 percent, for nonbiological brothers at 9 percent and for adopted brothers at 11 percent. Since the coordinance rate was higher among identical twins, this study correlated homosexuality with genetics. The study was based on self-classification as to sexual orientation, and when the second party was not available, the first party assumed what the sexual preference was for the second. However, the study can also be cited against the genetic argument since the adopted brothers' coordinance rate was higher than the nontwin biological brothers. There is no genetic link between adopted brothers. The only factor linking the two is environmental. "Moreover, since nontwin brothers share the same proportion of genes as fraternal twins, if homosexuality were genetically induced, the rates of homosexual coordinance should be the same for both groups, rather than the reported less than half for the nontwin brothers than for the fraternal twins reported."[90]

The studies on twins absolutely refute a genetic cause to homosexuality. "Identical twins have identical genes. If homosexuality was a biological condition produced inescapably by the genes (such as eye color), then if one identical twin was homosexual, in 100% of the cases his brother would be too."[91] Further refinement of twin studies, where the twins are randomly selected rather than a self-selected group, has now shown that where one twin is homosexual, only 10 percent of the time the other twin is also homosexual.[92] The twin studies underscore the fact that homosexuality is primarily environmental. For example, research teams "asked identical twins—one was homosexual, and one not—about their early family development, and found that the same family environment was perceived by the twins in quite different ways. These differences led later to homosexuality in one twin but not in the other. The scientific truth is—our genes do not force us into anything. But we can support or suppress our genetic tendencies. . . . We can foster them or foil them."[93]

As sociologist Steven Goldberg stated, "I know of no one in the field who argues that homosexuality can be explained *without* reference to environmental factors."[94] A study that examined identical (monozygotic) and fraternal (dizygotic) twins in the Minnesota Twin Registry found that environmental factors were a primary component in the formation of a person's sexual preferences.[95]

Hormonal studies attempting to link homosexuality to genetics are also flawed. If homosexuality were only hormonal, then increasing or decreasing certain hormones should increase or decrease one's sexual preferences. However, "hormonal therapies have failed to influence sexual orientation in adults, and there is also no evidence that sexual orientation is shifted in adults as a consequence of [hormonal] changes."[96]

A study involving fruit flies, testing reduction of serotonin, supports environmental, rather than genetic, homosexuality. Although some male fruit flies with decreased serotonin levels attempted to mate with other males, the female fruit flies were not similarly affected. Moreover, after a two-hour exposure with the treated male fruit flies, some of the nontreated fruit flies mimicked the treated fruit flies and began engaging in male mating activity. On the other hand, when the treated male fruit flies were surrounded by a majority of nontreated fruit flies, there was little or no male mating activity. The "later findings contradicted [the] genetic-determinant theory and suggests that environment can induce 'homosexual' behavior in previously nonhomosexual fruit flies."[97]

Research has shown that "there are no major genes for homosexuality."[98] Kinsey's colleague and biographer, Wardell Pomeroy, stated that "Kinsey was convinced that there was absolutely no evidence of inheritance."[99] There is little question that environmental factors play the predominant role in a person's sexual preference.[100] It is, therefore, legitimate for a state not to elevate personal sexual behavior to a preferred status. At any rate, the presence or absence of immutability is not determinative as to whether a law prohibiting a license to couples of the same gender is constitutional. For example, age and family relationship are immutable characteristics, meaning that these characteristics cannot be changed.

Yet it is perfectly legitimate for a state to prohibit marriage to an unemancipated, nonpregnant minor and to likewise prohibit incestuous marriage.

There is a growing body of academic literature explaining that one's sexual preference is fluid and ever-changing.[101] The growing frequency at which lesbians are entering into relationships with men confirms this fluidity. The "phenomenon" is becoming so commonplace that the term "hasbian"—"a woman who used to date women but now dates men"—has been introduced into the homosexual community.[102] Widely known examples include movie actress Anne Heche ending her relationship with Ellen DeGeneres to marry a man. Irish singer Sinead O'Connor declared herself lesbian, but in 2001 married a man. Julie Cypher broke off her relationship with singer Melissa Etheridge, declaring that she was never a lesbian. A 2000 survey in Australia similarly found that 19 percent of gay men reported having sex with a woman in the six months prior to the survey.[103] Numerous other studies confirm that "exclusive" homosexuality, among both males and females, is a myth.[104]

There is no scientific evidence that homosexuality is genetic and, therefore, immutable.[105] Significantly, Dr. Robert Spitzer, the man who was instrumental in pushing the American Psychiatric Association to declassify homosexuality as a mental disorder, has now acknowledged that homosexuals can become heterosexual.[106] The reason the "born that way" propaganda has been parlayed to the media is for purely political, rather than scientific, reasons. Homosexual advocates Marshall Kirk and Hunter Madsen, in their book, *After the Ball*, candidly set forth the homosexual media campaign, stating that "for all practical purposes, gays should be considered to have been *born gay*—even though sexual orientation, for most humans, seems to be the product of a complex interaction between innate predispositions and environmental factors during childhood and early adolescence. To suggest in public that homosexuality might be *chosen* is to open the can of worms labeled 'moral choice and sin.'"[107]

Since a person's sexual preference is fluid and subject to change, it is inappropriate to compare the same-sex marriage movement with the Supreme Court's decision that struck down interracial marriage in the case of *Loving v. Virginia*.[108] According to the Supreme Court, "Gender, like race, is a highly visible and immutable characteristic."[109] In contrast to the immutable characteristic of race, a person's sexual preference is not static; it is an ever-moving target and, as such, can never be considered immutable. The *Loving* case was more about institutionalized racism than it was marriage. The fundamental distinctive of the marriage institution was not disturbed in the *Loving* decision, namely, the relationship between one man and one woman. The *Loving* decision preserved the institution of marriage between one man and one woman but struck down institutionalized racism. In contrast, same-sex marriage would strike at the heart of the institution itself.

Fluidity of one's sexual preference and the lack of any evidence establishing its immutability preclude defining a class based on sexual preference. Common sense and human history have not undermined the self-evident truth—male and female relations are the fundamental foundation of all cultures.

CHAPTER 7
The Legal and Political Battle

*T*he assault on marriage is being waged in the political and judicial arenas. Some of the incremental legislative gains made by the homosexual movement are being used as legal arguments to push for same-sex marriage. These legislative gains have been designed to nibble at the edges of traditional marriage. When pro-family proponents argue that legislative efforts to elevate "sexual orientation" to the level of a protected civil right is a ruse to later push for same-sex marriage, homosexual advocates respond by labeling such argument as a scare tactic. However, once these laws have been enacted in a state, same-sex marriage activists point to them as the basis for their argument that same-sex marriage should be legalized.

The battle to preserve marriage must be waged and won in both the legislative halls and in the courtrooms. This battle is winnable, and it is certainly worth the effort.

The Legislature and Judiciary

The Legislative Agenda

In most states homosexual advocates are seeking a laundry list of new rights. These include the right to marry, adopt, engage in sodomy, obtain domestic partnerships, recognize "sexual orientation" and "gender identity" as a civil right and so-called hate crimes laws.[1] Transsexuals and homosexuals are also pushing for laws that eliminate gender, literally attempting to abolish the distinction between male and female. For example, transsexuals want gender to be eliminated from birth certificates, application forms, government records, and public restrooms.[2] Weslyan University no longer requires "M" or "F" on health clinic intake forms. Students are asked instead to "describe your gender identity history."[3]

The same-sex marriage agenda uses such words as *tolerance* and *nondiscrimination* and, thus, seeks to capitalize on themes that arose out of the Civil Rights era in order to force acceptance of sexually promiscuous lifestyles. The same-sex marriage agenda is not limited to the public legislative arena; it also includes private businesses. "In many regards, the workplace is the leading edge of change for the GLBT [gay, lesbian, bisexual, transsexual] Community. Company CEOs and executives can often wield even more power than state and local officials in creating significant changes that affect their employees' lives. They can enact new policies with the approval of a few board members rather than thousands or even millions of voters."[4]

Following on the heels of "sexual orientation" policies are domestic partnership benefits. The argument presented by homosexuals generally follows the reasoning that domestic partnership benefits (benefits that historically have been only for spouses and dependents) should be extended to same-sex couples in the same way they are extended to heterosexual couples because to do otherwise would allegedly discriminate on the basis of "sexual orientation." Once the benefits are achieved, the next logical step is to push for "civil unions" and especially for same-sex marriage. The legislative agenda also seeks the right of homosexuals to adopt in order to weaken the argument that heterosexual marriage is for procreation and child rearing. Even if adoption were available to homosexual couples, the fact remains that virtually every adopted child comes from the union of one man and one woman.

If same-sex marriage were legally sanctioned, public school curricula would "legitimize" a variety of homosexual, bisexual, and transsexual behavior as normal and healthy, even at the young age of five.[5] If the criterion for marriage is merely two consenting people with affection for each other, then there would be no legitimate basis to restrict marriage and thus no reason to prohibit polygamy (one man and several women), polyamory (multiple sexual unions), incestuous marriage, or pedophilia. Private and public employers would have to provide "family" health benefits to homosexual couples. Religious organizations would find themselves in a tremendous conflict. These organizations will be required to provide health benefits, including the cost of transsexual surgeries, to homosexual partners and transsexual employees on the terms provided to traditional families. The speech of those who believe in traditional marriage and who oppose homosexuality as normative will be labeled as hate speech and, as such, will be subject to punishment.

Children in a same-sex marriage culture would be just as easily adopted by homosexual and transsexual couples as by heterosexual couples. Even worse, boys and girls would be exposed to the idea that they "might be" gay, lesbian, bisexual, or transsexual during the most critical identity development phase of their lives. Accepting same-sex marriage would radically redefine our cultural and moral values.

The Judicial Agenda

Liberal social engineers are fond of using the judicial system to shape public policy when there is not enough clout in the political arena to command a majority. One such example occurred in Hawaii. The Hawaii Supreme Court sent a same-sex marriage case back to the trial court where the state was ordered to present evidence to prove the government had a compelling interest to deny marriage to same-sex couples.[6] Before the case could be heard at the trial court, the people responded by amending the state constitution by a vote of the citizenry to remove same-sex marriage from the jurisdiction of the courts.

Liberty Counsel successfully defeated an attempt by homosexuals to force Georgia into recognizing same-sex marriage. In the case of *Burns v. Burns*,[7] a husband and wife divorced after having three children. The husband had primary custody, and the ex-wife had visitation rights. However, due to the ex-wife's lesbian affairs, a judge entered an order stating that neither party could have overnight visits with the children while they were cohabiting with a person to whom he or she was not married or related within the second degree. On July 1, 2000, the state of Vermont passed a law authorizing same-sex couples to enter into a so-called civil union, similar to marriage.[8]

Following the passage of the bill, the ex-wife entered into another lesbian relationship, and she and her new partner traveled to Vermont where they obtained a civil union license on July 4, 2000. The two returned to Georgia where the ex-wife contended that she was legally "married." She argued in court that Georgia's Defense of Marriage Act, which limits marriage to one man and one woman, was unconstitutional and that the Federal Defense of Marriage Act ("DOMA"), which allows each state to define its own marriage policy, did not apply. The Georgia court rejected these arguments, stating that (1) a civil union in Vermont is not marriage, (2) even if Vermont had purported to legalize same-sex marriage, such would not be recognized in Georgia because state law defines marriage as one man and one woman, and (3) the Federal Defense of Marriage Act does not require one state to recognize an out-of-state, same-sex marriage.[9] The *Burns* court exercised judicial restraint when it declared the following: "What constitutes a marriage in the state of Georgia is a legislative function, not a judicial one, and as judges we are duty bound to follow the clear language of the statute."[10]

Same-sex marriage ought to be debated by the people, not a few judges. "Vigorous, robust interchange on issues of public importance is one of the pillars of self-government. The full exchange of views not only informs ultimate decisions, but tempers and refines the character of the persons who participate in the debate."[11] Indeed, a "broad dissemination of principles, ideas, and factual information is crucial to the robust public debate and informed citizenry that are 'the essence of self-government.'"[12] "Free and open debate is vital to informed decision-making by the electorate."[13] "Robust debate of public issues" is of "essential First Amendment value"[14] and "essential to our democratic society."[15] Public debate permits "the continued building of our politics and culture,"[16] facilitates reforms through peaceful means,[17] and maintains a system of government that is "responsive to the will of the people."[18]

Supreme Court Justice Antonin Scalia stated that it was "no business of the court (as opposed to the political branches) to take sides in this culture war."[19] On an issue that is as socially important and radically redefining as same-sex marriage, the people, not the courts, should have the final say. If judges attempt to remove "the ball from the legislators' court," such action will only prolong "divisiveness" and "defer stable settlement of the issue" which should be decided by the people.[20] Justice Holmes similarly cautioned that the judiciary should "confine" itself to "molecular motions" because "doctrinal limbs too swiftly shaped . . . may prove unstable."[21] Marriage has been traditionally left to the legislative, not to the judicial branch of government. The debate on same-sex marriage should be argued by the voters and debated from the political and spiritual pulpits. This important issue should not be left to a few judges. The judiciary is not a super legislature; it must not replace the will of the people with its own social theory.[22] The decision to officially adopt one social theory over another is best left to the people.[23]

Advancing the Homosexual Agenda by Adopting Innocent Children

A number of states, like Florida, ban same-sex adoption.[24] Utah prohibits adoption by any single person who is "cohabiting in a relationship that is not a legally valid and binding marriage under the laws of this state."[25] Mississippi prohibits adoption by same-sex couples, as couples,[26] and Arizona[27] also bans same-sex adoptions. Other states, like Colorado,[28] ban same-sex, second-parent adoptions. A Nebraska court upheld Nebraska's ban on homosexual adoption[29] and the Alabama Supreme Court denied custody to a lesbian mother because of her homosexuality.[30] A concurring opinion from the Alabama Supreme Court states that a parent's homosexuality "creates a strong *presumption of unfitness* that alone is sufficient justification for denying that parent custody of his or her own children or *prohibiting the adoption of the children of others*."[31] Only a handful of states specifically allow homosexual adoption.[32] Most states have never addressed the issue. When the state statutes were drafted, homosexual adoption was not a concern.

Advancing the Homosexual Agenda through Same-Sex Unions

The ultimate prize of the homosexual movement is to win the right of same-sex marriage. Most homosexuals, particularly males, do not seek same-sex marriage as an end but merely as a means to an end.

Same-Sex Marriage

The Supreme Court has long recognized the importance of marriage to society. In 1878, the High Court addressed polygamous marriages when Utah sought admission to the United States. The Court noted: "Marriage, while from its very nature a sacred obligation, is nevertheless, in most civilized nations, a civil contract, and usually regulated by law. Upon it society may be said to be built, and out of its fruits spring social relations and social obligations and duties, with which government is necessarily required to deal."[33]

On another occasion the Supreme Court recognized the importance of marriage consisting of one man and one woman. "No legislation can be supposed more wholesome and necessary in the founding of a free, self-governing commonwealth, fit to take rank as one of the co-ordinate States of the Union, than that which seeks to establish it on the basis of the idea of the family as consisting in and springing from the union for life of *one man* and *one woman* in the holy estate of matrimony; the sure foundation of all that is stable and noble in our civilization."[34]

Although involving consenting adults, polygamy is prohibited in all fifty states because it stands in direct conflict with the idea of "family as consisting and springing from the union for life of one man and one woman." Similarly, many states prohibit adultery.[35] State regulations legitimately extend beyond the one-man-and-one-woman proscription to also prohibit incestuous marriages.[36]

Although the right to marry may be constitutionally recognized as a fundamental liberty interest,[37] there is no such fundamental right to same-sex marriage. The United States Supreme Court has noted that a fundamental right depends not on personal and private action but on "the 'traditions and . . . conscience of our people' to determine whether a principle is 'so rooted [in history] . . . as to be ranked as fundamental.' The inquiry [is] whether a right involved 'is of such a character that it cannot be denied without violating those "fundamental principles of liberty and justice which lie at the base of all civil and political institutions."'"[38]

Therefore, in order to classify a right as fundamental, the court must consider the following question: "Whether the practice or relationship is deeply rooted in the common law traditions of the American people or whether it is essential to the very concept of ordered liberty."[39]

"Marriage and procreation are fundamental to the very existence and survival of the race."[40] The Supreme Court has described marriage as "the most important relation in life" and recognized that the marriage institution "has always been subject to the control of the legislature."[41] In 1967, in the case of *Loving v. Virginia*, the Supreme Court ruled unconstitutional a Virginia antimiscegenation (anti-interracial) statute that prohibited marriage between two people of a different race.[42] This case cannot be used by same-sex marriage proponents to champion their cause because the case was more about race than marriage. The central feature of marriage was left undisturbed by the decision, namely, the union of one man and one woman. Shortly after the Virginia case, the Supreme Court emphasized that "marriage involves interests of basic importance in our society."[43]

Same-sex marriage is not a fundamental right or liberty interest. There is no long-standing history in this country, or for that matter the world, to show societal support for same-sex marriage. Same-sex marriage cannot be compared to the *Loving* decision, which struck down a ban on interracial marriage. In *Loving*, the foundation of marriage between one man and one woman remained intact. The only issue before the Supreme Court was whether a person's immutable birth characteristic of race would act as a barrier to restrict marriage between an adult man and woman of different races. Race, *unlike* a person's sexual preference, is an immutable, unchangeable characteristic for which we have amended the United States Constitution no less than three times (by ratifying the Thirteenth, Fourteenth and Fifteenth Amendments). Before and after the *Loving* decision, marriage remains consistent with the natural order of one man and one woman.

While governments are "obliged to show equal respect to persons *qua* persons," they are not obliged to show equal respect "to all of the persons' acts and choices."[44] Prohibiting behavior deemed unacceptable or immoral is precisely what law does: it limits one's freedom to act in ways that cause harm to the individual or to society. States are justified in enforcing a societal morality as a means of self-preservation because "social bonds constituted by shared moral beliefs are placed in peril when the law tolerates actions that are generally considered to be wicked."[45] "Without morality, the foundations of our liberty will crumble, because there will be no moral compass differentiating between right and wrong."[46]

Moral visions of the various states have led to laws criminalizing fornication (sexual relations between unmarried persons), bestiality (sexual relations with animals), necrophilia (sexual relations with dead bodies), adult-minor consensual sexual relations, consensual adult incestuous sexual relations, and sodomy. "There has never been any doubt that the legislature, in the exercise of its police power, has authority to criminalize the commission of acts which, without regard to the infliction of any other injury, are considered immoral. Simply put, commission of what the legislature determines as an immoral act, even if consensual and private, is an injury against society itself."[47]

Most cultures generally recognize three categories of social behavior. The first and least favorite is prohibited conduct, which includes activities and associations that are prohibited by law. The second category includes permitted behavior, which encompasses activities and associations that are tolerated and condoned. The third category may be referred to as preferred conduct, which includes activities and associations that society singles out for "special approval, encouragement, and preference."[48] According to law professor, Lynn Wardle: "The boundary line between the first and second categories is the line of tolerance. On one side the association of behavior is deemed socially intolerable (prohibited), but on the other side of the line it is tolerated (permitted). The boundary line between the second and third categories is the line of preference. Associations in the permitted category are deemed reasonably acceptable, but not uniquely important, while those in the preferred category are essential to the success of our society."[49]

Historically homosexual conduct has been in the prohibited category while the male-female marriage relationship has universally been in the preferred category. The United States Supreme Court once observed: "Proscriptions against [sodomy] have ancient roots. Sodomy was a criminal offense at common law and was forbidden by the laws of the original 13 States when they ratified the Bill of Rights. In 1868, when the Fourteenth Amendment was ratified, all but 5 of the 37 States in the Union had criminal sodomy laws. In fact, until 1961, all 50 States outlawed sodomy."[50]

Removing homosexual conduct from what historically has been a prohibited category to a preferred category is a quantum leap. It is one thing to keep the government out of the bedroom, but it is quite another to require government to publicly endorse and promote a historically and overwhelmingly disfavored sexual practice.

Legalizing same-sex marriage would ignore the distinction between tolerance and preference by extending the highest legal preferences to relationships which our society historically has condemned and which, even now, the most sympathetic states have chosen only to tolerate. The confusion comes when proponents of same-sex marriage assert that because homosexual relations are tolerated they are entitled to a state-endorsed preferred status. This blurs the distinction between the two categories contrary to the reality of all state law schemes'—states universally draw distinctions between tolerance and preference.[51]

There is good reason to prefer heterosexual marriage. In the words of former Supreme Court Chief Justice Earl Warren, traditional marriage is of critical importance because it is "fundamental to our very existence and survival."[52] Nature and common sense teach us that male and female are biologically designed to propagate the human race. Without the male-female relationship the human race would cease to exist. Andrew Sullivan, the former editor of *New Republic* and outspoken homosexual activist, concedes that the "timeless, necessary, procreative unity of a man and a woman is inherently denied homosexuals."[53] Mr. Sullivan also concedes, as he must, that "no two lesbians and no two homosexual men can be parents in the way that a heterosexual man and a heterosexual woman with a biological son or daughter can be."[54]

Society has legitimate reasons for confining marriage to one man and one woman. Statistically, sexual promiscuity is increased among those who engage in homosexual conduct, the result of which is disease found predominantly, if not exclusively, among homosexuals.[55] A far-ranging study published in 1978 revealed that 75 percent of self-identified, white, gay men admitted to having sex with more than one hundred different males in their lifetime, with 28 percent claiming more than one thousand lifetime male sex partners.[56] A study published in 1997 produced similar results: of 2,583 homosexuals, only 2.7 percent claimed to have had sex with only one partner; the most common response, given by 21.6 percent of the respondents, was of having 101 to 500 lifetime sex partners.[57] The U.S. Centers for Disease Control similarly reported an upswing in promiscuity in San Francisco: from 1994 to 1997, the percentage of homosexual men reporting multiple partners and unprotected anal sex rose from 23.6 percent to 33.3 percent, with the largest increase among men under twenty-five.[58] A 1994 survey of twenty-five hundred homosexual men published by a pro-homosexual magazine revealed that in the previous five years, 48 percent of the men had engaged in "three-way sex" and 24 percent had engaged in "group sex (four or more)."[59]

A long-term monogamous relationship also has a different meaning among those who engage in homosexual conduct. "Gay magazines are . . . celebrating the bigger bang of sex with strangers or proposing 'monogamy without fidelity'—the latest Orwellian formulation to excuse having your cake and eating it too."[60] One author praises gay male couples for realizing that sexual fidelity is not necessary to show their love for each other and advocates that gay male couples can "provide models and materials for rethinking family life and improving family law."[61] A recent study reveals that although 46 percent of gay men attending "circuit parties" claimed to have a "primary partner," 27 percent of those men "had multiple sex partners (oral or anal) during their most recent circuit party weekend."[62]

Given these staggering statistics of sexual promiscuity, the number of diseases found predominantly (and in some instances, exclusively) among homosexual practitioners comes as no surprise. One study found that nearly 64 percent of men with AIDS had sex with men.[63] "Reports at a national conference about sexually transmitted diseases indicate that gay men are in the highest risk group for several of the most serious diseases."[64] The list of diseases found with extraordinary frequency among male homosexual practitioners as a result of anal sex include: anal cancer, chlamydia trachomatis, cryptosporidium, giardia lablia, herpes simplex virus, HIV, HPV, isospora belli, microsporidia, gonorrhea, viral Hepatitis types B and C, and syphilis.[65] *"Sexual transmission of some of these diseases is so rare in the exclusively heterosexual population as to be virtually unknown."*[66] Another disease found almost exclusively among homosexual practitioners is "Gay Bowel Syndrome."[67]

As for the diseases that are also found among heterosexuals, individuals engaged in homosexual conduct constitute the largest percentage of many of those diseases, including anal cancer, HIV, HPV (a collection of viruses that can cause warts, or papillomas, on various body parts), and syphilis. For example, 85 percent of the syphilis cases reported in the Seattle area of Washington in 1999 were among self-identified homosexual practitioners.[68] Syphilis among male homosexual practitioners is at epidemic levels in San Francisco,[69] and HPV also is "almost universal" among those men who have sex with men.[70] While the incidence of anal cancer in the United States is only .9/100,000, the number soars to 35/100,000 for those engaged in homosexual conduct.[71]

Lesbians are also at increased risk for certain diseases, including cancer, Hepatitis C, and bacterial vaginosis, predominantly because they are "significantly more likely to report past sexual contact with a homosexual or bisexual man and sexual contact with an IDU (intravenous drug user)."[72] A Philadelphia woman tested positive for HIV as a result of "shared sex toys" with her HIV-positive, bisexual female partner.[73]

Based on the long history of American tradition, social mores, and public health, there are many compelling reasons for restricting marriage to those of the opposite sex.

1. Protecting marriage by the Federal Defense of Marriage Act

In response to the failed judicial attempt in Hawaii to recognize same-sex marriage, Congress passed what is known as the Federal Defense of Marriage Act.[74] This law became effective on September 21, 1996, and states: "No state, territory, or possession of the United States, or Indian tribe, shall be required to give effect to any public act, record, or judicial proceeding of any other State, territory, possession, or tribe respecting a relationship between persons of the same sex that is treated as a marriage under laws of such other State, territory, possession, or tribe, or right or claim arising from such relationship."[75]

The intent of DOMA is to allow the battle over same-sex marriage to be waged among the states.[76] If a homosexual couples obtains a marriage license in one state they will ask a sister state to give legal recognition to the license under the Full Faith and Credit Clause of the United States Constitution. The Full Faith and Credit Clause states: "Full Faith and Credit shall be given in each State to the public Acts, Records, and Judicial Proceedings of every other state. And the Congress may by general Laws prescribe the Manner in which such Acts, Records, and Proceedings shall be proved, and the Effect thereof."[77]

The Federal DOMA specifically traces the language of the Full Faith and Credit Clause, stating that no state or territory shall be required to recognize a marriage consummated in another state if that marriage is between two people of the same sex. While judgments are entitled to full faith and credit, marriages are not judgments and are not required to be recognized.[78]

Prior to the United States Supreme Court's ruling that statutes prohibiting marriage on the basis of race were unconstitutional, some states allowed miscegenational (interracial) marriages while other states did not. Interracial couples who were validly married in one state found that after moving to other states their marriages were not legally recognized and their children were considered illegitimate.[79] Similarly, while polygamy was recognized by one jurisdiction, the same marriage was invalidated by another state.[80] Finally, an incestuous marriage recognized by one state has also been invalidated by another state.[81]

The basic rule relating to one state recognizing a marriage of another state is that "a marriage valid where celebrated is valid everywhere . . . [except] marriages deemed contrary to the laws of nature [and] marriages positively forbidden by statute because [they are] contrary to local public policy."[82] One reputable legal document regarding the conflict of laws between states recognized: "A marriage which satisfies the requirements of the state where the marriage was contracted will everywhere be recognized as valid unless it violates the strong public policy of another state."[83]

The Federal DOMA does not prohibit same-sex marriage; it is designed to place the issue with the individual states. It is up to the states to pass legislation regulating marriage. The Federal DOMA provides that if one state chooses not to recognize a marriage validated in another state between two people of the same sex, then the state will not be forced to do so under the Full Faith and Credit Clause. "Congress was intended to have broad power to create statutes like DOMA under the Effects Clause" of the Full Faith and Credit Clause.[84]

Under the Full Faith and Credit Clause, the Constitution gives Congress the power to determine the "effects" of an act, record, or judicial proceeding of another state. During the Constitutional Convention, the "Effects Clause" became the subject of controversy. The issue was whether the Full Faith and Credit Clause would include the power to govern the effects not only of state court judgments but also of the legislative acts of the states.[85] Justice Joseph Story noted in his commentary that the "effects" are "expressly subjected to the legislative power."[86]

The First Congress enacted the Full Faith and Credit Act to "prescribe the mode in which the public Acts, Records and judicial Proceedings in each State, shall be authenticated so as to take effect in every other state."[87] The Act went on to state that the "records and judicial proceedings, authenticated as aforesaid, shall have such faith and credit given to them in every court within the United States, as they have by law or usage in the courts of the state from which the said records are or shall be taken."[88] Today the Full Faith and Credit Act remains essentially unchanged.[89] "It follows that not every statute of another state will override a conflicting statute of the forum by virtue of the Full Faith and Credit Clause."[90]

Professor Ralph Whitten argues that "the evidence is compelling that Congress was intended to have broad power to create statutes like DOMA under the Effects Clause," and the historical evidence of the Full Faith and Credit Clause indicates that DOMA may not even be necessary, but is certainly within Congress's authority.[91]

The Supreme Court stated that the "Full Faith and Credit Clause does not compel 'a state to substitute the statutes of other states for its own statutes dealing with the subject matter concerning which it is competent to legislate.'"[92] Professor Lynn Hogue of the Georgia State University College of Law, commenting on Georgia law, stated that "homosexual unions will likely be held violative of the state's public policy."[93] Recognizing that a number of states have adopted statutes prohibiting the recognition of same-sex unions, Professor Hogue noted that these "statutes will control in states which have them. In instances in which a state lacks a statute, the common law (through the public-policy exception) will continue to supply the appropriate rule."[94] "The public policy exception, which protects states against the application of foreign laws repugnant to the principles upon which the forum state is grounded, is rooted in the principles of federalism and the protection of sovereignty which inheres in the Tenth Amendment."[95]

Commenting on the right of a state to legislate its own marriage policy, the Supreme Court noted: "No State can assume comprehensive attention to the various and potentially conflicting interests that several States may have in the institutional aspects of marriage [because] to do so would impair 'the proper functioning of our federal system.' The necessary accommodation between the right of one State to safeguard its interest in the family relation of its own people and the power of another state to grant divorces [or recognize marriage] can be left to neither State."[96]

Professor Hogue correctly notes that in "states which have adopted [same-sex] anti-recognition statutes such as Georgia's," the state courts will lack jurisdiction to adjudicate rights arising as a result of or in connection with out-of-state, same-sex unions.[97] Professor Lynn Wardle, who testified before Congress during the adoption of the Federal DOMA, stated:

There is no serious doubt that Congress has the power to enact legislation defining the "effect" of one state's laws, records and judgments in other states. . . . The Congressional Research Service of the Library of Congress has stated: "Congress has the power under the Clause to decree the effect that the statutes of one State shall have in other States." A host of scholarly authority for many decades concurs with this assessment.[98]

The Supreme Court has observed that Congress has a "substantial interest" in "balancing the interests" of the several states by preventing one state's policy from dictating what the legal policy of other states will be.[99] Even Professor Mark Strasser, who is an advocate of same-sex marriage, has conceded that a "marriage which would be treated as void in the domicile at the time of the marriage need not be recognized, notwithstanding it's being valid in the state of celebration."[100]

The Supreme Court has explained that "marriages not polygamous or incestuous, or otherwise declared void by statute, will, if valid by the law of the State where entered into, be recognized as valid in every other jurisdiction."[101] It is clear, therefore, that one state does not have to recognize an out-of-state, same-sex union or same-sex marriage recognized by another jurisdiction if (1) the out-of-state union is contrary to the state's public policy or (2) the out-of-state union is prohibited by the domicile state's statute and the domicile state has the jurisdiction to enact its own legislation on the matter.

2. Protecting marriage by state Defense of Marriage Acts

The vast majority of states have taken steps to enact legislation specifically prohibiting same-sex marriage. While some states may not have specific legislation using words such as *same-sex marriage*, the wording of the legislation may already be enough to prohibit a marriage license to couples of the same sex. However, it is recommended that each state enact legislation that expressly bans same-sex marriage. A sample piece of legislation may be drafted as follows: "Only marriage between one man and one woman shall be valid or recognized within this state. The uniting of persons of the same sex in marriage, or other similar same-sex relationship in this state or in any jurisdiction is void and shall not be valid or recognized in this state."[102]

Liberty Counsel successfully defended Georgia's marriage law. Quoting the state's Defense of Marriage Act, which was passed in 1996, the Georgia court declared that "it is the public policy of Georgia 'to recognize the union only of man and woman.' Marriages between persons of the same sex are prohibited in this state."[103]

3. Protecting marriage by amending the United States Constitution

In light of the Federal Defense of Marriage Act and the many states that have passed their own laws banning same-sex marriage, one might question the need to amend the United States Constitution to declare that marriage is between one man and one woman. The answer is simple—in light of so much judicial activism, we cannot afford to leave such an important issue to the courts. The litigation to advance same-sex marriage is increasing, and despite the many court victories, the Federal DOMA and the numerous state DOMAs, some judges will disregard the law and common sense. An amendment to the United States Constitution is the only way to once and for all remove the marriage battle from activist judges and securely place it in the hands of the people. As chapter 1 sets forth, marriage between one man and one woman is, and has always been, a national concern. Either we allow a few judges to set our national marriage policy, or "we the people" exercise our right to define marriage through the constitutional amendment process. Once a proposed amendment is passed by two-thirds of the U.S. House and Senate, three-fourths of the states (38) must ratify it. Thus, amending the Constitution to preserve marriage between one man and one woman is an exercise of states' rights.

Civil Unions

In response to a 1999 Vermont Supreme Court decision known as *Baker v. State of Vermont*,[104] the Vermont legislature passed the Civil Union Bill that became law on July 1, 2000.[105] All commentators agree that the Vermont Supreme Court created a new recognition of same-sex relationships in the state of Vermont. This legal relationship did not exist before, and it is unlike anything that existed in the other forty-nine states or territories. Although a civil union is not marriage, it is a parallel system that mimics marriage for same-sex couples. However, it must be clearly stated that the Vermont Supreme Court did not mandate same-sex marriage. In fact Judge Johnson dissented because she wanted the Vermont Supreme Court to sanction same-sex marriage.[106] However, the majority of the judges refused to do so, stating: "We hold only that plaintiffs are entitled under . . . of the Vermont Constitution to obtain the same benefits and protections afforded by Vermont law to married opposite-sex couples."[107]

The Vermont Supreme Court noted that a "sudden change in the marriage laws of the statutory benefits traditionally incidental to marriage may have disruptive and unforeseen consequences."[108] Responding to Judge Johnson's dissenting opinion, which argued in favor of same-sex marriage, the court stated the following:

We believe the argument is predicated upon a fundamental misinterpretation of our opinion. It appears to assume that we hold plaintiffs are entitled to a marriage license. We do not. We hold that the State is constitutionally required to extend to same-sex couples the common benefits and protections that flow from marriage under Vermont law. That the State could do so through a marriage license is obvious. But it is not required to do so, and the mandate proposed by our colleague is inconsistent with the Court's holding.[109]

In response to the decision in *Baker*, the state legislature passed what is now known as the Vermont Civil Union Law. The legislative findings indicate that "civil marriage under Vermont's marriage statutes consists of a union between a man and a woman. This interpretation of the state's marriage laws was upheld by the Supreme Court in *Baker v. State*."[110] The civil union law specifically stated that while "a system of civil unions does not bestow the status of civil marriage, it does satisfy the requirements of the Common Benefits Clause [under the Vermont Constitution]."[111] Even the definition section of the Vermont Civil Union Law states that "'marriage' means the legally recognized union of one man and one woman."[112]

To recognize a Vermont civil union outside of Vermont as the equivalent of marriage is akin to asking one state to recognize a driver's license issued by a sister state as the equivalent of a pilot's license. The only commonality between the two is that both are licenses and both provide most of the same benefits, rights, and obligations, but that's where the similarity ends because one is for opposite-sex and the other for same-sex couples.[113]

The difficulty in other jurisdictions recognizing a Vermont civil union as marriage has been acknowledged even by the proponents of same-sex marriage. Professor Greg Johnson of the Vermont Law School stated that the "weakest case would be out-of-state couples who come to Vermont for a civil union and then go back to their home states seeking not so much the benefits or protections of marriage but simply judicial recognition of their union."[114] Professor Barbara Cox, who has been an advocate of same-sex marriage and longs for the day when little children playing with dolls will accept the idea that two girl dolls or two boy dolls can marry each other, concedes that the portability of Vermont civil unions is highly questionable.[115] Professor Cox concedes that

the portability of marriages entered into both by Vermont couples who later move to other states and by non-Vermont couples who marry in Vermont and then return to their home states is uncertain. This uncertainty is due to the "public policy" exception to the general choice of law principle that marriages valid in the state of celebration are valid everywhere and due to the various Defense of Marriage Acts passed by Congress and the numerous state legislatures. That uncertainty is even greater now that same-sex couples may only enter into civil unions, rather than marriages, thus perhaps making it more difficult for them to use prior marriage recognition cases that would have supported the portability of their marital status. . . .[116]

Professor Cox recognizes that the "uncertainty" of civil unions "is even greater for non-Vermont couples who travel to Vermont, enter into civil unions, and then return to their domiciles. By requiring same-sex couples to enter into civil unions instead of marriages, Vermont has increased the uncertainty that out-of-state, same-sex couples would face concerning the interstate recognition of their marriages."[117] Professor Cox further recognizes that even if Vermont had recognized same-sex marriages, "the portability of their marriages still would have been more uncertain than the marriages of opposite-sex couples due to the . . . public policy exception which permits courts to refuse to recognize marriages that they find to be 'odious.'"[118] She concludes that "even if Vermont had provided its citizens with the right to marry, their legal status would have been unclear once they left the state's borders. With civil unions that status is all the more indefinite."[119]

Homosexual advocates wove a tangled web when the state of Vermont created civil unions. Vermont imposes no residency requirements in order to enter into a civil union.[120] However, in order to dissolve a civil union, the party seeking the dissolution must reside within the state for a period of six months or more, and the decree of dissolution may not be granted unless the plaintiff or the defendant has resided within the state for one year preceding the date of final hearing.[121] In other words, while Vermont does not require residency to enter into a civil union, the party seeking to dissolve a civil union must live in the state a minimum of six months, or, if the responding party does not already live in the state, at least twelve months must pass before the dissolution can be effective.

This tangled web has come home to roost for same-sex couples who obtained a Vermont civil union. In *Rosengarten v. Downes,*[122] two male homosexuals from Connecticut traveled to Vermont and obtained a civil union license. The two then traveled back to Connecticut, and thereafter the relationship broke down. After Mr. Downes moved out of the state of Connecticut, Mr. Rosengarten filed a petition in the Connecticut courts to dissolve the civil union. However, the Connecticut courts ruled that the state had no jurisdiction to dissolve a Vermont civil union because no such similar entity existed within the state. The court noted that a Vermont civil union is not marriage even in Vermont and that Connecticut recognizes only the marriage of one man and one woman. Thus, Connecticut had no authority to dissolve this civil union.[123]

Some politicians casually say they oppose same-sex marriage but favor civil unions. This statement reveals duplicity or ignorance. Although a Vermont-style civil union is not marriage, the only primary difference is that a civil union is for same-sex couples. Other than this difference, a civil union in Vermont mimics marriage. If Vermont-style civil unions were enacted outside of Vermont, in a few years same-sex marriage advocates would argue that the name *civil union* should be replaced with the name *marriage* since the two are parallel schemes. Thus, those who support traditional marriage must also oppose civil unions. In other words, it is disingenuous to say you are opposed to same-sex marriage but favor civil unions.

Domestic Partnership Benefits

In the legislative agenda of the same-sex marriage movement, domestic partnership benefits typically follow implementation of a "sexual orientation" nondiscrimination policy. For example, regarding the workplace environment, the Human Rights Campaign, a multimillion dollar homosexual lobbying organization headquartered in Washington, D.C., states:

Sexual orientation policies are an important first step that should come before any effort to organize a domestic partner benefits proposal. The nondiscrimination policy will be valuable in lobbying your employer for DP benefits. DP benefits are a logical extension of an employer's commitment to provide a workplace free of sexual orientation discrimination. Also, guarantee of fair treatment is essential if employees are expected to reveal their relationships in order to seek health care coverage for their domestic partners.[124]

In addition to arguing equality, homosexual advocates also argue that in order to attract the best and the brightest employees, the private and public sector must be "progressive" by affording domestic partnership benefits to same-sex couples. Of course, there is no evidence to back up such an argument. In fact, after General Motors adopted its domestic partnership policy, 1/100 of 1 percent of its employees, or 166 out of 1,330,000, chose the benefits during the year 2001.[125]

The push for domestic partnership benefits is an important legislative agenda in the march toward same-sex marriage. In the words of same-sex marriage advocates, "DP [domestic partnership] benefits are not the final step in the GLBT [gay, lesbian, bisexual, transsexual] quest for equality, but they are integral to its achievement. Equal protection for our relationships, whether through marriage or DP benefits, is a key goal for millions of GLBT people."[126]

Lambda Legal Defense Fund, a homosexual public interest law firm, has advanced domestic partnership benefits through the courts in order to crack the foundation of marriage. Although the Chicago Board of Education provided domestic partnership benefits to same-sex couples, Lambda argued that the same benefits should also be provided to unmarried cohabiting couples. The court rejected this argument by noting the following:

> Lambda is concerned with the fact that state and national policy encourages (heterosexual) marriage in all sorts of ways that domestic partner health benefits cannot begin to equalize. Lambda wants to knock marriage off its perch by requiring the Board of Education to treat unmarried heterosexual couples as well as it treats married ones, so that marriage will lose some of its luster.
>
> This is further evidence of the essentially symbolic or political rather than practical significance of the Board's policy [which grants domestic partnership benefits to same-sex couples]. Lambda is not jeopardizing a substantial benefit for homosexuals because very few of them want or will seek the benefit.[127]

As the court noted, domestic partnership benefits are often sought more for their symbolic statement than for their practical need. Obtaining domestic partnership benefits is an attempt to grasp benefits traditionally associated with marriage without the commitment of marriage. As the above example illustrates, sometimes same-sex marriage advocates argue that domestic partnership benefits should include both same-sex and opposite-sex partners. While such tactics might appeal to family members desiring to include a relative in a benefits package or to cohabiting, opposite-sex partners, such a broad domestic partnership policy is no less a ruse to undermine traditional marriage as a more narrow one designed solely for same-sex couples. As chapter 1 discussed, equalizing cohabitation with marriage weakens marriage, and as such, will open the door to same-sex marriage and the abolition of marriage altogether.

A Hill Worth Dying For

Marriage must be defended. The battle to preserve traditional marriage must be waged and won on many fronts. We must be aware of incremental steps designed to weaken the institution of marriage. One incremental advance by the same-sex marriage movement will only lead to another, and, before long, same-sex marriage will seem like only another small step. We must draw a line in the sand because once we cross the same-sex marriage line, it will be difficult to turn back. We are living at a critical time in human history. We are confronted with two separate and distinct roads for our future, and these roads diverge over the issue of marriage. We have a choice to preserve marriage and family, and by God's grace I firmly believe this is a winnable battle.

CHAPTER 8

In the Image of God

*I*n the early morning hours of April 26, 1986, a nuclear explosion occurred at Chernobyl that rocked the world.

The accident took place at reactor number four. The crew operating the nuclear plant had planned to test whether the turbines could produce enough energy in the event of a loss of power until the emergency generators were activated. The reactor was powered down to 25 percent of capacity, but the procedure did not go according to plan. For some reason the nuclear power level fell to less than 1 percent. When that occurred, the power had to be gradually increased, but only thirty seconds after the power was increased, a sudden and unexpected surge of power occurred. The reactor's emergency shutdown was designed to halt the chain reaction that occurred, but that too failed.

Almost immediately the power level and temperature rose, causing a thousand-ton steel cap on the reactor building to blow. The temperature reached over 3,600 degrees Fahrenheit (1,000 degrees more than necessary to melt steel), and thus the fuel rods melted. The graphite cover in the reactor then ignited into a ball of flame, and the radioactive fission products released during the core meltdown were jettisoned into the atmosphere.[1] Between April 26 and May 5, clouds of radioactive fallout were carried from Chernobyl to Scandinavia, to Poland, Czechoslovakia, Austria, Northern Italy, the Balkans, Greece, and Turkey.

Two decades after the nuclear catastrophe, berries, certain types of mushrooms, and game in Southern Bavaria and the Bavarian Forest continue to show significant levels of contamination. Certain by-products of splitting uranium nuclei become aspirated like an aerosol. When the cells of the body are exposed to such radiation particles, free radicals are produced. These free radicals or ions can impair cellular function and cause damage to the DNA. The DNA carries the genetic blueprint for cellular replication, structure, and function, and such damage can cause a weakening of the immune system and result in many forms of cancer.

Some people exposed to the radiation at Chernobyl died within a matter of months. Others continue to suffer from physical damage years later. This damage includes tumors and genetic mutation. In addition to the cancer that appeared in adults, the unborn children of women who were pregnant at the time were also affected. Even after-born children began developing thyroid cancer and leukemia. Many people suffered psychological trauma.

The Chernobyl disaster affected not only humans but also the environment. Radioactive fallout in Belarus contaminated approximately 22 percent of the agricultural land and 21 percent of the forests. The aftereffects included not only physiological, psychological, environmental, and agricultural damage, but some traditional cultural influences and practices were devastated and some significantly changed. The language, music, and art in the surrounding rural areas began reflecting the horrible results of radiation contamination.

Within seven months after the explosion, the ruined reactor building and its molten core were enclosed with a reinforced concrete casting. The entire complex was eventually closed on December 12, 2000.

Radioactive material such as uranium presents a paradox similar to many elements we experience in the natural world. When contained in a nuclear reactor, radioactive material can produce power and energy. Chernobyl supplied electrical power for the capital, Kiev. The inhabitants of Kiev came to rely upon the energy produced by Chernobyl. Those who live near a nuclear power plant take for granted the light that fills the room after flipping a switch, the warm comfort of a hot shower, or the convenience of electrical appliances. When properly contained in a nuclear reactor, radioactive material has the potential to produce positive benefits. However, as Chernobyl has taught us, when the nuclear reactor becomes cracked and the radioactive material leaks out, that which was designed to produce power and energy produces destruction and death. The effects are long-term and widespread, wreaking havoc not only on current but also on future generations. Not only are there physical health consequences, but there are also emotional, agricultural, and environmental consequences.

Human sexuality is analogous to radioactive material, and the marriage of a man and a woman is the equivalent of a nuclear reactor. When sex is contained within the confines of a husband and wife as man and woman, the result is the production of life and the emotional bonding of two people into one.

In order to set our moral compass in a sea of conflicting ideas, we must understand the origin and destination of our journey. The origin of our human history begins with creation, and the destiny ends with God creating a new heaven and a new earth. An airline pilot seeking to travel from Orlando to New York must chart the point of takeoff and the point of landing. A navigational chart will then set forth the specific direction of the compass. As long as the pilot flies in accordance with the compass, the plane will reach its intended destination.

To place in context the debate over same-sex unions, consider the story of creation. Contemplate for a moment the wonders of the created world. Standing on the edge of the Grand Canyon, the sight is surreal. Between one edge and the other side snakes a jagged scar in the depths of the earth a mile wide. The breadth of the landscape as you survey the horizon is too large to comprehend. The majesty of the Grand Canyon is awesome.

In a completely different environment, at forty feet under crystal blue water off the coast of Grand Cayman, are the most brilliantly colored coral painted in red, yellow, blue, and green. Surrounding this magnificent structure are thousands of fish. Some are yellow. Others are shiny as they speed through the water. Other fish are multicolored and spotted with black, yellow, or blue. Some are completely red. A moray eel slithers into the coral with its bright green skin. At one hundred feet under, literally on the edge of a tectonic plate, you stare downward into a black abyss.

Whether gazing at the Swiss Alps with their towering mountains, a field of drooping trees covered with freshly fallen snow, a magnificent sunrise on the east coast or a breathtaking sunset on the west, the stars on a clear night, multicolored birds or the animals in the plain, there is only one creation that was bestowed with God's highest appellation, that of being created in the image of God—the creation of man and woman.

The creation story tells it this way: "Then God said, 'Let us make man in our image, in our likeness, and let them rule over the fish of the sea and the birds of the air, over the livestock, over all the earth, and over all the creatures that move along the ground.' So God created man in his own image, in the image of God he created him; male and female He created them" (Gen. 1:26–27).

The Hebrew word used for "man" in Genesis 1:26 is the generic noun *adham* or *Adam*, which means "mankind." Genesis 1:27 states that God created "mankind" in his own image as "male" and "female."

Creating man and woman was God's crowning act of creation. Elevating the union of man and woman above every other created thing in the universe, God declared man and woman to be made in his own image. Nothing else in creation reflects the image of God except man and woman, and nothing is more central to the created order than the union of one man and one woman.

There is something fundamentally important about man and woman in God's creation. An image is a counterpart or a model. While image may connote physical resemblance, image may also connote characteristics. A son who is the image of his father may reflect characteristics of his father other than physical resemblance. Stating that someone is the image of good health refers to more than just physical characteristics; it refers to a state of being.[2] The model or image of God is unique and only found in the creation of, and the relationship between, a man and a woman. The creation story continues with the declaration that "a man will leave his father and mother and be united to his wife, and they will become one flesh" (Gen. 2:24).

Jesus spoke of the relationship of husband and wife when he declared to the Pharisees: "Haven't you read," he replied, "that at the beginning the Creator 'made them male and female,' and said, 'for this reason a man will leave his father and mother and be united to his wife, and the two will become one flesh'?" (Matt. 19:4–5).

The apostle Paul, in the book of Ephesians, also talks about the union of husband and wife as one. "'For this reason a man will leave his father and mother and be united to his wife, and the two will become one flesh'" (Eph. 5:31).

Writing about sexual immorality, Paul warned that sexual relations united two human beings into one. Speaking of this unity, he wrote:

> Do you not know that your bodies are members of Christ himself? Shall I then take the members of Christ and unite them with a prostitute? Never! Do you not know that he who unites himself with a prostitute is one with her in body? For it is said, "The two will become one flesh." But he who unites himself with the Lord is one with him in spirit.
>
> Flee from sexual immorality. All other sins a man commits are outside his body, but he who sins sexually sins against his own body. Do you not know that your body is a temple of the Holy Spirit who is in you, whom you have received from God? You are not your own; you were bought at a price. Therefore honor God with your body (1 Cor. 6:15–20).

There is a significant difference between being sexually intimate with a person of the opposite sex and being emotionally close platonic friends. Sexuality between a man and a woman forms the basis for the survival of future generations. God created sexual intimacy between a husband and wife as a means of strengthening the human bond of two people into one. Premarital or extramarital sex fractures this bond because sex unites two people into one and thereby drives a wedge between the relationship of a husband and wife by inserting a third party into that union.

Of all the known passions, human sexuality is closely analogous to radioactive material. Confining sex in the union of a man and a woman as husband and wife produces power, energy, unity, and lays the groundwork for the survival of future generations. A husband-and-wife model is akin to the Chernobyl nuclear reactor. Like radioactive material, if the sexual urge is allowed to seep outside of the human reactor of husband and wife, then instead of producing power and posterity, it produces destruction and death. This is true whether the sexual activity occurs before marriage (premarital sex), during marriage (adultery), or in alternative relationships (homosexuality or bestiality).

The reason the issue of same-sex marriage is so critical to our culture and religious freedom is that it contorts the very image of God and is contrary to the natural order. When the image of God is broken or the natural order rearranged, then we experience cultural, moral, physical, and psychological consequences. Among teens who have sex, eight thousand will contract sexually transmitted diseases every day. That is one every ten seconds. Of the approximately 1.5 million abortions that occur each year, 20 percent involve teenagers.

Sexual abuse of a minor, whether homosexual or heterosexual, fractures the image of God and the created order. Walk through the corridors of any prison and speak with those who are incarcerated for violent crimes. You will find an alarming number of inmates who have been sexually abused during their infant or adolescent years. I have encountered many people trapped in the clutches of the homosexual lifestyle who have experienced sexual abuse from a parent or close relative.

Sex during marriage with someone other than one's spouse is one of the primary causes for divorce. Well-known political and religious leaders have had their careers ruined because they came in contact with the radioactive sexual drive outside of marriage. Presidential candidate Gary Hart had to withdraw from his presidential race after the national media revealed he had a sexual affair. The ministry of Jimmy Swaggart has never been the same since it became known that he had slept with prostitutes. The flourishing religious empire of Jim and Tammy Faye Baker fell apart when Jim Baker had sex in a hotel with a woman who was not his wife.

Homosexuality is out of sync with God's creation, and it is contrary to the natural order. A homosexual relationship is exactly the opposite of what God ordained. Take anything that was created or designed to operate one way and reverse the sequence of operation, and the inevitable result is destruction. Same-sex unions strike at the very image of God and the natural order.

One doesn't need to believe in the Bible or subscribe to Judeo-Christian theology to conclude that human sexuality is like radioactive material, that it has the potential to produce as much good as it can be destructive, and that sex between a man and a woman is self-evident in the natural order. Whether you believe in a Creator God or a humanistic evolutionary model, the fact remains that human sexuality is best suited to occur between a man and a woman. To ignore this obvious fact is nonsensical. To sanction the opposite through same-sex marriage is cultural suicide.

CHAPTER 9

Sinners in the Hand of a Loving God

*J*onathan Edwards (1703–1758), a powerful preacher of the evangelical revival known as the Great Awakening, was notably remembered for his sermon delivered in 1741 entitled "Sinners in the Hand of an Angry God."[1] While not his typical sermon, his revival message painted a picture of God holding sinners over the pit of hell with flames lapping at their feet, as a spider holds a bug. Edwards vividly described the following:

> The God that holds you over the pit of hell, much as one holds a spider, or some loathsome insect over the fire, abhors you, and is dreadfully provoked: his wrath towards you burns like fire; he looks upon you as worthy of nothing else, but to be cast into the fire; he is of purer eyes than to bear to have you in his sight; you are ten thousand times more abominable in his eyes than the most hateful venomous serpent is in ours. You have offended him infinitely more than ever a stubborn rebel did his prince; and yet it is nothing but his hand that holds you from falling into the fire every moment.[2]

Sinners are doomed to hell, Edwards exclaimed, dangled by a thin spiderweb over this raging inferno. The people sat on the edge of their pews and began to sweat from the visual imagery of the hot flames. After bringing the congregants to the verge of eternal torment, the great preacher turned their eyes from the dreadful fate that awaited them to a rescuing God. "Therefore, let every one that is out of Christ, now awake and fly away from wrath to come. The wrath of Almighty God is now undoubtedly hanging over a great part of this congregation: let every one fly out of Sodom: 'Haste and escape for your lives, look not behind you, escape to the mountain, lest you be consumed'" (Gen. 19:17).[3]

Although Jonathan Edwards's sermon emphasized the separation between God and humanity and thus portrayed God as *angry*, the point of his message was that a *loving* God reaches out his hand to rescue each one of us despite our wickedness and sin.

Balancing Love and Justice

When considering homosexuality and same-sex marriage, we must remember to balance God's justice with his love. While God is just, he is also a God of love. On the topic of homosexuality especially, we err by emphasizing one of God's attributes to the neglect or exclusion of the other. Homosexuality or same-sex marriage evokes strong emotions on both sides. Some are quick to condemn to hell and damnation those involved in the homosexual lifestyle, while some involved in the lifestyle seek to justify their behavior by focusing on the love of God and ignoring his justice. Those on both sides of this cultural debate should remember that "all have sinned and fall short of the glory of God" (Rom. 3:23). God indeed is love, but he is also a God of justice, and thus he sent his Son to pay the penalty for our sin. The Bible says that we "are justified freely by his grace through the redemption that came by Christ Jesus. God presented him as a sacrifice of atonement, through faith in his blood. He did this to demonstrate his justice, because in his forbearance, he had left the sins committed beforehand unpunished—he did it to demonstrate his justice at the present time, so as to be just and the one who justifies those who have faith in Jesus" (Rom. 3:24–26).

The apostle Paul then rhetorically asks, "Where, then, is boasting? It is excluded" (Rom. 3:27). The book of Romans states that because Christ died for our sins, our position with God is made right when we accept the sacrifice of his son Jesus, and thus "we have peace with God through our Lord Jesus Christ" (Rom. 5:1). The penalty of our sin is erased as Christ stands in the gap between God and mankind. To those who would use God's grace as a license for sin, Paul quickly writes: "What shall we say, then? Shall we go on sinning so that grace may increase? By no means! We died to sin; how can we live in it any longer?" (Rom. 6:1–2).

Sin is always sin. There is only one sin that cannot be forgiven, namely, what the Bible refers to as blasphemy against the Holy Spirit (see Mark 3:29). Apparently, blasphemy against the Holy Spirit is the hardening of one's heart to the point that God's Holy Spirit is no longer recognized but is instead deemed to be evil.[4] Other than this one sin, every other known sin comes within the grace of God through his Son Jesus Christ.

God's grace and love are always balanced by inevitable consequences. To the Christian church in Corinth, Paul wrote: "Do you not know that the wicked will not inherit the kingdom of God? Do not be deceived: Neither the sexually immoral nor idolaters nor adulterers nor male prostitutes nor homosexual offenders nor thieves nor the greedy nor drunkards nor slanderers nor swindlers will inherit the kingdom of God. And that is what some of you *were*. But you were washed, you were sanctified, you were justified in the name of the Lord Jesus Christ and by the Spirit of our God" (1 Cor. 6:9–11).

Paul identifies three kinds of sexual immorality: (1) adulterers, (2) male prostitutes, and (3) males who practice homosexuality. In Romans 1:26, Paul also condemns female homosexuality. People who engage in such practices, including the other categories of misbehavior listed, will not inherit the kingdom of God. However, God's grace reached to those in the church of Corinth because some of them *were* engaged in these various practices until they were forgiven, and their lives were changed (see 1 Cor. 6:11).

Why should Christians, or those concerned with moral values, care whether someone else engages in homosexual activity or wants to enter into a same-sex marriage? The reason is the same as stated by Jesus to his disciples when he declared, "I have come that they may have life and have it more abundantly" (John 10:10). Misuse of our physical bodies, particularly in the area of sexual activity, limits the full life that God has destined for us. As the apostle Paul said, "The body is not for sexual immorality but for the Lord, and the Lord for the body" (1 Cor. 6:13). Homosexuality hurts adults, children, and the culture. As I said in chapter 1, hurting people hurt people.

In the created order there are certain metaphysical laws that, if violated, have known and specific consequences. Some of these laws include the Laws of Thermodynamics. Energy exists in many forms including heat, light, chemical, and electrical. Thermodynamics is the study of energy. The First Law of Thermodynamics states that energy can be changed from one form to another, but it cannot be created or destroyed. Thus, the total amount of energy and matter in the universe remains constant, merely changing from one form to another.

The Second Law of Thermodynamics states that in all energy exchanges, if no energy enters or leaves the system, the potential energy of the state will always be less than that of the initial state. This is sometimes referred to as entropy. This law is best illustrated by our everyday activity of eating. The potential energy locked in food is converted into kinetic energy through the marvels of the body, and that energy is converted to heat and dissipated. Complete entropy occurs when our cells cease taking in energy and die.

Sir Isaac Newton developed three Laws of Motion. The First Law states that every object in a state of uniform motion tends to remain in that state of motion unless an external force is applied to it. In the absence of gravitational pull, a missile launched into outer space will continue in motion until an external force is applied to slow its speed.

Newton also popularized the Second Law of Motion, which states that the relationship between an object's mass (m), its acceleration (a), and the applied force (F) is the mathematical formula of $F=ma$. In other words, the speed and size of an object is equivalent to the force of the impact.

Newton's Third Law of Motion is familiar to everyone. This law states that for every action there is an equal and opposite reaction. This law, like the other laws already mentioned, is constant and unchanging. The results are fixed and immutable.

In addition to these laws, there is also the law we commonly refer to as gravity. If you are stupid enough to walk off the roof of your house with nothing below to catch you, you will suffer the inevitable consequences of the sudden stop at the end of your fall. If you get hurt, should you blame God? Absolutely not! Ignore the law of gravity and you will suffer the consequences.

Like these metaphysical laws, there are also moral and spiritual laws of the created order. In the context of human sexuality, the Bible speaks of the inevitable consequences of rejecting God. In the book of Romans, Paul wrote:

> The wrath of God is being revealed from heaven against all the godlessness and wickedness of men who suppress the truth by their wickedness, since what may be known about God is plain to them, because God has made it plain to them. For since the creation of the world God's invisible qualities—his eternal power and divine nature—have been clearly seen, being understood from what has been made, so that men are without excuse.
>
> For although they knew God, they neither glorified him as God nor gave thanks to him, but their thinking became futile and their foolish hearts were darkened. (Rom. 1:18–21)

Just like Newton's Laws of Motion or the Laws of Thermodynamics, the consequences of disobedience to God affects our moral behavior. Paul continues: "Therefore God gave them over in their sinful desires of their hearts to sexual impurity for the degrading of their bodies with one another. . . . God gave them over to shameful lusts. Even their women exchanged natural relations for unnatural ones. In the same way men also abandoned natural relations with women and were inflamed with lust for one another. Men committed indecent acts with other men, and received in themselves the due penalty for their perversion. (Rom. 1:24, 26–27)

Sexual immorality is not the only consequence of pushing God from the center of our lives; other consequences follow.

Furthermore, since they did not think it worthwhile to retain the knowledge of God, he gave them over to a depraved mind, to do what ought not to be done. They have been filled with every kind of wickedness, evil, greed and depravity. They are full of envy, murder, strife, deceit and malice. They are gossips, slanderers, God-haters, insolent, arrogant and boastful; they invent ways of doing evil; they disobey their parents; they are senseless, faithless, heartless, ruthless. Although they know God's righteous decree that those who do such things deserve death, they not only continue to do these very things but also approve of those who practice them. (Rom. 1:28–32)

In the book of Deuteronomy, Moses set forth two options for the children of Israel as they concluded forty years of wandering in the wilderness. When God's people were on the verge of ending their vagabond lifestyle to become permanent residents in the promised land, Moses set forth a path of blessing and one that would lead to curses. Chapter 28, verses 1 through 14, speaks of the blessings, while verses 15 through 68 describe the inevitable curses. The difference between the two paths is a choice to follow God and his commandments or to disobey him. The section begins by declaring: "If you fully obey the LORD your God and carefully follow all his commands I give you today, the LORD your God will set you high above all the nations on earth. All these blessings will come upon you and accompany you if you obey the LORD your God." (Deut. 28:1–2)

The path of obedience to God includes blessing in the city and the country. The fertility rate of women and families will be blessed, and the production of crops and livestock will flourish. The nation will be strong against its enemies, and the people will prosper in every profession they pursue. They will be innovative and productive. As a result of fully obeying the Lord, the environment will even reap the blessings of God.

"However, if you do not obey the Lord your God and do not carefully follow all his commandments and decrees I am giving you today, all these curses will come upon you and overtake you" (Deut. 28:15). Instead of being blessed in the city and country, the people will be cursed. The fertility rate will drop, and agricultural endeavors and livestock production will suffer. People will become confused in their thinking and will be plagued with many new and incurable diseases, including sexually transmitted diseases.[5] The people of God who could have been blessed will become the target of many enemies. The marital bond will be stressed, and the divorce rate will increase.[6] Women, who normally would extend tender mercy to their children, will kill them out of distress or because of convenience.[7] Borrowing will increase, and debt will plague the land. The environment will suffer.

The blessings and curses portrayed in Deuteronomy depict the same immutable principles governing morality and the culture that govern the laws of motion or thermodynamics. Every decision we make has consequences, either for good or for evil. The two attributes of love and justice are two sides of the same coin. While Jonathan Edwards' famous sermon focused on the justice of God, his intent was to show God's overwhelming love. The fact is that God knows the results of bad choices. He has set before us two roads to follow. The first is the path of relationship with him. This path has inevitable positive consequences. Not everyone chooses the right path because of selfishness, brokenness, and sinful desires that always attempt to twist and turn our destiny.

The second path is the choice not to follow God or the choice of giving less than our full commitment to him. When we choose this path, our self-centeredness controls our destiny. That destiny has inevitable negative consequences. When God created man and woman in his image, he knew what he was doing. The relationship between a husband and wife is one of the most desirous and uplifting human relationships this side of eternity, except for our relationship with God.

God ordained that we should have a close relationship with him. A right relationship with God fills our spiritual emptiness and provides security. Acceptance provides stability and self-worth. Rejection is just the opposite; it provides instability and self-deprecation. Acceptance or rejection plays an important role in the development of who we are as men and women. Children raised in an environment with a mother and father, who not only love each other but also love them, are the most secure and well-adjusted children. However, children or adults who face rejection can become damaged in their human sexuality, and if that rejection is not healed by the love of Christ, the person's sexuality can become a lethal and self-destructive coping mechanism.

Alan Chambers, the executive director of Exodus International, an organization that ministers to people who desire freedom from homosexuality, shares his heart-wrenching testimony that illustrates my point.

> I dreamed about everything good. I dreamed about being loved, accepted, and secure. I dreamed about commitment and relationship, but I knew lonely. I knew what it was like not to fit in and to be teased to tears. I knew what it was like to watch the boys on the playground and feel such anxiety and insecurity about joining them I literally would do anything to avoid it. I knew what it was like to play with the girls with whom I outwardly had more in common. I knew what it was like to be different from the other boys my age and have an insatiable need to be accepted and liked by them. I knew the pain of molestation. I knew what it was like to believe

the lie that molestation was my fault because I let it happen. I knew what it was like to feel shame and pain because a part of me wanted it to happen again because if nothing else, he had chosen me! I knew what it was like to feel important and desirable to an older guy, even if it was only for a moment behind a locked door, under the guise of secrecy, confusion and stolen innocence. I knew what it was like to be so emotionally hungry for male love, affirmation and attention that the dirtiest acts satisfied a portion of my hunger. I knew what it felt like to believe that my longing for male love and acceptance wore the name "sex." I knew what it was like to come to the realization that I was a homosexual even though I had never asked for my same sex attractions. I knew what it was like to be called "homo," "fag," and "queer" until I believed it was the truth. I dreamed of more, but lived on less.[8]

Alan says that by the time he was ten or eleven he began "to hear at church that 'homosexuals could not share in God's kingdom,' but under no circumstances did I hear that 'such were some of you' (1 Cor. 6:9–11) which was two thousand-year-old evidence that homosexuals could change."[9]

In 1990 Alan attended a youth conference where the speaker stated that there was a young man sitting in the audience who thinks he is gay, that he had been molested, and that he thinks the only way out is suicide. Alan went forward and heard for the first time from this preacher that "God loves you—no matter what."[10] Alan began attending support groups in late 1990 at the age of eighteen. He wanted to leave his homosexual lifestyle, but six months later he reverted back to his old ways. He came across a place where anonymous sexual encounters occurred. Although the sex did not involve a relationship, he felt that he was at least desirable to someone for ten minutes. He says that "sex was a counterfeit to the love and security I desired. I became addicted. Later I would learn the scripture, 'to the hungry, even what is bitter tastes sweet' (Prov. 27:7)."[11]

In 1991 on Easter Sunday, Alan was alone in a gay bar waiting for his friends who never came. At that time God began to impress upon him what he had heard during the youth conference—that God loved him no matter what. At that moment when he felt he desperately needed help, two friends from his church walked through the doors of the bar, paid the cover charge, and told Alan that God had prompted them to come and help him. Together they walked out of that bar. "That Easter Sunday night in 1991 the Lord personally sent a brother and sister in the flesh to walk beside me on my journey out of homosexuality."[12] Alan recommitted himself to God. He found a church that gave him love and support. He stated, "Gradually my will and then my desires changed. I no longer needed gay sex. . . . Today I am experiencing what I used to only dream about but never found in the gay life. I have a loving wife, a wonderful relationship with my family, godly friendships, a church which stands for the truth and understands God's grace, and a ministry where I can serve Him who made all of my dreams come true. . . . We cannot help but be changed as we make Him Lord of our life and experience His love for us."[13]

The story of Alan Chambers is repeated in the many testimonies on the Web site of Exodus International. Some experience rejection in childhood. Rejection often may arise from a physically or sexually abusive relationship with parents or close family members. Sometimes rejection comes about merely because the parent—particularly the one who is the same sex as the child—was too busy to spend quality time and to express true love for the child. Rejection may also arise out of relationships with the opposite sex that go sour, either because of rejection or because of rape or some other emotional trauma. The resulting behavior following rejection may become manifest through a variety of coping mechanisms, including drugs or alcohol and even same-sex relationships.

Growing up in a home with a loving mother and father is critically important to the sexual development of children. When God created man and woman, he indeed knew what he was doing. Sexual intimacy between a man and a woman, in the context of husband and wife, is good. However, when human sexuality is taken outside of the relationship of husband and wife, it breeds destruction and death. Someone is inevitably rejected, and someone inevitably feels dirty, guilty, and shameful. Children suffer most particularly, and these fragile human beings who are on loan to us from God may carry deep scars. Whether our torment comes from something we chose or something that was forced upon us, the end result is the same. In order to break the continuing cycle of destruction, we must understand the immeasurable love of God. As Christians we must model God's justice and his love to those who appear most undeserving because it is precisely for these people that Christ suffered and died. His forgiveness covers every sin.

We are all sinners in the hand of a loving God. God's grace is greater than all of our experiences of rejection. We are born sinners, and as such, we are inherently alienated from God. God bridged that gulf by sending his Son to die in our place. He washes us clean of all our filth and establishes us in a right relationship with him.

Shedding Our Moral Laryngitis

At a time when silence was generally accepted and complicity was the norm of the day, one man stood out above all the other religious leaders. His name was Dietrich Bonhoeffer (1906–1945). Executed by hanging in the Flossenberg

Concentration Camp for his role in resisting Hitler, Bonhoeffer wrote some of his most profound words in prison.

Upon completing his academic study, he began teaching theology in Berlin. After Adolf Hitler ascended to power in January 1933, the German Evangelical Church, which Bonhoeffer attended, entered a difficult time of history. A group called the Deutsche Cristen ("German Christians") began trumpeting Nazi ideology within the evangelical church. This liberal socialist faction even advocated removing the Old Testament from the Bible. Relying upon a state law that barred all non-Aryans from civil service, the Deutsche Cristen group proposed the idea of preventing non-Aryans from becoming ministers or religious teachers. The controversy threatened to split the German Evangelical Church. While many within the Evangelical Church still promoted the notion that Jews should be evangelized and become part of the church through baptism, the Deutsche Cristen group believed that Jews should be considered a separate race and that they could never become associated with the church. Bonhoeffer opposed the efforts of the Deutsche Cristen, but by the fall of 1933, the Deutsche Cristen gained control of many Protestant church governments throughout Germany. The policy of excluding Jews from the ministry was eventually approved in September 1933 by the national church senate in Wittenberg.

Bonhoeffer escaped imprisonment by fleeing to London, England. There he worked with two German-speaking congregations. He later returned to Germany and began teaching young clergy in the so-called Confessing Church. By August 1937 the Himmler Decree declared the education and examination of confessing ministry candidates illegal, and many of Bonhoeffer's students were arrested. Bonhoeffer then spent the next few years traveling undercover, teaching secretly within the borders of Germany. The Gestapo banned Bonhoeffer from Berlin in January 1938 and in September 1940 issued an order forbidding him from delivering any public speech. He could have fled to a comfortable life in the United States in 1939, but instead he decided to remain in Germany. He explained to the German Lutheran, Reinhold Niebuhr, that he must return in order to stand up for the Christian civilization.

Bonhoeffer was imprisoned and eventually executed in 1945, but while he was in prison, he wrote many letters, including the December 1942 Christmas letter entitled "After Ten Years." He asked a poignant question that every Christian today must ponder: "We have been silent witnesses of evil deeds: We have been drenched by many storms; we have learnt the arts of equivocation and pretense; experience has made us suspicious of others and kept us from being truthful and open; intolerable conflicts have worn us down and made us cynical. Are we still of any use?"[14]

The question Bonhoeffer asked, "Are we still of any use?", is just as powerful now as it was during the Nazi regime. Jesus said that we should be the salt of the earth and the light of the world.

"You are the salt of the earth. But if the salt loses its saltiness, how can it be made salty again? It is no longer good for anything, except to be thrown out and trampled by men.

"You are the light of the world. A city on a hill cannot be hidden. Neither do people light a lamp and put it under a bowl. Instead they put it on its stand, and it gives light to everyone in the house. In the same way, let your light shine before men, that they may see your good deeds and praise your Father in heaven." (Matt. 5:13–16)

Salt is used for flavoring and, more particularly, for preserving. Light dispels darkness and gives guidance. A false notion of tolerance has been the crutch that many use as an excuse to say nothing about the cultural debate over same-sex marriage. My friend, Reverend Howard Eddington, once said that pastors, leaders, and others concerned about marriage and the family have been plagued with "moral laryngitis" when it comes to homosexual issues.

As Christians we operate under the command of two commissions: the cultural commission and the Great Commission. The cultural commission is set forth in the book of Genesis. After God created Adam and Eve, he blessed them and told them to be fruitful and multiply, to fill the earth and exercise dominion over the earth (see Gen. 1:28–30). Having dominion does not mean to exercise unyielding power. Rather, Adam and Eve and their descendants are the caretakers of the earth, which not only includes the plants, the animals, and the environment but certainly the culture and well-being of our fellow brothers and sisters. The Great Commission is found in the gospel of Matthew, where Jesus Christ commissions every believer to make disciples and to teach God's commandments (see Matt. 28:18–20).

These two commissions have never been revoked. The cultural commission requires God's people to (1) spread throughout the earth and (2) care for God's creation. The Great Commission requires God's people to (1) bring people to a right relationship with God through Jesus Christ and (2) teach God's will to all people. The cultural commission and the Great Commission mean that God's people must impart God's will and extend his blessing throughout all the earth.

In the article, "Future Shock," published in a pro-homosexual magazine, Patricia Warren writes, "Whoever captures the kids owns the future."[15] At stake in this battle over same-sex marriage are children, the culture, and freedom of expression. A false notion of tolerance combined with selfishness, where we are only concerned about the small bubble of reality that surrounds us, has paralyzed the

Christian and pro-family community. Many have failed to act in this cultural war for several reasons, none of which are legitimate.

One reason some are apathetic is a misunderstanding of tolerance. Tolerance does not mean that everything must be accepted. While individuals have differences of opinions, there are certain moral absolutes that cannot be breached. Tolerance can be used to silence any opposition whether it be to polygamy, prostitution, incest, or pedophilia. All of our laws derive from some kind of moral understanding. By respecting another person's property or protecting their physical well-being, these policy choices are grounded in our moral understanding of right and wrong. Tolerance does not mean that we lose our convictions.

My father was an alcoholic, but while I accept him as my father, I do not accept his alcoholism. Close relatives or friends who are involved in the homosexual lifestyle, and who may be nice people, should have no effect on whether we accept homosexual behavior or same-sex marriage as normative. While those who do not understand the grace of Christ think "loving the sinner but hating the sin" is a cliché, it is a biblical truism. We must love the homosexual, but we cannot accept homosexual activity as correct behavior or same-sex marriage as marriage.

Another reason some people don't get involved in speaking the truth is selfishness. We often are too wrapped up in our small worlds of work, home, and personal pleasures. Whether we help the poor by standing in the soup kitchen line or e-mail our government leaders regarding our convictions, these activities take time—time that some are not willing to share. We sometimes fool ourselves into thinking that if we ignore the problem, it will go away because one day will follow another and another and so on. Or we sooth our conscience by thinking that we don't have to get involved because someone else will.

Some people don't get involved in the culture battles because they misunderstand God's love. By emphasizing God's grace, these people think God's love will overlook sexual misadventures. Yet, while God's love does cover a multitude of sins, love is also demanding and life changing. While a wife might forgive her husband for many shortcomings, persistent adultery is typically not one of them.

Another reason some are silent is that they fail to understand what is at stake in this cultural war over same-sex marriage. Most people are motivated to make decisions out of a desire either to experience pleasure or to avoid pain. I am compelled to be involved in this cultural war for moral and religious values, first and foremost because I want to please my Lord who gave his life for my sins. Additionally, it would be horribly painful to know that I could have freed someone from sexual bondage, that I could have made a positive impact on a person's life and the culture, but instead chose to do nothing. I would receive no greater joy than knowing I had some positive role to play in helping another human being experience an abundant life.

The church has a tremendous opportunity to impact the culture for good. No other group of people gathers together in such massive numbers on a weekly basis like those who attend churches or synagogues. If clergy were cured of their "moral laryngitis," if the people in the pews were concerned about those sitting next to them, let alone those outside the four walls, then America, and the world, would be a better place. Our children and our very existence are at stake. Are we of any use? The answer to that question lies not with community leaders, politicians, or even friends, but with you.

The reason it is so important for Christians and the community to be concerned with homosexuality and same-sex unions is that so many people are trapped within the clutches of this sexually destructive behavior. If we have no compassion for those involved in the homosexual lifestyle, if we prefer not to get involved to stop same-sex unions from gobbling up the beautiful lives of those who are created in God's image, then we do not understand, nor have we begun to experience, the depths of Christ's love.

CHAPTER 10

Drawing a Line in the Sand

*F*ollowing the surprise attack on Pearl Harbor, the Japanese naval commander, Isoroku Yamanoto, is credited with saying, "I fear all we have done is to awaken a sleeping giant and fill him with a terrible resolve." I believe this is what's happening with the majority of Americans in response to the aggressive, same-sex marriage movement.

On June 26, 2003, when the United States Supreme Court shocked the country by "discovering" a so-called constitutional right to engage in homosexual sodomy,[1] I issued a press release on behalf of Liberty Counsel declaring: "Today's decision has awakened a sleeping giant and will galvanize and reinvigorate the majority of Americans who believe in traditional marriage but have ignored the radical agenda of the same-sex marriage movement."[2] Most of the public statements made by leaders of other pro-family organizations bellowed gloom and doom. My statement stood out in stark contrast to the gloomy predictions, and the media wire services carried my message throughout the country. Eventually other leaders began picking up on the same theme of awakening the sleeping giant.

Was my message designed merely to capture headlines? Or was the sleeping giant theme the product of naivety? Neither! The vast majority of Americans continue to believe in the sanctity of marriage between a man and a woman. The problem is that so many remain silent and watch from the sidelines while the cultural battle rages. Thus, the primary voices in the debate have been liberal media fueled by a promiscuous entertainment industry and a radical agenda advanced by a vocal minority.

I continue to remain optimistic regarding the future. Life is a series of choices. How can a tragedy push one person to greatness and another to miserable depression? The difference is not the event. The event remains the same. The difference is

115

how the person reacts. We can choose whether the historical events will control our lives or whether we will use them to positively shape our destiny.

My optimism about the future is not mere psychological well-wishing. It is encompassed in my biblical worldview, grounded in fact, and watered by reality. I was addressing an audience in Midland, Texas, giving one success story after another of people whom Liberty Counsel has had the privilege of representing. During the question-and-answer period, a gentleman raised his hand and asked, "How can you be so optimistic when so many bad things are happening in the world?" I responded by posing a hypothetical illustration. "Suppose," I said, "you were not able to watch your favorite football team on television because of a prior commitment, so you recorded the game. However, before you were able to watch the game, someone unfortunately told you the score, and you learned that your favorite team won. Nevertheless, for mere entertainment purposes, you sat down and watched the game anyway." I then said, "Let me ask you a question. If your team was down by twenty-one points in the second quarter, would you get depressed?" The answer is obviously "No!" Why? Because you know the outcome. I then said, "I know who wrote the last chapter of the book, and therefore, I never get discouraged when I see evil attacking our culture."

Ironically, the day after I gave this illustration, I flew to Lynchburg, Virginia, where that Saturday evening I watched the Liberty Flames' football team compete against Virginia Military Institute (VMI) during the Liberty University homecoming game. My wife and I left the game at the beginning of the third quarter when VMI had just scored on a long pass, making the score 28 to 3. To my surprise, when I woke up Sunday morning, I learned that Liberty came back in the fourth quarter and won the game in the last few seconds by a score of 31 to 28! God has a sense of humor. He emblazed my own illustration into my soul forever.

Some people may erroneously take my illustration to mean that there's no point engaging the culture since God already knows what will happen in the end. "So, relax, don't worry, God has everything in control," some might say. The point of my story is not to deactivate you but, rather, to motivate you to action. Yes, God knows how human history will end. He also knew that the young nation of Israel would eventually enter into the promised land after leaving Egypt. But you must remember that, except for Joshua and Caleb, the entire generation of people who saw God's miraculous deliverance from the tyrannical rule of the Egyptians never saw the promised land. Why? Because they did not believe that God could deliver them from the giants of the land (see Num. 14:1–23). So, these people, who saw first-hand God's intervention in human history, who could have trekked in a matter of months from bondage in Egypt to "a land flowing with milk and honey,"[3] wasted their lives and died in the desert without a permanent home. God's ultimate plan was completed. The nation of Israel was rescued from Egypt and established in a new home, but God's plan was accomplished with different people at a later date. My point is this: we can squander our lives in the desert eking out a miserable existence, or we can enter the promised land.[4]

After the Jewish people entered the promised land, they faced many threats from outside forces. They had to battle for their land (see the book of Joshua). Once settled, the Jews encountered multiple threats from the inside. They were often influenced by the surrounding culture, and some even assimilated the pagan religious rituals into their own worship. The book of Judges pictures a seesaw period during which the Israelites moved away from God, became depressed and oppressed by their moral and cultural decay, and then cried out to God for help. When the people repented, God raised up new leaders, whom the Bible refers to as "Judges."[5] These judges typically called the people back to God, and some, more than others, brought positive reform to the land. For a while the people were satisfied, but slowly they slipped back into their old habits. The book of Judges clearly illustrates that history is affected by the attitude and actions of the people and their leaders.

Take American history as another example. Since the founding of this great country, we have experienced two national religious revivals. The First Great Awakening occurred between the 1720s and 1740s. Jonathan Edwards, of whom I wrote in the last chapter, was a great preacher during the First Great Awakening, and his sermon, "Sinners in the Hand of an Angry God," is often pointed to as a key event. The Second Great Awakening started in New England in the 1790s. Now suppose you lived between the 1740s and 1790s, a period of fifty years. You would have read about the First Great Awakening, and you might have longed for the days of religious revival, but your theology was such that you acted like a pacifist, seeing no point being involved in the culture. Well, maybe you could relate to the generation of people who squandered their lives in the unforgiving desert. Perhaps, instead of you being the next Jonathan Edwards, God would move on, allow you to moan about the times, and bring revival to a future generation. Who knows that the promised land or a Third Great Awakening is not just around the corner? Can you really be so certain that you have no role in bringing about an awakening?

I'm not saying that through our own efforts we will establish God's kingdom here on earth. I am not a Reconstructionist. Nor am I saying that preserving marriage between one man and one woman is the "promised land" or the "Third Great Awakening." What I am saying is that God has called us to action. God is active. He is creative. His followers should be no less. We must have concern for people. We must engage the culture now not later.

Each morning I eagerly look forward to serving my Lord. Yes, bad things do happen, but even during the dark times when it "appears" evil might triumph,

I am comforted knowing who holds the future. Time and time again, I have seen God use events that were meant for evil and turn them around into good (see Gen. 50:20).

We live in a unique epoch of American and world history. We were not born for this day by mere chance. God is not surprised by current events. Each day is an opportunity to do good, to play some role in shaping the future of America and the world. While we all have different roles to play, each person is important in fulfilling God's plan. As for me, I have no doubt that I was born for such a time as this.

Esther in the Bible found herself in a unique place in the history of the Jewish people. After she was chosen to be the queen of King Ahasuerrus, Haman, who had been elevated by the king to his cabinet, plotted to kill the queen's cousin, Mordecai. Haman convinced the king that the Jewish people were plotting the overthrow of the kingdom. He persuaded the king to issue a decree to set aside a specific day on which all the Jews would be killed. Being Jewish herself, even Queen Esther was at risk.

The custom of the Persian kingdom at the time forbade the queen from entering the king's presence unless she was first summoned. If she appeared before the king without his blessing, she herself could be killed. The king had not summoned her for several weeks. To save her people, she would have to risk her life by going to the king in order to avert the slaughter of her own people. After she had exchanged several written communications with Mordecai, Mordecai sent this message to Queen Esther: "Do not think that because you are in the king's house you alone of all the Jews will escape. For if you remain silent at this time, relief and deliverance for the Jews will arise from another place, but you and your father's family will perish. And who knows but that you have come to royal position for such a time as this?" (Esther 4:13–14).

The story of Esther continues with her entering the presence of the king's room despite the fact she had not been summoned. When King Ahasuerrus laid eyes on her, he stretched forth his royal scepter, indicating that he accepted her presence. This action then set in motion a series of events that ultimately resulted in the irony of the story. The Jewish people were spared, and Haman, who plotted their destruction, was hanged upon a gallows he had made for Mordecai.

I have learned by experience that God has a sense of humor, and he loves irony. That which the enemy intends for evil, God can change for good. The difference between evil triumphing and being defeated is the presence of one person willing to take a stand. Yes, God can work without our human participation, but most of the time he chooses human instrumentalities. I truly believe that Satan is stupid and that he always overgorges himself. The only reason he wins is because we allow him to win. I count it a privilege to be born for such a time as this. I am thrilled that

I am not sitting on the sidelines of this culture war. Our head coach has called us onto the field and placed us right in the midst of the game. We can never give up.

You might say, "I'm only one person." "How can I make a difference?" Let me ask you a question: If a second grader can make a difference, then don't you think you can? The story of Morgan Nyman is illustrative of literally thousands of stories I have encountered since 1989, when I founded Liberty Counsel. Morgan was a second-grade student at an elementary school in Wisconsin. The teacher instructed the class to bring in Valentine cards so the children could exchange them with their friends on Valentine's Day. Morgan created three of her own cards. The first card had a puppy at the top with the letters "DOG." The bottom of the card stated, "Depend on God." The second card had a hopping frog with the letters "FROG." This card read at the bottom: "Freely rely on God." The third Valentine card Morgan created said, "Jesus loves you—pass it on." She presented these cards to her teacher, but the teacher, seeing that they were religious in nature, consulted with the principal. The principal issued a letter to Morgan's parents stating that she could not pass out the Valentine cards because of the so-called "separation of church and state."

After considering the circumstance and being unable to resolve the matter with the school officials, Liberty Counsel filed a federal lawsuit on behalf of Morgan and her parents. The evening news on all the major networks in the greater Milwaukee area ran as their top story the Morgan Nyman case. One television broadcast showed a picture of the school Morgan attended, stating, "School officials were unavailable for comment." The next scene focused on little Morgan Nyman, a cute, blond-haired, second-grade girl. The third scene showed one of the cards that Morgan wanted to pass out to her friends, and the entire television screen focused on the words, "Jesus loves you—pass it on."

Instead of Morgan being able to pass out a few Valentine cards to about twenty-five students, her Valentine message was broadcast to literally hundreds of thousands of people, perhaps even millions. The story was then picked up by the wire services and carried throughout the country, and even more people were reached with the message. We ultimately won the case, resulting in a new school board policy that favorably accommodated a wide array of religious activities for students.

The following year on Valentine's Day, I was in Los Angeles arguing in federal court on behalf of an after-school program called the Good News Club, which is sponsored by Child Evangelism Fellowship. On the flight back from Los Angeles to Orlando, I wondered whether Morgan had passed out her Valentine cards a year after the lawsuit. When I returned to my office in Orlando, on the top of my desk sat a Valentine card from Morgan to me.

As I said, Satan is stupid. He should have known better than to pick on a cute, second-grade girl who wanted to pass out Valentine's cards. Morgan and her family had a choice. They could forego the opportunity to pass out the Valentine cards to twenty-five second graders, or they could stand up for their civil liberties and fight. Morgan and her parents chose to share the gospel and thus to obey God. In doing so, Morgan learned a valuable lesson to stand up for Jesus Christ and do what is right. Instead of the message about Christ ("Jesus loves you") being suppressed, it was seen and heard across the country.

The story of Morgan Nyman is typical of many people Liberty Counsel has represented over the years. It breaks my heart whenever we receive a call from someone whose freedom has been threatened and who is in a position to make a choice to change the situation but chooses not to do so. However, we are fortunate to work with so many people who are willing to stand in the gap, restore the culture, and be a testimony for Jesus Christ. Why am I optimistic about the future? Because of thousands of stories like Morgan Nyman's. I have literally seen this same story, changed only by the person and the facts, repeated over and over again. My optimism about the future is, therefore, not illusory; it is based in reality.

As I said earlier, Satan is a glutton. He always overgorges himself. He always bites off more than he can chew. Like any human pleasure or desire taken to excess, Satan is never satisfied. When he overplays his hand, we must be willing to stand in the gap at that critical moment.

Some of the decisions by courts or governmental authorities illustrate evil gorging on the culture. When the United States Supreme Court issued the *Lawrence v. Texas* decision on June 26, 2003, regarding the Texas homosexual sodomy statute, the reasoning in the case was absolutely ludicrous. Only seventeen years earlier in the case of *Bowers v. Hardwick*,[6] the United States Supreme Court surveyed the same Constitution and at that time was unable to find any constitutional right to same-sex sodomy. Indeed, there is none. So how did the right get in the Constitution a mere seventeen years later? It didn't. The justices invented this so-called homosexual sodomy right out of thin air. A few of the justices seemed to think it was important to rely on the European Court of Human Rights for guidance, apparently forgetting the Revolutionary War and our own Constitution.

Supreme Court Justice Sandra Day O'Connor once candidly admitted that the power of the Supreme Court resides solely in the perception of its legitimacy by the people.[7] She acknowledged that "the Court cannot buy support for its decisions by spending money and, except to a minor degree, it cannot independently coerce obedience to its decrees."[8] She continues, "The Court's power lies, rather in its legitimacy, a product of substance and perception that shows itself in the people's acceptance of the Judiciary as fit to determine what the Nation's law means and to declare what it demands."[9] While courts may issue orders, they literally have no power to enforce them. They must rely on the executive branch to enforce their written decrees.[10] The people still have the real power in America, and it is "we the people" who can shape the destiny of this great nation.

Consider the recent history of the same-sex marriage battle. While some who support marriage between one man and one woman might get discouraged, and some might be ready to give up the battle, I urge you to take heart and draw a line in the sand. Now is not the time to wave the white flag. To the contrary, now is the most important time in history to preserve the culture. The battle over traditional marriage is one we can win.

Consider the events of the past decade. In the mid-1990s, a Hawaii court ruled that the state must show a compelling reason why it should be permitted to ban same-sex marriage. Prior to the completion of the litigation, the people of Hawaii, in a statewide referendum, voted to amend their constitution to prevent the courts from undermining traditional marriage.[11] In 1996 the U.S. Congress passed what is known as the Federal Defense of Marriage Act, which declares that the states may refuse to recognize an out-of-state, same-sex marriage.[12] Between 1996 and February 2004, thirty-eight states passed their own state Defense of Marriage Acts.[13] Of these states that passed DOMAs during this time, in addition to Hawaii, three states passed Defense of Marriage Acts by statewide referenda between 1998 and 2000 (Alaska, California, and Nebraska).[14]

Before the Massachusetts Supreme Judicial Court ruled in a 4 to 3 decision on November 18, 2003, that the state constitution confers a "right" to same-sex marriage,[15] almost twenty other state courts had rejected same-sex marriage in favor of traditional marriage.[16] Between November 18, 2003 and the end of January 2004, approximately fourteen states filed legislation to amend their state constitutions to protect traditional marriage. All this activity took place in spite of the Thanksgiving, Christmas, and New Year's holidays, when the state legislatures are typically not in session.

Then on February 12, 2004, San Francisco Mayor Gavin Newsom began illegally issuing so-called same-sex marriage licenses. The next day Liberty Counsel filed suit to stop Mayor Newsom. Before the California Supreme Court put a stop to the mayor's illegal activity, several other mayors and governmental officials began imitating Mayor Newsom. Liberty Counsel filed suit in each case to defend marriage. This series of events led to President George W. Bush's announcement that he supported an amendment to the United States Constitution to preserve marriage as a union between one man and one woman. Other legislatures joined the battle and more states filed legislation to amend their state constitutions to protect marriage. The polls reflected the opinions of the people. What they saw happening in America did not sit well with them. Complacency was turned into activism, and the overwhelming sentiment in America swung decidedly to the side of traditional marriage.

Had the radical same-sex marriage movement patiently waited several years, perhaps they would have won this battle. It is conceivable that the propaganda of the media would have fooled the majority of Americans and desensitized them to the threat of the same-sex marriage movement. However, the radical agenda became too aggressive, too greedy, and advanced too fast. The majority of Americans realized how easy our liberty and family values could be pulled from under us by the whim of judges, and, when they saw the lawlessness of Mayor Newsom, many began to understand for the first time the radical nature of the same-sex marriage agenda. Thus, I believe, in light of these events, the battle over marriage can be won. The majority of Americans firmly believe in marriage between one man and one woman. I not only believe that the same-sex marriage movement will be defeated; I also believe that we have been forced to consider the importance of our own marriages, and, in the end, the institution of traditional marriage will be strengthened.

So what can one person do? We can be thankful that at this time in our history, all we are being asked to do is pick up a pen instead of a musket. The founding fathers were willing to sign their own death warrants when they penned their names at the bottom of the Declaration of Independence. If they were told all they had to do was send an e-mail to their political representatives from the safety of their home or office computer, write a letter, or perhaps even make a call from their cell phones, they would have thought the challenge too easy and would mock those who refused to participate. Our governmental representatives do listen. When an issue is of great concern, then one person can organize a telephone or e-mail chain by calling their local radio or television stations, write a letter to the editor, activate their churches and Sunday schools, or contact a few friends. In other words, each person is like a domino lined up in a row. One domino leans against another and a chain reaction begins. Each church should have a social concerns committee. One person can monitor the agendas of the local city, county, and school governments by checking the postings on the Internet or requesting the meeting agendas. When an important issue is before the government officials, then be sure to show up and voice your opinion. The same holds true for state and national politics and is no less true for certain large corporate politics.

Another way to be involved in this cultural war is to be like a sentinel, acting as a guardian to your local community. Whenever an issue arises that affects religious freedom, the sanctity of human life, or the traditional family, then contact Liberty Counsel (800-671-1776). Liberty Counsel is a religious liberty litigation, education, and policy organization dedicated to restoring the culture by advancing religious freedom, the sanctity of human life and the traditional family. We have hundreds of affiliate attorneys throughout the United States. We are pleased to partner with Liberty University School of Law. At the law school, and through the ministry of Liberty Counsel's Center for Constitutional Litigation and Policy, we are training the next generation of lawyers, clergy, community leaders, educators, politicians, policy makers, and world leaders. If you want to become involved in these cultural battles to preserve the heritage of the family, and to preserve the culture itself, many training opportunities are available. Liberty Counsel provides free legal representation, but we are ineffective if we are unaware of an important issue in your community. If we do not know that an issue of religious and moral importance is taking place in your community, then we cannot get involved. And if we don't show up, we can't win.

To build a house takes three things: (1) a person, (2) a tool, and (3) money. You may be the person in your community that we represent, or you may be the person who alerts us to an important matter. I believe God has created Liberty Counsel as a tool that you can use in order to extend your reach into every significant cultural battle. While you may not be able to be at every court hearing or policy debate, God has equipped Liberty Counsel with the skills. However, we cannot show up unless we know there is an issue to defend or a cause to advance. This brings us to the third item. A house cannot be built without money. Liberty Counsel represents individuals all over the world free of charge. We do not charge for any of our legal services. We can only show up because of the prayers and support of people concerned about the religious and moral values of the culture.

Liberty Counsel has numerous educational materials, not the least of which is our Web site (www.lc.org), along with many other educational resources. In order to impact the culture and affect the debate on same-sex marriage, you need to be informed about the issues so that you are not swayed by the one-sided, liberal slant of the media. Then, when an issue arises, you will be able to detect a problem and know where to go for the solution.

We must act now to draw a line in the sand. Enough is enough. We must once and for all time preserve marriage between one man and one woman, and in the process, we must strengthen the marriage institution. The battle for the culture is not optional; it is our duty!

We are living in a unique time in history. I know our parents and grandparents have sometimes told us that we do not have it as hard as they did in their generation. We oftentimes hear that history repeats itself, and indeed, that is frequently true. However, there is one thing we can say for sure: not one of our ancestors in America lived to see the day when society came to the brink of accepting same-sex marriage. We truly live in a unique time. God has placed us here at this time in human history for a reason, and he expects us to take advantage of the moment. We can never give up.

The Christian does not have the option of noninvolvement. Future generations depend on how we live and act today. We are here for such a time as this. We can react to our surroundings in one of two ways. We can acquiesce with apathy, or we can choose to make a difference. I choose the latter. I feel privileged that God has raised me up for this moment in human history. Each day I wake up, I have the anticipation like I did a few minutes before football games, when I was suited up in pads anxiously awaiting the locker room door to open so that I could run on the field and begin the battle. Why am I so optimistic about the future? Why do I believe that we can make a difference and preserve marriage between one man and one woman? Because I know that with God all things are possible, that the only difference between good and evil is one Christian willing to take a stand for Jesus, and I know who wrote the last chapter of the book.

Notes

Chapter 1

1. Maggie Gallagher, "What Is Marriage For? The Public Purposes of Marriage Law," *Louisiana Law Review*, 62 (2002), 773–75.

2. Ibid., 776.

3. Harry D. Krause, "Marriage for the New Millennium: Heterosexual, Same Sex, or Not at All?," *Family Law Quarterly*, 34 (2000), 271, 276.

4. Gallagher, "What Is Marriage For?," 781–82. See also William J. Doherty, William A. Glaston, Norval D. Glenn, John Gottman et al., *Why Marriage Matters: Twenty-one Conclusions from the Social Sciences* (New York: Institute for American Values, 2002), 8–9 ("Marriage exists in virtually every known human society. . . . At least since the beginning of recorded history, in all the flourishing varieties of cultures documented by anthropologists, marriage has been an institution. As a virtually universal human idea, marriage is about the reproduction of children, families, and society. . . . Marriage across societies is a publicly acknowledged and supported sexual union which creates kinship obligations and sharing of resources between men, women, and the children that their sexual union may produce.").

5. Maggie Gallagher, "What Is Marriage For?," *Weekly Standard*, 11 August 2003, 23.

6. Ibid., 22.

7. Ibid.

8. Ibid., 24.

9. Ibid., 25.

10. Gallagher, "What Is Marriage For?," *Louisiana Law Review*, 789.

11. Ibid.

12. Ibid., citing Population Division of the Department of Economic and Social Affairs, United Nations, "Replacement Migration: Is It a Solution to Declining and Aging Populations?" (2000). Available at http://www.un.org/esa/population/publications/migration.htm.

13. http://www.un.org/esa/population/publications/wpp2002/WPP2002HIGHLIGHTSrev1.PDF.

14. Ibid., at v. Six countries currently account for half of the annual population increase. These include India (21 percent), China (12 percent), Pakistan (5 percent), Bangladesh (4 percent), Nigeria (4 percent), and the United States (4 percent). See vi.

15. Louise Rafkin, ed., *Different Mothers: Sons and Daughters of Lesbians Talk About Their Lives* (Pittsburgh: Cleis Press, 1990), 10.

16. Kyneret Hope, "Of Lesbian Descent," in ibid., 59.

17. Michael, "Out of the Pain," in ibid., 110–16.

18. Kathleen Hill, "Change in Consistency," in ibid., 150.

19. Carey Conley, "Always Change," in ibid., 157.

20. Adam Levy, "Mom Breaks the Big Rule," in ibid., 164. See also Sprigg and Dailey, *Getting It Straight*, 95–120.

21. Gallagher, "What Is Marriage For?," *Louisiana Law Review*, 782.

22. See Essie M. Rutledge, "Black Parent-Child Relations: Some Correlates," *Journal of Comparative Family Studies*, 21 (1990), 369. Young black women who have close relationships with their father are typically happier than their peers who do not. Jonathen L. Sheline, Betty J. Skipper, and W. Eugene Broadhead, "Risk Factors for Violent Behavior in Elementary School Boys: Have You Hugged Your Child Today?" *American Journal of Public Health*, 84 (1994), 661.

23. See G. C. Mireault, T. Thomas, and K. Baror, "Maternal Identity Among Motherless Mothers and Psychological Symptoms in Their Firstborn Children," *Journal of Family Studies*, 11 (2002), 287–97.

24. Tim Dailey, *Dark Obsession* (Nashville: Broadman & Holman, 2003), 81–139.

25. Paula Ettelbric, quoted in B. Rubenstein, "Since When Is Marriage a Path to Liberation," *Lesbians, Gay Men, and the Law* (New York: The NY Press, 1993), 398, 400.

26. Michelangelo Signorile, *Life Outside* (New York: Harper Collins, 1997), 213.

27. Michelangelo Signorile, "Bridal Wave," *Out*, December/January 1994, 161.

28. Michelangelo Signorile, "I Do, I Do, I Do, I Do, I Do," *Out*, May 1996, 30.

29. Tom Stoddard, "Approaching 2000: Leading the Challenges to San Francisco's Families," quoted in Roberta Achtenberg, et al., *The Final Report of the Mayor's Task Force on Family Policy, City and County of San Francisco*, 13 June 1990, 1.

30. M. Pollak, "Male Homosexuality," in *Western Sexuality: Practice and Precept in Past and Present Times*, Anthony Forster, trans., P. Aries and A. Bejin, eds. (New York: B. Blackwell, 1985), 40–61.

31. See M. Pollak, "Male Homosexuality," in *Western Sexuality*, 40–60.

32. M. Saghir and E. Robins, *Male and Female Homosexuality* (Baltimore: Williams & Wilkins, 1973), 225.

33. See Steve Bryant and Demian, "Relationship Characteristics of American Gay and Lesbian Couples: Findings from a National Survey," *Journal of Gay and Lesbian Social Services* (1994), 101–17.

34. David P. McWhirter and Andrew M. Mattison, *The Male Couple: How Relationships Develop* (Inglewood Cliffs: Prentice-Hall, 1984), 252–53.

35. Ibid., 3.

36. A. P. Bell and M. S. Weinberg, *Homosexualities: A Study of Diversity among Men and Women* (New York: Simon & Schuster 1978), 308–09; A. P. Bell, M. S. Weinberg, and S. K. Hammersmith, *Sexual Preference* (Bloomington, Ind.: Indiana University Press, 1981).

37. See Paul Van de Ven, et al., "A Comparative Demographic and Sexual Profile of Older Homosexual Active Men," *Journal of Sex Research*, 34 (1997), 354; "Sex Survey Results," *Genre*, October 1996, quoted in "Survey Finds 40 Percent of Gay Men Have Had More Than 40 Sex Partners," *LAMBDA Report*, January 1998, 20.

38. See Michael W. Wiederman, "Extramarital Sex: Prevalence and Correlates in a National Survey," *Journal of Sex Research*, 34 (1997), 170; E. O. Laumann et al., Table 5.5, *The Social Organization of Sexuality: Sexual Practices in the United States*, (Chicago: University of Chicago Press, 1994), 216; M. Clements, "Sex in America Today: A New National Survey Reveals How Our Attitudes Are Changing," *Parade*, 7 August 1994, 4–6.

39. David M. Fergusson, John L. Horwood, and Annette L. Beautrais, "Is Sexual Orientation Related to Mental Health Problems in Suicidality in Young People?," *Archives of General Psychiatry*, 56 (1999), 876.

40. Ibid.

41. Ibid.

42. J. Michael Bailey, "Homosexuality and Mental Illness," *Archives of General Psychiatry*, 56 (1999), 883.

43. Theo G. M. Sandfort, et al., "Same-Sex Sexual Behavior and Psychiatric Disorders: Findings from the Netherlands Mental Health Survey and Incidence Study (NEMHSIS)," *Archives of General Psychiatry*, 58 (2001), 85–87.

44. J. Bradford, et al., "National Lesbian Healthcare Survey: Implications for Mental Healthcare," *Journal of Consulting and Clinical Psychology*, 62 (1994), 239.

45. See Lettie L. Lockhart, et al., "Letting Out the Secret: Violence in Lesbian Relationships," *Journal of Interpersonal Violence*, 9 (1994), 469–92.

46. Gwat Yong Lie and Sabrina Gentlewarriar, "Intimate Violence in Lesbian Relationships: Discussion of Survey Findings and Practice Implications," *Journal of Social Services Review*, 15 (1991), 41–59.

47. D. Island and E. Letelliar, *Men Who Beat the Men Who Love Them: Battered Gay Men and Domestic Violence* (New York: Haworth Press, 1991), 14.

48. Gregory L. Greenwood, et al., "Battering Victimization among a Probability-Based Sample of Men Who Have Sex with Men," *American Journal of Public Health*, December 2002, 92.

49. "Violence between Intimates," *Bureau of Justice Statistics Selected Findings*, November 1994, 4.

50. Richard Herrell, et al., "Sexual Orientation and Suicidality: A Co-twin Control Study in Adult Men," *Archives of General Psychiatry*, 56 (1999), 867–74.

51. Theo G. M. Sandfort, et al., "Same-Sex Sexual Behavior and Psychiatric Disorders: Findings From the Netherlands Mental Health Survey and Incidence Study (NEMHSIS)," *Archives of General Psychiatry*, 58 (2001), 88.

52. See *Harvard Mental Health Letter*, 18 (2001), 4.

53. *Centers for Disease Control Semiannual HIV/AIDS Surveillance Report* vol. 13, no. 1 (Midyear 2001), 33.

54. Robert S. Hogg, et al., "Modeling the Impact of HIV Disease on Mortality in Gay and Bisexual Men," *International Journal of Epidemiology*, 26 (1997), 657.

55. "Studies Point to Increased Risk of Anal Cancer," *Washington Blade*, 2 June 2000 (available at http://www.washblade.com/health/000602htm).

56. For studies documenting the significant increase in each one of these diseases, see Sprigg and Dailey, *Getting It Straight* (Washington, D.C.: Family Research Council, 2004), 75–86.

57. Stanley Kurtz, "The End of Marriage in Scandinavia," *Weekly Standard*, 2 February 2004, 26–33; see also Declaration of Stanley Kurtz, filed in *Lewis v. Alfaro*, Case No. S122865. (Cal. S. Ct. 2004) (This affidavit was filed in support of the litigation to stop San Francisco Mayor Gavin Newsom and City Clerk Nancy Alfaro from illegally issuing same-sex marriage licenses.)

58. Declaration of Kurtz, paragraph 32, 10.

59. Ibid., paragraphs 35–37, 11.

60. Kurtz, "The End of Marriage in Scandinavia," 26.

61. Declaration of Kurtz, paragraph 16, 4.

62. Kurtz, "The End of Marriage in Scandinavia," 27.

63. Ibid., 29.

64. Ibid., 30.

65. Ibid., 29.

66. Ibid., 31.

67. Ibid., 32.

68. Ibid.

69. Ibid., 33.

70. Ibid.

71. Ibid.

72. See example, Julie A. Greenberg, "Deconstructing Binary Race and Sex Categories: A Comparison of the Multiracial and Transgendered Experience," *San Diego Law Review*, 39 (2002), 917; Julie A. Greenberg, "When Is a Man a Man, and When Is a Woman a Woman?" *Florida Law Review*, 52 (2000), 725; Julie A. Greenberg, "Defining Male and Female: Intersexuality and the Collision Between Law and Biology," *Arizona Law Review*, 41 (1999), 265.

73. See *Late Corporation of the Church of Jesus Christ of Latter-Day Saints v. United States*, 136 U.S. 1, 19 (1890).

74. 98 U.S. 145 (1878).

75. Ibid., 164.

76. Ibid., 166.

77. *Late Corporation of the Church*, 136 U.S. at 19. See also *Davis v. Beason*, 133 U.S. 333 (1890).

78. See *Toncray v. Budge*, 14 Idaho 621, 95 P. 26 (Idaho 1908).

79. See Arizona Enabling Act, 36 Stat. 569; New Mexico Enabling Act, 36 Stat. 558; Oklahoma Enabling Act, 34 Stat. 269; Utah Enabling Act, 28 Stat. 108.

80. See *Romer v. Evans*, 517 U.S. 620, 648–49 (1996) (Scalia, J., dissenting).

81. Act of Admission of Idaho, 26 Stat. 215.

82. See Arizona Constitution art. XX, paragraph 2; Idaho Constitution art. I, paragraph 4; New Mexico Constitution art. XXI, paragraph 1; Oklahoma Constitution art. I, paragraph 2; Utah Constitution art. III, paragraph 1.

83. See *Witherspoon v. Illinois*, 391 U.S. 510, 536 (1968) (citing *Reynolds*, 98 U.S. at 147, 157).

84. See 8.U.S.C. paragraph 1182(A).

85. Stanley Kurtz, "Beyond Gay Marriage," *Weekly Standard*, 11 August 2003, 26.

86. Ibid., 27.

87. Ibid.

88. Ibid., 28.

89. Ibid., 29.

90. Ibid.

91. Ibid., 30.

92. Ibid., 31.

93. Fern Shen, "Defining Marriage: The BIG Story—an Occasional Look at What Everyone Is Talking About," *Washington Post*, 17 March 2004, at C16; see also Fern Shen, "What's Best for Kids," *Washington Post*, 17 March 2002, C16.

94. "Parents Angered by Book about Gay Princes" (available at http://www.cnn.com/2004/EDUCATION/03/18/gay.princes.ap/index/html).

95. *City of New Orleans v. Dukes*, 427 U.S. 297, 303 (1976).

96. See Linda J. Waite and Maggie Gallagher, *The Case for Marriage: Why Married People Are Happier, Healthier, and Better Off Financially* (New York: Doubleday, 2000).

97. *Cleveland v. United States*, 329 U.S. 14, 19 (1946).

98. *Goodridge v. Dep't of Pub. Health*, 798 N.E. 2d 941 (Mass. 2003). See also In re Opinions of the Justices to the Senate, 802 N.E. 565 (Mass. 2004).

99. 28 U.S.C. paragraph 1738C.

100. Waite and Gallagher, *The Case for Marriage*, 186.

101. Jackii Edwards with Nancy Kurrack, *Like Mother Like Daughter? The Effects of Growing Up in a Homosexual Home* (Vienna, Va.: Xulon Press, 2001), 8.

Chapter 2

1. This statement was posted on Alan Chambers' blog on January 23, 2004. See http://alan-chambers.blogspot.com/archives/2004_01_alanchambers_archive.html.

2. Exodus International is an international nonprofit organization that ministers to those individuals desiring to leave the homosexual lifestyle. Their Web site is http://www.exodusinternational.org.

3. Joseph Nicolosi, *A Parents' Guide to Preventing Homosexuality* (Downers Grove, Ill.: InterVarsity Press, 2002), 22.

4. A. P. Bell, N. S. Weinberg, and S. K. Hammersmith, *Sexual Preference: Its Development in Men and Women* (Bloomington, Ind.: Indiana University Press, 1981), 76.

5. http://www.peoplecanchange.com/Rott_Problems.htm.

6. Nicolosi, *Preventing Homosexuality*, 31.

7. S. Fisher and G. Greenberg, *Freud Scientifically Reapprised: Testing the Theories in Therapy* (New York: Wiley, 1996), 135.

8. Nicolosi, *Preventing Homosexuality*, 23.

9. Ralph R. Greenson, "Dis-identifying from Mother: Its Special Importance for the Boy," *International Journal of Psychoanalysis*, 40 (1968), 370.

10. Marvin Siegelman, "Parental Background of Male Homosexuals and Heterosexuals," *Archives of Sexual Behavior,* 3 (1974), 3–4. See also Daniel G. Brown, "Homosexuality and Family Dynamics," Bulletin of the Menninger Clinic, September 1963, 229–30. (Reporting on a study of nineteen actively homosexual children and finding a grossly deficient or very negative relationship with his same-sex parent, coupled with an overly intimate attachment to the opposite-sex parent.)

11. Nicolosi, *Preventing Homosexuality,* 71–72.

12. Irven Bieber, et al., *Homosexuality: A Psychoanalytical Study* (New York: Vintage Books, 1962), 172. Bieber's study was confirmed by a study published in Great Britain in 1964. See P. J. O'Connor, "Aetiological Factors in Homosexuality as Seen in Royal Air Force Psychiatric Practice," *British Journal of Psychiatry,* 110 (1964), 384–85.

13. Leif J. Braaten and C. Douglas Darling, "Overt and Covert Homosexual Problems among Male College Students," *Genetic Psychological Monographs,* 71 (1965), 302–03 ("The present authors feel that the function of the *detached* father in the psychogenesis of male homosexuality deserves a more important place than hitherto it has been given.").

14. Ray B. Evans, "Childhood Parental Relationships of Homosexual Men," *Journal of Counseling and Clinical Psychology,* 33 (1969), 133.

15. See Evelyn Hooker, "Parental Relations and Male Homosexuality in Patient and Nonpatient Samples," *Journal of Counseling and Clinical Psychology,* 33 (1969), 140–41.

16. See John R. Snortum, James F. Gillespie, John E. Marshall, John P. McLaughlin, and Ludwig Mossberg, "Family Dynamics and Homosexuality," *Psychological Reports,* 24 (1969), 763 (noting that the "present findings lend strong support to the earlier results obtained by Bieber" and "the pathological interplay between a close-binding controlling mother and a rejecting and detached father"); Marvin Siegelman, "Parental Background of Male Homosexuals and Heterosexuals," *Archives of Sexual Behavior,* 3 (1974), 10; William Byne and Bruce Parsons, "Human Sexual Orientation: The Biologic Theories Reapprised," *Archives of General Psychiatry,* 50 (1993), 236 ("The literature suggests that many, perhaps a majority, of homosexual men report family constellations similar to those suggested by Bieber et al. to be causally associated with the development of homosexuality—e.g., overly involved, anxiously over controlling mothers, poor father-son relationships.").

17. Daniel G. Brown, "Homosexuality and Family Dynamics," *Bulletin of Menninger Clinic,* September 1963, 232.

18. Joseph Nicolosi, *Reparative Therapy of Male Sexuality* (Northvale, N.J.: Jason Aronson, Inc., 1991), 25.

19. Bob Davies and Lori Rentzel, *Coming Out of Homosexuality* (Downers Grove, Ill.: InterVarsity Press, 1993), 44.

20. David Blankenhorn, *Fatherless America* (New York, N.Y.: Basic Books, 1995), 219.

21. David Popenoe, *Life without Father* (Cambridge: Harvard University Press, 1996), 144.

22. Ibid., 146.

23. See A. P. Bell, N. S. Weinberg, and S. K. Hammersmith, *Sexual Preference: Its Development in Men and Women* (Bloomington, Ind.: Indiana University Press, 1981).

24. Nicolosi, *Preventing Homosexuality,* 49.

25. See Kenneth Zucker and Susan Bradley, *Gender Identity Disorder and Psychosexual Problems in Children and Adolescents* (New York: Guilford, 1995).

26. Richard Fitzgibbons, "The Origins and Therapy of Same-Sex Attraction Disorder," in *Homosexuality in American Public Life,* Christopher Wolfe, ed. (Dallas: Spence, 1999), 86–97.

27. http://www.peoplecanchange.com/Root_Problems.htm.

28. See James R. Bramblett, Jr., and Carol Anderson Darling, "Sexual Contacts: Experiences, Thoughts, and Fantasies of Adult Male Survivors of Child Sexual Abuse," *Journal of Sex and Martial Therapy,* 23 (1977), 313 (Gender identity confusion and gender preference are often accompanied by a history of child sexual abuse.).

29. See Daryl Bem, "Exotic Becomes Erotic: A Developmental Theory of Sexual Orientation," *Psychology Review,* 103 (1966), 327. Bem's theory is that the developing young boy faces rejection by his peers, and, over time, the fear and anger habituate, and later during adolescence the boy

begins feeling a positive response to that which he feared, eventually resulting in an eroticized response.

30. Nicolosi, *Preventing Homosexuality*, 150–51.

31. Elaine Siegel, *Female Homosexuality, Choice without Violation: A Psychoanalytic Study* (Hillsdale, N.J.: Analytic, 1988).

32. Richard Fitzgibbons, "The Origins and Therapy of Same-Sex Attraction Disorder," in *Homosexuality in American Public Life*, Christopher Wolfe, ed. (Dallas: Spence, 1999), 85–97.

33. Nicolosi, *Preventing Homosexuality*, 156.

34. See Zucker and Bradley, *Gender Identity Disorder*, 252–53. A study of twenty-six girls with gender identity disorder revealed that nearly 77 percent of the mothers had histories of depression, and all had been depressed during the infancy of their daughters.

35. Ibid., 253.

36. Nicolosi, *Preventing Homosexuality*, 148.

37. Zucker and Bradley, *Gender Identity Disorder*, 252.

38. Anita Worthen and Bob Davies, *Someone I Love Is Gay* (Downers Grove, Ill.: InterVarsity Press, 1996), 83.

39. Andria Sigler-Smalz, "Understanding the Lesbian Client," *NARTH Bulletin*, April 2000, 12.

40. Nicolosi, *Preventing Homosexuality*, 158.

41. Ibid., 44.

42. Ibid.

43. Carol Brockmon, "A Feminist View of Sado-Masochism in the 90s," *In the Family*, April 1998, 11.

44. Jamie Malernee, "S. Teen Girls Discovering 'Bisexual Chic' Trend," *Sun-Sentinel*, 30 December 2003, A–1.

45. Ibid.

46. Ibid.

47. Ibid.

48. Laura Sessions Stepp, "Part Way Gay?" *Washington Post*, 4 January 2004, D–1.

49. Ibid.

50. Ibid.

51. Ibid.

52. Ibid.

53. Ibid.

54. See Mathew D. Staver and Kevin Tang, "The Genetic and Physiological Relationship between Diabetes and Obesity," *The Advocate*, September 1997, 1–4; Mathew D. Staver and Erin E. Kelling, "Obtaining a Rated Annuity through Medical Data Indicating Reduced Life Expectancy," *The Advocate*, October 1996, 1–4.

55. Nicolosi, *Preventing Homosexuality*, 39.

Chapter 3

1. Patricia Neil Warren, "Future Shock," *The Advocate*, 3 October 1995, 80.

2. Leslie Newman, *Heather Has Two Mommies* (Los Angeles, Calif.: Alyson Publications, 1989). This book is written for young children portraying a little girl by the name of Heather who has two lesbian parents, Mama Jane and Mama Kate. In the book Mama Jane and Mama Kate decided to have children and therefore visited a "special doctor" who "put some sperm into Jane's vagina." Heather is the result of this in vitro fertilization. Heather eventually learns through day care that many other children have fathers. When Heather feels sad that she has no father, her teacher, Molly, assures her that she has two mommies and that's "pretty special."

3. Michael Willhoite, *Daddy's Roommate* (Los Angeles, Calif.: Alyson Publications, 1990). The main character in this picture book for children is a boy whose heterosexual parents divorce. However, soon after the divorce someone new came to Daddy's house. This new "roommate" by the name of Frank lives, works, eats, and sleeps with Daddy. The book states that being "gay is just one more kind of love, and love is the best kind of happiness."

4. See Midge Decter, "Homosexuality in the Schools," *Commentary*, March 1993, 19–20.

5. *The Wanderer*, 21 March 1996, 1. See also Mark Mueller, "Parents Rip Class on Gay Tolerance," *Boston Herald*, 1 March 1996, 1. To read a transcript describing the program, see NARTH, "'Making Schools Safe' Means 'Refashioning Values'" in Massachusetts" (available at http://www.narth.com/docs/makingsafe.html). The Massachusetts-based Parents Rights Coalition published a transcript of a pro-homosexual indoctrination program in the Massachusetts public schools (available at http://www.parentsrightscoalition.org). In the case of *Brown v. Hot, Sexy and Safer Productions, Inc.*, 68 F.3d 525 (1st Cir. 1995), *cert. denied*, 516 U.S. 1159 (1996), a federal appeals court upheld the right of a public school to require students to attend a sex education program in which several monologues and skits were performed graphically discussing male and female genitals, excretory functions, anal sex, oral sex, masturbation, and homosexuality.

6. See www.starsinc.org/outright.html.

7. See "Institutional Heterosexism in Our Schools: A Guide to Understanding & Undoing It," 2 May 2002 (available at www.glsen.org/templates/resources/record.html?section=18&record=1313).

8. See www.pflag.org/publications/BeYourself.PDF.

9. Linnea Due, *Joining the Tribe: Growing Up Gay and Lesbian in the 90s* (Los Angeles, Calif.: Anchor Books, 1995), 111.

10. *Revolutionary Voices: A Multicultural Queer Youth Anthology*, Amy Sonnie, ed. (Los Angeles, Calif.: Alyson Books, 2000), 167. See also Ellen Bass and Kate Kaufman, *Free Your Mind: A Book for Gay, Lesbian, Bisexual Youth and Their Allies* (New York: HarperPerennial, 1996), 6–7.

11. *Two Teenagers in Twenty: Writings of Gay and Lesbian Youth*, Ann Heron, ed. (Los Angeles, Calif.: Alyson Books, 1995), 134, 167, 171.

12. Ibid.

13. See www.pflag.org/publications/BeYourself.PDF, 4–5.

14. *Growing Up Gay/Growing Up Lesbian: A Literary Anthology*, Bennett L. Singer, ed. (New York: New Press, 1994), 100. GLSEN recommends this book for students in seventh through twelfth grades.

15. Ibid., 111.

16. Ibid., 6–87.

17. Alex Sanchez, *Rainbow Boys* (New York: Simon & Schuster, 2001), 148. GLSEN recommends this reading for students in grades seven through twelve.

18. Ibid., 43–44.

19. *Bi Any Other Name: Bisexual People Speak Out*, Loraine Hutchins and Lani Kaahumanu, eds. (Los Angeles, Calif.: Alyson Books, 1991), 179–80 (The same book also describes this statement by another homosexual as follows: "By age twelve, I had become a porn aficionado, since the couple for whom I babysat and my older brother kept copies of the magazines around. I must say that I came in touch with my bisexuality, or my bisexual feelings, through men's pornography."). Ibid., 292 (Also describing the following: "Well, I am politically radical . . . and I am also sexually radical. I support all people's rights, all lifestyles that are consensual and not coercive. I have many friends in the S and M community and in the transsexual and transvestite communities. . . . I am a prostitute's rights advocate."). Ibid., 206.

20. *Queer 13: Lesbian and Gay Writers Recall Seventh Grade*, Clifford Chase, ed. (New York: Rob Weisbach Books, 1998), 43–44. "The whole world of rest-room sex had opened itself up to me."

21. Singer, *Growing Up Gay/Growing Up Lesbian*, 110–11.

22. Mary L. Gray, *In Your Face: Stories from the Lives of Queer Youth* (Binghamton, N.Y.: Harrington Park Press, 1999), 37–38.

23. Heron, *Two Teenagers in Twenty*, 81, 91.

24. Gray, *In Your Face*, 23.

25. Sonnie, *Revolutionary Voices*, 171–72 (describing an interview with a young man who was a cross-dresser and works as a prostitute specializing in sadomasaochism).

26. Ibid., 43.

27. Bass and Kaufman, *Free Your Mind*, 6–7. This book is recommended by GLSEN for seventh graders.

28. Sonnie, *Revolutionary Voices,* 167.

29. Gray, *In Your Face,* 32.

30. Sonnie, *Revolutionary Voices,* 43-44.

31. This quote is taken from a lesson entitled "Bisexual Basics" designed for middle school as part of a curriculum manual published by GLSEN for educators. The manual title is *Tackling Gay Issues in School: A Resource Module* by Leif Mitchell, 78. This publication is cosponsored by GLSEN, 1999, Planned Parenthood, and Leif Mitchell.

32. Gray, *In Your Face,* 42.

33. Bass and Kaufman, *Free Your Mind,* 279.

34. Romans 1:26. See also Timothy Dailey, *Dark Obsession: The Tragedy and Threat of the Homosexual Lifestyle* (Nashville: Broadman & Holman, 2003), 35–80 (discussing homosexuality in the Old and New Testaments and in the writings of the early church).

35. For a listing of additional quotations from the recommended reading sources of both GLSEN and PFLAG, see http://www.missionamerica.com.

36. See Stephen Daniels, "Intolerant Tolerance: The Weapon of Moral Relativism." Available at www.ncfamily.org/PolicyPapers/Findings%200212-Tolerance.pdf, 2.

37. See Cheryl Wetzstein, "Nation Divided on Gay Parents," *Washington Times,* 21 March 2002, A02; 2001 CA AB 25 (permitting registered same-sex domestic partners to jointly adopt a child).

38. See "Rosie O'Donnell Works with ACLU Overturning Adoption Ban," *Gay Today,* 18 February 2002 (available at www.gaytoday.badpuppy.com/garchive/events/021802ev.htm, 1).

39. See press release from ACLU, "ACLU Challenges NJ's Resistence to Joint Adoption by Lesbian and Gay Couples," 19 June 1997 (available at www.aclu.org/news/n061997a.html).

40. Gallagher, "What Is Marriage For?" *Los Angeles Law Review,* 62, 782.

41. See Alfred A. Messer, "Boys' Father Hunger: The Missing Father Syndrome," *Medical Aspects of Human Sexuality,* 23 (1989), 44.

42. Carol Z. Garrison, "Epidemiology of Depressive Symptoms in Young Adolescents," *Journal of the American Academy of Adolescent Psychiatry,* 28 (1999), 343 (study of seven hundred junior high school students showed that symptoms of depression showed up significantly less often in children raised by both natural parents than among their peers living with only one parent, or one parent and a step-parent).

43. See Pamela Bekier, et al., "Role Reversals in Families of Substance Misusers: Transgenerational Phenomenon," *International Journal of Addictions,* 28 (1993), 613; Seessie Manual Rutledge, "Black Parent-Child Relations: Some Correlates," *Journal of Comparative Family Studies,* 21 (1990), 369 (finding the "general happiness" of young women to increase when they have a close relationship with their father); Janet Gross and Mary E. McCauley, "A Comparison of Drug Use and Adjustment in Urban Adolescent Children of Substance Abusers," *International Journal of Addictions,* 25 (1991), 495 (Inner-city youth living in a single-sex home are more likely to engage in drug abuse.).

44. See Olle Lundberg, "The Impact of Childhood Living Conditions on Childhood Illness and Mortality in Adulthood," *Social Science and Medicine,* 36 (1993), 1047; Carmen N. Velez and Jane A. Ungemack, "Drug Use among Puerto Rican Youth: An Exploration of Generational Status Differences," *Social Science and Medicine,* 29 (1989), 779 (finding a greater vulnerability to drug use among children raised in a home where the father is absent); Robert L. Flewelling and Karl Bauman, "Family Structure as a Predictor of Initial Substance Abuse and Sexual Intercourse in Early Adolescence," *Journal of Marriage and Family,* 52 (1990), 171; Paul R. Amato, "Parental Absence during Childhood and Depression in Later Life," *Social Science Quarterly,* 32 (1991), 543.

45. Patricia L. McCall, "Adolescent and Elderly White Male Suicide Trends: Evidence of Changing Well-Being," *Journal of Gerontology: Social Science,* 33 (1991), 543; Scott J. South and Stewart E. Tolnay, "Relative Well-Being among Children and the Elderly: The Effects of Age Group Size and Family Structure," *Social Science Quarterly,* 33 (1992), 115; Patricia McCall and Kenneth Land, "Trends in White Male Adolescent, Young Adult and Elderly Suicide: Are There Common Underlying Structural Factors?" *Social Science Review,* 23 (1994), 57.

46. Ibid. See also Paul R. Amato and Bruce Keith, "Parental Divorce and Adult Well-Being: A Meta-analysis," *Journal of Marriage and Family,* 53 (1991), 43; Scott J. South and Stewart E. Tolnay, "Relative Well-Being Among Children and the Elderly; The Effect of Age Group Size and Family Structure," *Social Science Quarterly,* 33 (1992), 115 (concluding that the degree to which children reside is "traditional families" in positively related to their well-being); Judith S. Wallerstein, Julia M. Lewis, and Sandra Balkeslee, *The Unexpected Legacy of Divorce: A 25 Year Landmark Study* (N.Y.: Hyperion, 2000).

47. See, eg., Richard Herrell, et al., "Sexual Orientation and Suicidality: A Co-twin Control Study in Adult Men," *Archives of General Psychiatry,* 56 (1999), 867. See also Gary Remafedi, "Suicide and Sexual Orientation," *Archives of General Psychiatry,* 56 (1999), 885; Richard C. Friedman, "Homosexuality, Psychopathology, and Suicidality," *Archives of General Psychiatry,* 56 (1999), 887.

48. J. Bradford, et al., "National Lesbian Health Care Survey: Implications for Mental Health Care," *Journal of Consulting and Clinical Psychology,* 62 (1994), 239.

49. See Richard Herrell, et al., "Sexual Orientation and Suicidality: A Co-twin Control Study in Adult Men," *Archives of General Psychiatry,* 56 (1999), 867–74.

50. Theo G. M. Sandfort, et al, "Same-Sex Sexual Behavior and Psychiatric Disorders: Findings from the Netherlands Mental Health Survey and Incidence Study (NEMHSIS)," *Archives of General Psychiatry,* 58, (2001), 85, 88.

51. See *Harvard Mental Health Letter,* 18 (2001), 4.

52. Robert Lerner, Ph.D. and Althea K. Nagai, Ph.D., *No Basis* (Washington, D.C.: Marriage Law Project, Ethics and Public Policy Center, 2001), 6.

53. Ibid., 118–23.

54. Ibid., 13–16.

55. Ibid., 27.

56. Ibid., 66.

57. Ibid., 75–77.

58. Ibid., 83.

59. See Stacey and Biblarz, "(How) Does the Sexual Orientation of Parents Matter," 159, 174.

60. Ibid., 166.

61. See Diana Baumrind, "Commentary on Sexual Orientation: Research and Social Policy Implications," *Developmental Psychology,* 31 (1995), 130, 133–34.

62. Ibid., 134.

63. Lerner and Nagai, *No Basis,* 69. See Charlotte J. Patterson, "Lesbian and Gay Parenting: A Resource for Psychologists," *American Psychological Association Public Interest Directorate,* 1995 (available at http://www.apa.org/pi/parent.html, 8); Charlotte J. Patterson, "Children of Lesbian and Gay Parents," *Child Development,* 63 (1992), 1025; Charlotte J. Patterson, "Children of the Lesbian Baby Boom," in *Lesbian and Gay Psychology,* Beverly Greene and Gregory M. Herek, eds. (Thousand Oaks, Calif.: Sage Publications 1994), 156; Charlotte J. Patterson and Raymond W. Chan, "Gay Fathers," in *The Role of the Father in Child Development,* M. E. Lamb, ed., 3d ed. (Hoboken, N.J.: Wiley Canada, 1996); Charlotte J. Patterson and Richard E. Redding, "Lesbian and Gay Families with Children: Implications of Social Science Research for Policy," *Journal of Social Issues,* 52 (1996), 29; Charlotte Patterson, "Families of the Lesbian Baby Book: Parent's Division of Labor and Children's Adjustment," *Developmental Psychology,* 31 (1995), 122.

64. Ibid., 74.

65. Ibid., 103.

66. Charlotte J. Patterson, "Lesbian and Gay Parenting: A Resource for Psychologists," *American Psychological Association Public Interest Directorate,* 1995 (available at http://www.apa.org/pi/parent .html, 2).

67. *Amer v. Johnson,* 4 Fla. L. Wlky. Supp. 845b (Fla. 17th Cir. 1997).

68. Ibid.

69. See Lerner and Nagai, *No Basis,* 75.

70. Ibid., 16.

71. Ibid., 43.

72. Ibid., 40.

73. Ibid., 40–42.

74. David Cramer, "Gay Parents and Their Children: A Review of Research and Practical Implications," _Journal of Counseling and Development,_ 64 (1986), 506. See also Frederick W. Bozett, "Gay Fathers: A Review of the Literature," in _Homosexuality and the Family,_ Frederick W. Bozett, ed. (New York: Harrington Park Press, 1989), 152; Peter Sprigg and Timothy Dailey, _Getting It Straight: What the Research Shows About Homosexuality_ (Washington, D.C.: Family Research Council, 2004), 95–102.

75. See, e.g., L. Keopke, et al., "Relationship Quality in a Sample of Lesbian Couples with Children and Child-Free Lesbian Couples," _Family Relations,_ 41 (1992), 225 ("fraught with methodological problems"); S. L. Huggins, "A Comparative Study of Self-esteem of Adolescent Children of Divorced Lesbian Mothers and Divorced Heterosexual Mothers," _Journal of Homosexuality,_ 18 (1989), 134 (admitting that the "small sample size makes any interpretation of these data difficult"); J. M. Bailey, et al., "Sexual Orientation of Adult Sons of Gay Fathers," _Developmental Psychology,_ 31 (1995), 124 ("available studies [are] insufficiently large to provide much statistical power"); Susan Golombok and Fiona L. Tasker, "Do Parents Influence the Sexual Orientation of Their Children? Finds from a Longitudinal Study of Lesbian Families," _Developmental Psychology,_ 32 (1996), 9 (stating the "small sample size resulted in an underestimate of the significance of group difference as a result of low statistical power"); Fiona L. Tasker and Susan Golombok, "Adults Raised as Children in Lesbian Families," _Developmental Psychology,_ 31 (1995), 213 (cautioning against drawing conclusions due to "small sample size"); Ghazala A. Javid, "The Children of Homosexual and Heterosexual Single Mothers," _Child Psychiatry and Human Development,_ 23 (1993), 245 ("the numbers are too small in this study to draw conclusions"); Jerry J. Bigner and R. Brooke Jacobson, "Adult Responses to Child Behavior and Attitudes Toward Fathering: Gay and Nongay Fathers," _Journal of Homosexuality,_ 23 (1992), 99–112 ("It is practically impossible to obtain a representative sample of gay fathers."); Patterson, "Families of the Lesbian Baby Book," _Developmental Psychology,_ 31, 122 ("No claims about representativeness of the present sample can be made."); Norman L. Wyers, "Homosexuality in the Family: Lesbian and Gay Spouses," _Social Work,_ 32 (1987), 144 (admitting that the study "cannot be considered representative," that the findings "cannot be generalized beyond the sample itself," and the findings are "vulnerable to all the problems associated with self-selected research participants"); Laura Lott-Whitehead and Carol T. Tully, "The Family Lives of Lesbian Mothers," _Smith College Studies on Social Work_ 63 (1993), 265 (study had "methodological flaws," lacked "representativeness," "probability random sampling . . . was impossible," and cannot be generalized); Susan Golombok, et al., "Children in Lesbian and Single-Parent Households: Psychosexual and Psychiatric Appraisal," _Journal of Child Psychology and Psychiatry,_ 24 (1983), 569 (lacks random sampling and thus "it is impossible to know what biases are involved in the method of sample selection"); Mary B. Harris and Pauline H. Turner, "Gay and Lesbian Parents," _Journal of Homosexuality,_ 12 (1985), 104, 111–12 (most gay parents who participate in parenting studies are concerned about parenting their children and thus those less concerned with parenting do not volunteer, and noted that complete anonymity of the subjects has turned up opposite results); Nanette Gartrell, et al., "The National Lesbian Family Study: Interviews with Prospective Mothers," _American Journal of Orthopsychiatry,_ 66 (1996), 279 (since the subjects volunteered, "the study findings may be shaped by self-justification and self-presentation bias"); Peter Sprigg and Timothy Dailey, _Getting It Straight,_ 95–102.

76. See, e.g., David Crary (AP), "Kids of Gay Parents Arguably Different, 2 Say; More Likely to Explore Homosexuality," _Commercial Appeal_ (Memphis, Tn.), 17 June 2001, A17.

77. Ibid.

78. One article summarizes research on the effect of loving fathers on children's well-being, concluding that "fathers clearly play an important role in the psychological and social survival of their kids." Douglas Carlton Abrams, "The Daddy Dividend," _Psychology Today,_ March/April 2002, 40. This finding and similar ones about mothers have obvious implications for the claim that the sexes are essentially fungible in regard to parenting.

79. Sotirios Sarantakos, "Children in Three Contexts: Family, Education and Social Development," *Children Australia*, 21 (1996), 23. All these children were being raised by couples, not single parents. The study found that the children of married couples did the best, and the children of homosexual couples did the worst in nine out of thirteen categories.

80. Note: personal autonomy is not necessarily good. In fact, children from divorced homes are more likely to separate themselves from their parent(s) and thus become more autonomous in the sense of being more likely to reject the values of their parents, and such behavior often leads to delinquency. See e.g., Jeanne E. Jenkins, Dale El Hedlund, and Richard E. Ripple, "Parental Separation Effects on Children's Divergent Thinking Abilities and Creativity Potential," *Child Study Journal*, 18 (1988), 149; Denise Kandel and Emily Rosenbaum, "Early Onset of Adolescent Sexual Behavior and Drug Involvement," *Journal of Marriage and Family*, 52 (1990), 783; Birgitte R. Mednick, Robert L. Baker, and Linn E. Carothers, "Patterns of Family Instability and Crime: The Association of Timing of the Family's Disruption with Subsequent Adolescent and Young Adult Criminality," *Journal of Youth and Adolescence*, 19 (1990), 201.

81. Ibid., 29.

82. Judith Stacey and Timothy J. Biblartz, "(How) Does the Sexual Orientation of Parents Matter," 174, 179; Richard Herrell, et al., "Sexual Orientation and Suicidality: A Co-twin Control Study in Adult Men," 867. See also Gary Remafedi, "Suicide and Sexual Orientation," *Archives of General Psychiatry*, 56 (1999), 885; Richard C. Friedman, "Homosexuality, Psychopathology, and Suicidality," *Archives of General Psychiatry*, 56 (1999), 887.

83. Ibid., 170.

84. Richard Green, et al., "Lesbian Mothers and Their Children: A Comparison with Solo Parent Heterosexual Mothers and Their Children," *Archives of Sexual Behavior*, 15 (1986), 167–84.

85. Stacey and Biblartz, "(How) Does the Sexual Orientation of Parents Matter," 174, 179.

86. See Robert T. Michael, John H. Gagnon, Edward O. Laumann, and Gina Kolata, *Sex in America: A Definitive Survey* (Boston: Little Brown & Co., 1994), 176–77. A valuable resource regarding the sexual behavior and identity of the American population is the National Health and Social Life Survey (NHSLS) which is designed by scholars at the University of Chicago and conducted by the National Opinion Research Center (NORC). Results of this survey are published in the book cited herein, *Sex in America*, and also in Edward O. Laumann, John H. Gagnon, Robert T. Michael, and Stuart Michaels, *The Social Organization of Sexuality: Sexual Practices in the United States* (Chicago: The University of Chicago Press, 1994), 311, Table 8.3B. Even the Human Rights Campaign, the largest pro-homosexual lobbying organization in America, confirmed these figures from the NHSLS in its amicus brief before the United States Supreme Court. See *Lawrence v. Texas*, Docket No. 02–012 (U.S. Supreme Court), brief of amicus curiae Human Rights Campaign et al., Jan. 16, 2003, 16 n.42.

87. See Fiona L. Tasker and Susan Golombok, "Adults Raised as Children in Lesbian Families," *Developmental Psychology*, 31 (1995), 213.

88. J. M. Bailey, et al., "Sexual Orientation of Adult Sons of Gay Fathers," *Developmental Psychology*, 31 (1995), 124, 127–28.

89. Susan Golombok and Fiona L. Tasker, "Do Parents Influence the Sexual Orientation of Their Children? Findings from a Longitudinal Study of Lesbian Families," *Developmental Psychology*, 32 (1996), 7.

90. Richard Green, et al., "Lesbian Mothers and Their Children: A Comparison of the Solo Parent Heterosexual Mothers and Their Children," *Archives of Sexual Behavior*, 15 (1986), 67–84. See also Stacey and Biblartz, "(How) Does the Sexual Orientation of the Parents Matter?," 179 ("recent studies indicate that a higher proportion of children of lesbigay parents are themselves apt to engage in homosexual activity").

91. See, e.g., Flewelling and Bauman, "Family Structure as a Predictor of Initial Substance Abuse and Sexual Intercourse in Early Adolescence," *Journal of Marriage and Family*, 52 (1990), 171; Denise Kandel and Emily Rosenbaum, "Early Onset of Adolescent Sexual Behavior and Drug Involvement," *Journal of Marriage and Family*, 52 (1990), 783; Arland D. Thornton, "Influence of the Marital History of Parents on the Marital and Cohabitational Experiences of Children," *American Journal of*

Society, 96 (1991), 68; Joan Kahn and Kay Anderson, "Intergenerational Patterns of Teenage Fertility," *Demography,* 29 (1992), 39; Nancy Lee Leland and Richard P. Barth, "Gender Differences and Knowledge, Intentions, and Behaviors Concerning Pregnancy and Sexually Transmitted Disease Prevention among Adolescents," *Journal of Adolescent Health,* 13 (1992), 589.

92. P. Cameron and K. Cameron, "Homosexual Parents," *Adolescence,* 72 (1996), 731. See also Peter Sprigg and Timothy Dailey, *Getting It Straight,* 121–42 (presents compelling information to show that there is a link between homosexuality and child sexual abuse); Timothy Dailey, *Dark Obsession,* 111–21.

93. J. A. Gaudino, Jr., et al., "No Fathers' Names: A Risk Factor for Infant Mortality in the State of Georgia," *Social Science and Medicine,* 48 (1999), 253; C. D. Siegel, et al., "Mortality from Intentional and Unintentional Injury among Infants of Young Mothers in Colorado 1986–1992," *Archives of Pediatric and Adolescent Medicine,* 150 (1996), 1077; Trude Bennett and Paula Braveman, "Maternal Marital Status as a Risk Factor for Infant Mortality," *Family Planning Perspectives,* 26 (1994), 252.

94. See Trude Bennett, "Marital Status and Infant Health Outcomes," *Social Science and Medicine* 35 (1992), 1179; Jeremy Schuman, "Childhood, Infant and Perinatal Mortality, (1996) Social and Biological Factors in Deaths of Children Aged Under Three," *Population Trends,* 92 (1998), 5–14; A. Armtzen, et al., "Marital Status as a Risk Factor for Fetal and Infant Mortality," *Scandanavian Journal of Social Medicine,* 24 (1996), 36 (reviewing mortality rates in Sweden); E. Frossas, et al., "Maternal Predictors of Perinatal Mortality: The Role of Birthweight," *International Journal of Epidemiology,* 28 (1999), 475 (reporting infant mortality rates in Finland).

95. See Chris Coughlin and Samuel Vuchinich, "Family Experience in Preadolescence and the Development of Male Delinquency," *Journal of Marriage and Family,* 58 (1996), 491; Robert Zager, et al., "Developmental and Disruptive Behavior Disorders among Delinquents," *Journal of American Academy of Child and Adolescent Psychiatry,* 28 (1989), 437; Abbie K. Frost and Bilge Pakiz, "The Effects of Marital Disruption on Adolescents: Time as a Dynamic," *American Journal of Orthopsychiatry,* 60 (1990), 544; Arnold P. Goldstein, *Delinquents on Delinquency* (Champaign, Ill.: Research Press, 1990), 4, 33, 37; Darin Featherstone, Burt Cundick, and Larry Jensen, "Differences in School Behavior and Achievement Between Children from Intact, Reconstituted and Single-Parent Families," *Adolescence,* 27 (1992), 1; Peggy McGauhey and Barbara Starfield, "Child Health and the Social Environment of White and Black Children," *Social Science and Medicine,* 36 (1993), 867 (children raised in mother-only families are twice as likely to have behavioral problems than if raised with two biological parents).

96. Martin Daly and Margo Wilson, "Evolutionary Psychology and Marital Conflict: The Relevance of Step Children," in *Sex, Power, Conflict: Evolutionary and Feminist Perspectives,* David M. Buss and Neil N. Malamuth, eds. (New York: Oxford University Press, 1996), 9.

97. Martin Daly and Margo Wilson, "Child Abuse and Other Risks of Not Living with Both Parents," *Ethology and Sociobiology,* 6 (1985), 197; David Finkelhor, et al., "Sexual Abuse in National Survey of Adult Men and Women: Prevalence, Characteristics, and Risk Factors," *Child Abuse and Neglect,* 14 (1990), 19; Mark Errickson, "Rethinking Oedipus: An Evolutionary Perspective of Incest Avoidance," *American Journal of Psychiatry,* 150 (1993), 411.

98. Gallagher, "What Is Marriage For?" *Louisiana Law Review* 62, 787 (citing Paul Amato, "Children of Divorce from the 1990s: An Update of the Amato and Keith (1991) Meta-analysis," *Journal of Family Psychiatry,* 15 (2000), 355; William H. Jeynes, "The Effects of Several of the Most Common Family Structures on the Academic Achievement of Eighth Graders," *Marriage and Family Review,* 30 (2000), 73; Catherine Ross and John Mirosky, "Parental Divorce, Life Course Disruption, and Adult Depression," *Journal of Marriage and Family,* 61 (1999), 1034. See also Marianne D. Parsons, "Lone-Parent Canadian Families and the Socioeconomic Achievements of Children as Adults," *Journal of Comparative Family Studies,* 21 (1990), 353; Paul R. Amato and Bruce Keith, "Separation from a Parent during Childhood and Adult Socioeconomic Attainment," *Social Forces,* 70 (1991), 187; Featherstone et al., "Differences in School Behavior and Achievement between Intact, Reconstituted and Single-Parent Families," *Adolescence* 27 (1992), 1; Josefina Figueira-McDonough, "Residents, Dropping Out and Delinquency Rates," *Deviant Behavior* 14 (1993), 109; Roger

Wojtkiewicz, "Simplicity and Complexity in the Effects of Personal Structure on High School Graduation," *Demography,* 30 (1993), 701.

99. L. Keopke, et al., "Relationship Quality in a Sample of Lesbian Couples with Children and Child-free Lesbian Couples," *Family Relations,* 41 (1992), 228.

Chapter 4

1. Marshall Kirk and Hunter Madsen, *After the Ball: How America Will Conquer Its Fear and Hatred of Gays in the 90s* (New York: Penguin Books, 1990), back cover.

2. Ibid., 183

3. Ibid.

4. Ibid., 154.

5. Ibid., 149.

6. Ibid., 189.

7. Ibid.

8. Ibid.

9. Ibid., 179.

10. Ibid., 148.

11. Ibid., 149.

12. Ibid., 150.

13. Ibid., 150–53, 189–91.

14. Ibid., 153–54.

15. Ibid., 186–87.

16. Ibid., 146.

17. The document was first published in *Gay Community News,* February 1987, 15–21.

18. The text of the essay is available at http://libercratic.government.directnic.com/Journal/social/queer/homosexual_agenda.htm.

19. Ibid.

20. See, e.g., Alan Sears and Craig Osten, *The Homosexual Agenda: Exposing the Principal Threat to Religious Freedom Today* (Nashville: Broadman & Holman, 2003); Peter Sprigg and Timothy Dailey, *Getting It Straight: What the Research Shows about Homosexuality* (Washington, D.C.: Family Research Council, 2004).

21. See *Baker v. State,* 744 A.2d 864 (Vermont, 1999).

22. Ibid.

23. Ibid., 885–86.

24. See Kees Waaldjik, "The Law of Small Change: How the Road to Same-Sex Marriage Got Paved in the Netherlands," 3–4 (an address given at the Conference on National, European and International Law, Kings College, University of London, July 1–3, 1999). Waaldijk is a member of the Faculty of Law, Universiteit Leiden, the Netherlands (mailto:waaldijk@euronet.nl). The Netherlands passed the law in 2001 in Dutch Bill #22672 (available at http://www.lc.org/Resources/hate_crimes_article.html).

25. Ibid.

26. Ibid.

27. Michelangelo Signorile, "Bridal Wave," *Out,* December/January 1994, 161.

28. Ibid.

29. David Thorstad, "Man/Boy Love and the American Gay Movement," *Journal of Homosexuality,* 20 (1990), 255. See also Edward Brongersma, et al., *Male Intergenerational Intimacy: Historical, Socio-Psychological, and Legal Perspectives* (Binghamton, N.Y.: Hayworth Press, Inc., 1993).

30. Marshall Kirk and Hunter Madsen, *After the Ball: How America Will Conquer Its Fear and Hatred of Gays in the 90s* (New York: Penguin Books, 1990), 304.

31. Ibid., 326.

32. Ibid., 328.

33. Ibid., 330–31.

34. Ibid., 330.

35. William Aaron, *Straight* (New York: Bantam Books, 1972), 208.

Chapter 5

1. After the trial court ruling, Liberty Counsel filed an amicus brief before the Colorado appeals court on behalf of Ms. Clark urging the court to reverse the order as it collides with the First Amendment protections of free speech and free exercise of religion.

2. After the trial court rendered its ruling, Liberty Counsel agreed to represent Linda Kantaras on appeal.

3. See www.freerepublic.com/forum/a3628536b3717.htm.

4. Ibid.

5. See Letter from Gloria L. Young to various organizations (emphasis added).

6. See Resolution No. 873–98, City and County of San Francisco, Nov. 13, 1998.

7. Ibid (emphasis added).

8. Rachel Gordon, "The Battle over Same-Sex Marriage," San Francisco *Chronicle* (available at http://www.sfgate.com/cgi-bin/article.cgi?file=/chronicle/archive/2004/02/15/MNGMN51F8Q1.DTL).

9. Liberty Counsel immediately filed suit against Mayor Gavin Newsom and the City Clerk Nancy Alfaro to stop the issuance of these worthless licenses. The California Supreme Court intervened four weeks later and halted the illegal activity of the mayor and the city.

10. See *American Family Association, Inc. v. City and County of San Francisco*, 277 F.3d 1114 (9th Circuit, 2002).

11. See Canadian Charter of Rights and Freedoms § 15(1).

12. See CFYI-AM re: *The Dr. Laura Schlessinger Show*, CBSC Decision 99/00–0005 (Feb. 9, 2000) and CJCH-AM re: *The Dr. Laura Schlessinger Show*, CBSC Decisions 98/99–0808, 1003 and 1137 (Feb. 15, 2000) (available at http://www.cbsc.ca/english/decisions/decisions/2000/000510.htm) ("CBSC" stands for Canadian Broadcasts Standards Council).

13. See also Canadian Broadcast Standards Council, Prairie Regional Council, CKRD re: Focus on the Family CBSC Decision 1996/1997–0155, decided December 16, 1997.

14. See Joanne Laucius, "Bible Had Role in Exposing Gays to Hatred," *The Ottawa Citizen Online*, 20 June 2001.

15. Ibid.

16. Ibid.

17. See "Fredericton Mayor Faces Human Rights Tribunal for Refusing to Proclaim Gay Pride Week" (available at http://www.lifesite.net/ldn/1998/jul/98071003.html*); Richard Hudler v. City of London and Mayor Dianne Haskett* (1997 case summaries published by the Ontario Human Rights Commission) (available at http://www.ohrc.on.ca/english/cases/summary-1997.shtml). The mayor helped satisfy the $10,000 debt by stepping down and forfeiting salary for three weeks. See John Miner, "Haskett Shocker: The Mayor Steps Down for Three Weeks until Election Day," *London (Ontario) Free Press*, 22 October 1997, A-1. However, Mayor Haskett shortly thereafter prevailed in a landslide election against her opponent who backed homosexual rights. See Deborah van Brink, "Haskett Landslide," *London (Ontario) Free Press*, 11 November 1997. The Mayor received 61,908 votes to her opponent's 30,207. See also "Mayor of London Refuses to Bow to Human Rights Commission" (available at http://www.realwomenca.com/newsletter/1997_Nov_Dec/article_6.html).

18. At the time one British pound was the equivalent of $1.50 to $1.75 U.S. dollars.

19. See *London Sunday Telegraph*, 16 January 2000.

20. See "Dutch Court Will Not Pursue Pope for Homosexual Discrimination" (available at http://www.cwnews.com/news/viewstory.cfm?recnum=13480). See also George Neumayr, "Diabolizing the Pontiff," *American Spectator*, 23 May 2003 (available at http://www.spectator.org dsp_article.asp?art_id=4844); Christopher Ferrara, "Will the Pope Be Prosecuted for Hate Crimes?" *Fatima Retrospectives* (available at http://www.fatima.org/review/perspective344.htm).

21. See Alan Sears and Craig Osten, *The Homosexual Agenda: Exposing the Principal Threat to Religious Freedom Today* (Nashville: Broadman & Holman, 2003), 167–87.

22. Edmond Burke, "Letter to William Smith" (January 9, 1795), in *America's God and Country Encyclopedia of Quotations,* William Federer, ed. (St. Louis, Mo.: Amerisearch, Inc., 2000), 82.

Chapter 6

1. See Richard Duncan, "Homosexual Marriage and the Myth of Tolerance: Is Cardinal O'Conner a 'Homophobe'?" *Notre Dame Journal of Legal Ethics and Public Policy,* 10 (1996), 587, 602–07; Lynn Wardle, "A Critical Analysis of Constitutional Claims for Same-Sex Marriage," *Brigham Young University Law Review,* 1 (1996), 18–24; Richard Duncan, "Who Waits to Stop the Church: Homosexual Rights Legislation, Public Policy, and Religious Freedom," *Notre Dame Law Review,* 69, (1994), 393, 440–42; Ken Masters, "Here Is 'The Church:' Scenes from the Documentary PBS Yanked," *Washington Post,* 14 August 1991, C-1 (discussing producer and director Robert Hilferty's film, *Stop the Church,* which was shown at the Berlin International Film Festival. This film won an award for the "Best Commentary" at the Ann Arbor Film Festival. Mr. Hilferty is a member of Act-Up, the AIDS Coalition to Unleash Power. This film is filled with epitaphs against the Roman Catholic Church because of its position on homosexuality. The church is described as hypocritical and filled with hate. One man on the film states that the "Catholic church is an archaic, anachronistic, futilist leftover which practices ritual sacrifice on the bodies of gay men, lesbians, women, and people of color."). See also Alan Sears and Craig Osten, *The Homosexual Agenda: Exposing the Principal Threat to Religious Freedom Today* (Nashville: Broadman & Holman, 2003).

2. See www.ufmcc.com.

3. Ibid.

4. Ibid. In Genesis 19:1–25, the story of Sodom and Gomorrah clearly illustrates the sexual perversion of its inhabitants when a group of men wanted to have homosexual sex with two male visitors of Lot. There is nothing in the story that condemns Sodom and Gomorrah for their alleged failure to feed the poor.

5. The Bible clearly condemns homosexuality. Leviticus 18:22 states: "Do not lie with a man as one lies with a woman; that is detestable." Leviticus 20:13 similarly declares: "If a man lies with a man as one lies with a woman, both of them have done what is detestable." In the New Testament, Romans 1:26–27 states the following: "Because of this, God gave them over to shameful lusts. Even their women exchanged natural relations for unnatural ones. In the same way the men also abandoned natural relations with women and were inflamed with lust for one another. Men committed indecent acts with other men, and received in themselves the due penalty for their perversion." First Corinthians 6:9–11, states, "Do you not know that the wicked will not inherit the kingdom of God? Do not be deceived: Neither the sexually immoral nor idolaters nor adulterers nor male prostitutes nor homosexual offenders nor thieves nor the greedy nor drunkards nor slanderers nor swindlers will inherit the kingdom of God. And that is what some of you *were.* But you were washed, you were sanctified, you were justified in the name of the Lord Jesus Christ and by the Spirit of our God." The Qur'an also condemns homosexuality. See Qur'an 7:80–81 ("For you practice your lusts on men in preference to women: ye are indeed a people transgressing the unbounds."). See also Qur'an 26:165.

6. See William J. Doherty, William A. Galston, Norval D. Glenn, and John Gottman, et al., *Why Marriage Matters: Twenty-one Conclusions from the Social Sciences* (New York: Institute for American Value, 2002), 8–9; Joseph Daniel Unwin, an address given March 27, 1935, to the Medical Section of the British Psychological Society, reprinted in *Sexual Regulations and Cultural Behavior,* 5 (Trona, Calif.: Frank M. Darrow, 1969), 30–32. See also Pitirim A. Sorokin, *The Crisis of Our Age: The Social and Cultural Outlook* (New York: E.P. Dutton & Co., Inc., 1941) and Pitirim A. Sorokin, *The American Sex Revolution* (Boston: Porter Sargent, 1956).

7. See *The Documentary History of the Supreme Court of the United States, 1789–1800,* vol. 3, Maeva Marcus, ed. (New York: Columbia University Press, 1990), 347.

8. Ibid. A Westlaw research query of the United States Supreme Court database searching for the words "Blackstone" and "common law" in the same paragraph reveals over 136 separate Supreme Court cases referencing these terms from the 1940s to the present (date of search March 30, 2004).

9. *Ratcliff's Case*, Eng. Rep. 76 (K.B. 1592), 713, 726. Blackstone noted that natural law forms the basis of the common and that natural law is derived from the law of God. "The doctrines thus delivered we call the revealed or divine law, and they are to be found only in the Holy Scriptures. These precepts, when revealed, are found upon comparison to be really a part of the original law of nature." William Blackstone, *Commentaries on the Laws of England*, 1 (1769) (Oxford: Clarendon Press, 1765–1769), 42.

10. Ibid.

11. James Wilson, "Of the General Principles of Law and Obligation," in *The Works of the Honourable James Wilson*, 1, Byrd Wilson, ed. (Philadelphia: Bronson & Chauncey, 1804), 104–06.

12. Declaration of Independence (U.S. 1776), The Organic Laws of the United States of America.

13. Raymond B. Marcin, "Natural Law, Homosexual Conduct, and the Public Policy Exception," *Creighton Law Review*, 32 (1998), 67 (quoting *Corpus Juris Civilivis*, 58, 785). Justinian's collection served as the basis of canon law for the Christian church and European and English civil law.

14. St. Thomas Aquinas, *Summa Theological Secundae*, 4, Quest 154, Art. 11 (Benziger Bros. Press, 1947).

15. Vern L. Bullough, *Homosexuality: A History* (New American Library, 1979), 34.

16. Blackstone, *Commentaries on the Laws of England*, 1 (1769), 215.

17. Ronald M. Perkins and Ronald N. Boyce, *Criminal Law*, 3d ed. (New York: Foundation Press, 1982), 465.

18. *Black's Law Dictionary*, 2d ed. (1910), 1094.

19. *Bowers v. Hardwick*, U.S. 478 (1996), 186, 192 (citing "Survey on the Constitutional Right to Privacy in the Context of Homosexual Activity," *University of Miami Law Review*, 40 (1986), 521, 525). But see *Lawrence v. Texas*, 539 U.S. 558 (inventing a constitutional right to engage in homosexual sodomy and questioning whether there has been a long-standing history of laws directed at homosexual conduct).

20. *Bowers*, 478 U.S. 193–94.

21. See Charles Murray, *Losing Ground: American Social Policy, 1950–1980* (New York: Basic Books, 1984).

22. See Alfred C. Kinsey, Wardell B. Pomeroy, and Clyde E. Martin, *Sexual Behavior in the Human Male* (Philadelphia: W.B. Saunders Co., 1948).

23. See Edward O. Laumann, John H. Gagnon, Robert T. Michal, and Stuart Michaels, *The Social Organization of Sexuality: Sexual Practices in the United States* (Chicago: University of Chicago Press, 1994); D. Forman and C. Chilvers, "Sexual Behavior of Young and Middle-Aged Men in England and Wales," *British Medical Journal*, 298 (1989), 1137–1142; G. Remafedi, et al., "Demography of Sexual Orientation in Adolescents," *Pediatrics* 89 (1992), 714–21.

24. Judith A. Reisman and Edward W. Eichel, *Kinsey, Sex and Fraud: The Indoctrination of a People*, J. H. Court and J. Gordon Muir, eds. (Lafayette, La: Huntington House/Lochinvar 1990); Judith A. Reisman, *Kinsey: Crimes and Consequences* (Arlington, Va.: The Institute for Media Education, Inc., 1998, 2000).

25. James H. Jones, *Alfred C. Kinsey: A Public/Private Life* (New York: W.W. Norton & Co., 1997).

26. See William N. Eskridge, Jr. "Challenging the Apartheid of the Closet: Establishing Conditions for Lesbian and Gay Intimacy, Nomos, and Citizenship, 1961–1991," *Hofstra Law Review*, 25 (1997), 817.

27. Ibid., 934–35.

28. "The APA could only take the action it did by disregarding and dismantling hundreds of psychiatric and psychoanalytic research papers and reports that had been done on homosexuality over the previous two decades. . . . The APA ignored the science, and, for reasons that were nothing but political, 'cured' homosexuality by fiat." Charles W. Socarides, *Homosexuality: A Freedom Too Far* (Phoenix: Adam Margrave Books, 1995), 74.

29. Robert H. Knight, "'Sexual Orientation' in American Culture," July 10, 2002 (available at www.cultureandfamily.org/articledisplay.asp?id=2927&department=CFI&category=papers at 5).

30. Ibid.
31. 42 U.S.C. § 2000a, et seq.
32. 42 U.S.C. § 2000b, et seq.
33. 42 U.S.C. § 2000c, et seq.
34. 42 U.S.C. § 2000d, et seq.
35. 42 U.S.C. § 2000e, et seq.
36. 42 U.S.C. § 2000e–2.
37. See U.S. Const. amend. XIII.
38. See U.S. Const. amend. XIV.
39. See U.S. Const. amend. XV.
40. See U.S. Const. amend. XIX.
41. 163 U.S. 537 (1896).
42. 347 U.S. 483 (1954).
43. The First Amendment addresses freedom of religion. The Thirteenth Amendment abolishes slavery. The Fourteenth Amendment applies to all persons born or *naturalized* in the United States. The Sixteenth Amendment prohibits voting discrimination against someone because of race or color. The Nineteenth Amendment prohibits voting discrimination against someone on account of sex.
44. See *Engel v. Vitale*, 370 U.S. 421, 427–48 (1962).
45. See Alfred W. Meyer, "The Blaine Amendment and the Bill of Rights," *Harvard Law Review*, 64 (1951), 939. Despite its failure in the Senate, several states adopted similar Blaine amendments that arose out of clear anti-Catholic sentiment. Jews have also faced real discrimination. In *LeBlanc-Sternberg v. Fletcher*, 67 F.3d 412 (2d Cir. 1995), the court describes an attempt by a local "civic" association to gain control of a zoning area in an effort to prevent Orthodox and Hasidic Jews from moving into the community.
46. See *Locke v. Davey*, 124 S. Ct. 1307 (2004).
47. See *McDaniel v. Paty*, 435 U.S. 618 (1978). Thomas Jefferson initially advocated such a position in his 1783 draft of a constitution for Virginia. Jefferson later concluded that he was wrong to advocate that clergy should be barred from elected office. By the mid-1970s, Maryland and Tennessee continued to disqualify ministers from holding public office. See *Kirkley v. Maryland*, 381 F. Supp. 327 (D. Md. 1974). In 1978, the Supreme Court ruled that banning clergy from holding public office was unconstitutional. See *Paty*, 435 U.S. 618.
48. See Mathew D. Staver and Anita L. Staver, "Disestablishmentarianism Collides with the First Amendment: The Ghost of Thomas Jefferson Still Haunts Churches," *Cumberland Law Review*, 33 (2002), 43–105; *Falwell v. Miller*, 203 F. Supp. 2d, 624 (W.D. Va. 2002).
49. See John J. Donohue III and James Heckman, "Continuous versus Episodic Change: The Impact of Civil Rights Policy on the Economic Status of Blacks," *Journal of Economic Literature*, 29 (1991), 1603–43.
50. See Robert L. Nelson and William P. Bridges, "Paternalism and Politics in a University Pay System," in *Legalizing Gender Equality: Courts, Markets, and Unequal Pay for Women in the United States* (New York: Cambridge University Press, 1999).
51. See Mathew D. Staver and Anita L. Staver, "Disestablishmentarianism Collides with the First Amendment: The Ghost of Thomas Jefferson Still Haunts Churches," *Cumberland Law Review*, 33 (2002), 46–69. The disestablishment movement in Virginia included confiscation of church property by the government. Today, some of the government buildings in Virginia stand upon land illegally confiscated from churches without any compensation whatsoever being paid for the property. Although Liberty Counsel successfully struck down the restrictions on church incorporation (thus allowing churches to incorporate and hold and manage real and personal property), the same property restrictions are still being applied today on churches that do not incorporate. Similar restrictions continue to be enforced in West Virginia (where churches may not incorporate) and New York (property restrictions). Ibid., 52–53.
52. See *United States v. Carolene Produce Company*, 304 U.S. 144, 153 n.4 (1938); see also *Lyng v. Castillo*, 477 U.S. 635, 638 (1986); *Massachusetts Board of Retirement v. Murgia*, 427 U.S. 307, 312 n.4 (1976).

53. *Frontiero v. Richardson*, 411 U.S. 677, 686 (1973). "Gender, like race, is a highly visible and immutable characteristic." *Caban v. Mohammed*, 441 U.S. 380, 398 (1979).

54. Some members of the homosexual community who spoke at the April 16, 2002 hearing traveled from Ft. Lauderdale, Florida, a three-and-a-half to four-hour drive on the interstate highway.

55. Although Board member Hernan Castro admitted that there was no evidence of discrimination in public accommodation, he nevertheless made a motion to amend the City Code to include "sexual orientation," not only in the employment section but also in the public accommodation section. He stated that he had to "assume" that such discrimination existed, even though there was no evidence or testimony to support such discrimination.

56. Jeff Kunerth, "Orlando Welcomes Gays—Sort Of," *Orlando Sentinel*, 14 April 2002, A1, A11.

57. See Kelly Brewington, "Gays' Economic Clout Leaves Stamp on City," *Orlando Sentinel*, 13 April 2002, at A1, A6.

58. The study is reported in *The Wall Street Journal*, 18 July 1991, B1. Simmons Market Research Bureau's first survey was released in 1989. Their second survey, which was released in 1996, produced similar findings. The 1996 study found that 28 percent of gays earned more than $50,000 while 21 percent of gay households had incomes over $100,000. The survey was sponsored by several homosexual organizations. See www.rivendellmarketing.com; see also "The Gay Market: Substantial Spending Power" (available at http://www.rivendellmarketing.com/news/news_articles_set.html). A gay research group known as Overlooked Opinions reported similar findings following a survey released in 1993. See "Affluence of Gay Market Confirmed: Household Incomes Exceed $100,000 for More Than One-Fifth of Respondents" (available at http://www.rainbowreferrals.com/sponsors/marketstudy.asp); see also *Romer v. Evans*, 517 U.S. 620, 645 (1996) (Scalia, J., dissenting) (homosexuals "have high disposable income").

59. See http://www.glcensus.com.

60. See Howard Buford, "Understanding Gay Consumers," *Gay and Lesbian Review Worldwide* (Spring 2000), 26–28 (noting the competing images); Ronald Alsop, "Gay Affluence Data Contradicted; Are Homosexuals More Affluent Than Others? Some Activists Suggest That the Data Are Overstated," *Contracostas Times*, 16 January 2000, D1 (same); Gene Coretz, "Do Gays Have Higher Incomes?" *Business Week*, April 2003, 21 (same).

61. N. V. Lee Badgett, *Income Inflation: The Myth of Affluence Among Gay, Lesbian and Bisexual Americans* (National Gay and Lesbian Task Force and The Institute for Gay and Lesbians Strategic Studies, 1998), 2. See also N. V. Lee Badgett, "The Wage Effects of Sexual Orientation Discrimination," *Industry and Labor Relations Review*, 48 (1995), 726.

62. Donald C. Barrett, Lance N. Pollack and Mary L. Tilden, "Teenage Sexual Orientation, Adult Openness, and Status Attainment in Gay Males," *Social Perspectives*, 45 (2002), 168; Marieka M. Klawitter and Victor Flatt, "The Effects of State and Local Antidiscrimination Policies on Earnings for Gays and Lesbians," *Journal of Policy Analysis and Management*, 17 (1998), 662, 669 ("Regardless of the level of employment protection, male same-sex couples have the highest household incomes, followed by married couples, female same-sex couples, and unmarried different-sex couples.").

63. N. V. Lee Badgett, "The Wage Effects of Sexual Orientation Discrimination," *Industry and Labor Relations Review*, 48 (1995), 15.

64. Ibid., 25. See also Klawitter and Flatt, "The Effects of State and Local Antidiscrimination Policies," 674 (noting that women in same-sex couples earned about 18 percent more than married women).

65. Howard Buford, "Understanding Gay Consumers," *Gay and Lesbian Review Worldwide* (Spring 2000), 26–28.

66. Klawitter and Flatt, "The Effects of State and Local Antidiscrimination Policies," 676.

67. Robert T. Michael, John H. Gagnon, Edward O. Laumann, and Gina Kolata, *Sex in America: A Definitive Survey* (Boston: Little Brown & Company, 1994), 182. See also J. Schwartz, "Gay Consumers Come Out Spending," *American Demographics*, April 1992, 10–11 (finding the median educational attainment of gays to be 15.7 years compared with 12.7 years for the overall adult

population); Peter Sprigg and Timothy Dailey, *Getting It Straight: What the Research Shows about Homosexuality* (Washington, D.C.: Family Research Council, 2004), 55–68.

68. Over time the titles used to describe "sexual orientation" have evolved from "gay and lesbian," to "gay, lesbian, and bisexual," to "gay, lesbian, bisexual, and transsexual," to "gay, lesbian, bisexual, transsexual, and questioning youth." A "questioning youth" is a young person who is unsure of his or her sexual preference. A new term has now arisen—the term *hasbian*. This refers to someone like Anne Hesch, who called herself a lesbian while having an affair with Ellen DeGeneres but who is now married to a man.

69. Letter from Gen. Colin Powell to R. Patricia Schroeder (May 8, 1992), in David F. Burrelli, "Homosexuals and U.S. Military Personnel Policy," *Current Issues,* 14 January 1993, 25–26; see also "Assessment of the Plan to Lift the Ban on Homosexuals in the Military: Hearings before the Military Forces and Personnel Subcommittee of the House Committee on Armed Services," 103d Congress, 1st Session 31, 32 (1993) (statement of Gen. Colin Powell, Chairman, Joint Chiefs of Staff) ("[Homosexuality] is something quite different than the acceptance of benign characteristics such as color or race or background."). In 1971 Justice Peterson of the Minnesota Supreme Court stated in one of the first same-sex marriage cases: "In common sense and in a constitutional sense, there is a clear distinction between a marital restriction based merely upon race and one based upon the fundamental difference of sex." *Baker v. Nelson,* 191 N.W. 2d 185, 187 (Minn. 1971).

70. See William Byne and Bruce Parsons, "Human Sexual Orientation: The Biological Theories Reprised," *Archives of General Psychiatry,* 50 (1993), 228–39.

71. See Elizabeth R. Moberly, *Psychogenesis: The Early Development of Gender Identity* (London: Routledge & Kegan, 1983); Joseph Nicolosi, *Reparative Therapy of Male Homosexuality* (Northvale, N.J.: Jason Aronson, Inc., 1991); and Charles W. Socarides, *Homosexuality: Freedom Too Far* (Phoenix: Adam Margrave Books, 1995).

72. E. Mansell Pattison and Myrna Loy Pattison, "Ex-Gays: Religiously Mediated Change in Homosexuals," *American Journal of Psychiatry,* 137 (1980), 12 ("All subjects manifested major before-after changes. Corollary evidence suggests that the phenomenon of substantiated change in sexual orientation without exclusive treatment and/or long term psychotherapy may be much more common than previously thought.").

73. Mark F. Schwartz and William H. Masters, "The Masters and Johnson Treatment Program for Dissatisfied Homosexual Men," *American Journal of Psychiatry,* 141 (1984), 173–81. See also Starla Allen, "Uncovering the Real Me," *Exodus International Update,* February 1996. See also <http://www.exodus-international.org>.

74. Simon LeVay, "A Difference in Hypothalamic Structure between Heterosexual and Homosexual Men," *Science,* 253 (1991), 1034.

75. LeVay admitted "the existence of 'exceptions' in the present sample (that is, presumed heterosexual men with small INAH 3 nuclei, and homosexual men with large ones) hints at the possibility that sexual orientation, although an important variable, may not be the sole determinant of INAH 3 size." Ibid., 1035.

76. Ibid.

77. Wardle, "Critical Analysis," 65.

78. William Byne, "The Biological Evidence Challenged," *Scientific American,* May 1994, 50–55; Byne and Parsons, "Human Sexual Orientation," 228; Richard C. Freedman and Jennifer Downey, "Neurobiology and Sexual Orientation: Current Relationships," *Journal of Sexual Neuropsychiatry,* 5 (1993), 131; Stanton L. Jones and Don E. Workman, "Homosexuality: The Behavioral Sciences and the Church," *Journal of Psychology and Theology,* 17 (1989), 213–25; Stanton L. Jones, "1993 Addendum to Jones and Workman," in *Homosexuality in the Church: A Reader and Study Guide,* J. S. Siker, ed. (Louisville, Ky.: Westminster John Knox Press, 1994); Stanton L. Jones and M. Yarhouse, "Science and the Ecclesiastical Homosexuality Debates," *Christian Scholar's Review,* 26 (1997), 446.

79. Wardle, "Critical Analysis," 63–64.

80. LeVay, "A Difference in Hypothalamic Structure," 1034.

81. Ibid., 1036, n.7.

82. Though LeVay acknowledges this possibility, he found it not determinative. Ibid., 1036. See Byne, "The Biological Evidence Challenged," *Scientific American,* May 1994, 53.

83. LeVay himself admitted that the "results do not allow one to decide if the size of INAH 3 in an individual is the cause or consequence of that individual's sexual orientation, or if the size of the INAH 3 in sexual orientation co-vary under the influence of some third, unidentified variable." LeVay, "A Difference in Hypothalamic Structure," 1035. LeVay also admits that there is "the possibility that the small size of INAH 3 in homosexual men is the result of AIDS or its complications and is not related to the men's sexual orientation." Ibid., 1036. Other researchers have concluded that it is possible to "hypothesize a plausible mechanism by which human immunodeficiency virus infection" may account for reduction in the volume of INAH 3 in homosexual men. See also Byne and Parsons, "Human Sexual Orientation," 235.

84. David Nimmons, "Sex and the Brain," *Discover,* March 1994, 64–71.

85. D. H. Hammer, et al., "DNA Markers on the X Chromosome and Male Sexual Orientation," *Science,* 261 (1992), 21–27.

86. G. Rice, et al., "Male Homosexuality: Absence of Linkage to Microsatellite Markers That Xq28," *Science,* 284 (1999), 665–67.

87. John Horgan, "Gay Genes Revisited: Doubts Arise over Research on the Biology of Homosexuality," *Scientific American,* November 1995, 26.

88. D. Hammer and P. Copeland, *Living with Our Genes: Why They Matter More Than You Think* (New York: Bantam Doubleday Dell, 1998), 188.

89. J. Michael Bailey and Richard C. Pillard, "A Genetic Study of Male Sexual Orientation," *Archives of General Psychiatry,* 48 (1991), 1089; see also J. Michael Bailey, et al., "Heritable Factors Influence Sexual Orientation in Women," *Archives of General Psychiatry,* 50 (1993), 217 (female twins study).

90. Wardle, "Critical Analysis," 69.

91. Neil Whitehead, "The Importance of Twin Studies," *NARTH Bulletin,* April 2001, 26.

92. Neil Whitehead, "What Is the Genetic Contribution to Homosexuality?", *NARTH Bulletin,* December 1999, 22.

93. Ibid.

94. Steven Goldberg, *When Wish Replaces Thought: Why So Much of What You Believe Is False* (Buffalo, N.Y.: Prometheus, 1994), 636.

95. Scott L. Hershberger, "Twins Registry Study of Male and Female Sexual Orientation," *Journal of Sex Research,* 34 (1997), 212, 220–21. See also Miron Barron, "Genetic Linkage and Male Homosexual Orientation," *British Journal of Medicine,* 307 (1993), 337 (The "finding that the adoptive brothers of homosexual twins are more prone to homosexuality than the biological siblings suggest that male homosexuality may well be environmental."). For more information, see Sprigg and Dailey, *Getting It Straight,* 1–16.

96. Byne and Parsons, "Human Sexual Orientation," 230. "Currently, data pertaining to possible neurochemical differences between homosexual and heterosexual individuals are lacking." Ibid., 232.

97. Wardle, "Critical Analysis," 70.

98. J. Michael Bailey and Richard C. Pillard, "Genetic Study of Male Sexual Orientation," *Archives of General Psychiatry,* 48 (1991), 1095.

99. Wardell V. Pommeroy, *Dr. Kinsey and the Institute for Sex Research* (New York: Harper & Row, 1972), 76.

100. Ralph H. Gundlach, "Childhood Parental Relationships and the Establishment of Gender Roles of Homosexuals," *Journal of Consulting and Clinical Psychology,* 33 (1969), 137; Ralph R. Greenson, "Disidentifying from Mother: Its Special Importance for the Boy," *International Journal of Psychoanalysis,* 49 (1968), 370; Marvin Siegelman, "Parental Background of Male Homosexuals and Heterosexuals," *Archives of Sexual Behavior,* 3 (1974), 3–4; Herbert Bieber, et al., *Homosexuality: A Psychoanalytical Study* (New York: Vintage Books, 1962); Daniel G. Brown, "Homosexuality and Family Dynamics," *Bulletin of the Menninger Clinic,* 27 (1963), 232; P. J. O'Connor, "Aetiological Factors in Homosexuality As Seen in Royal Air Force Psychiatric Practice," *British Journal of Psychiatry,*

110 (1964), 384–85; Leif J. Braaten and C. Douglas Darling, "Overt and Covert Homosexual Problems among Male College Students," *Genetic Psychological Monographs,* 71 (1965), 302–03. See also Sprigg and Dailey, *Getting It Straight,* 16–34 (in addition to parental and other environmental factors, Sprigg and Daley cite studies regarding the effect of urbanization and education).

101. See, e.g., Naomi Mezey, "Dismantling the Wall: Bisexuality and the Possibilities of Sexual Identity Classification Based on Acts," *Berkeley Women's Law Journal,* 10 (1995), 98–109 (sexual orientation is "not fixed, but change[s] over time"; categories of heterosexual and homosexual "are rhetorical . . . because of a disjuncture between the concepts of homosexual and heterosexual and the sexual acts they claim to signify"); Andrew Sullivan, *Virtually Normal: An Argument about Homosexuality* (1995), 151–54 (for purposes of discrimination laws, race is different than sexual orientation because sexual orientation can be hidden and is a complex "mixture of identity and behavior").

102. See Amy Sohn, "Bi for Now" (available at www.newyorkmetro.com/nymetro/nightlife/sex/columns/nakedcity/n_8301/index.html).

103. See Julie Robotham, "Safe Sex by Arrangement as Gay Men Reject Condoms," *Sydney Morning Herald,* 7 June 2001.

104. See, e.g., Allison L. Diaman, Mark A. Schuster, Kimberly McGuigan, and Janel Lever, "Lesbians' Sexual History with Men: Implications for Taking a Sexual History," *Archives of Internal Medicine,* 159 (1999), 2730–31 (almost 80 percent of lesbians have had a male sex partner); Edward O. Laumann, John H. Gagnon, Robert T. Michael, and Stuart Michaels, *The Social Organization of Sexuality: Social Practices in the United States* (Chicago: The University of Chicago Press, 1994), 294–96 (only one in fifteen men who've had a homosexual experience are exclusively homosexual, and only one in twenty-one women with a homosexual experience has been exclusively homosexual); Sprigg and Dailey, *Getting It Straight,* 48–50.

105. See Michael Bronski, "Blinded by Science," *The Advocate,* 1 February 2000, 64 (Dr. Edward Stein explains that "there are serious problems with the science" claiming a biological origin to homosexuality).

106. See Pete Winn, "A Crack in the Wall? A Respected Psychiatrist Rethinks Homosexuality," *CitizenLink: Family Issues in Policy and Culture,* 21 February 2000 ("I'm personally convinced that many of these individuals have maintained and made major changes in their sexual orientation") (available at www.family.org/cforum/hotissues/a0009548.html); Dr. Warren Throckmorton, "Initial Empirical and Clinical Findings Concerning the Change Process for Ex-Gays," *Professional Psychology—Research and Practice,* 33 (2002), 242–48 ("sexual orientation, once thought to be an unchanging sexual trait, is actually quite flexible for many people, changing as a result of therapy for some, ministry for others and spontaneously for still others").

107. Marshall Kirk and Hunter Madsen, *After the Ball: How America Will Conquer Its Fear and Hatred of Gays in the 90s* (New York: Penguin Books, 1990), 184.

108. 388 U.S. 1 (1967).

109. "Cabin," 441 U.S. 398.

Chapter 7

1. See e.g., *Goodridge v. Department of Public Health,* 798 N.E.2d 941 (Mass. 2003) (same-sex marriage); *Lofton v. Security of the Department of Children and Family Services,* 358 F.3d 804 (11th Cir. 2004) (upholding Florida law banning homosexual adoption); Human Rights Campaign (available at www.hrc.org); Glen E. Lavy, "Behind the Rhetoric: The Social Goals of GLBT Advocacy in Corporate America" (available at www.corporateresourcecouncil.org/white_papers/Behind_The_Rhetoric.pdf) (each discussing the efforts to gain employee benefits); "HRC Applauds Cincinnati City Council for Vote Adding Sexual Orientation to Hate Crimes Law" (5 February 2003) (available at www.hrc.org/newsreleases/2003/030205hatecrimes.asp) (Cincinnati adds sexual orientation to hate crimes law, despite FBI crime statistics showing bias crimes as a result of race and religion far exceed those based on sexual orientation, www.fbi.gov/ucr/ ucr.htm). See also *S.D. Myers, Inc. v. City & County of San Francisco,* 253 F.3d 461 (9th Cir. 2001) (upholding San Francisco law that

requires all entities contracting with the city to provide benefits to partners of same-sex employees on the same basis as spouses of employees).

2. See *Goings v. West Group*, 635 N.W.2d 718 (Minn. 2001) (transsexual sued employer over gender designations on restrooms); see "Restrooms Bring Transgender Rights to the Forefront" (2 May 2002) (available at www.ntac.org/pr/release.asp?did=21) (restrooms); Human Rights Campaign (available at www.hrc.org) (search for "transsexual" or "transsexual rights"); www.ci.boulder.co.us/cao/brc/12-1.html (Boulder ordinance prohibiting employment discrimination based on actual or perceived gender identity). See also Julie A. Greenberg, "When Is a Man a Man, and When Is a Woman a Woman?", *Florida Law Review*, 52 (2000), 725.

3. Fred A. Bernstein, "On Campus, Rethinking Biology 101," *New York Times*, 7 March 2004, 9–1, 6.

4. Sally Kohn, *The Domestic Partnership Organizing Manual for Employee Benefits*, 1 (available at www.ngltf.org/downloads/dp/dp_99.pdf). This publication is provided by the Policy Institute of the National Gay and Lesbian Task Force, 1999.

5. Groups such as Parents and Friends of Lesbians and Gays (www.pflag.org) and Gay, Lesbian, Straight Education Network (www.glsen.org) advocate that it is healthy to discover your "sexual identity" by sexually experimenting with members of the same sex at the early age of five.

6. *Baehr v. Lewin*, 852 P.2d 44 (Haw.), reconsideration granted in part, 875 P.2d 225 (Haw. 1993). Interestingly, only two permanent members of the five-member Hawaii Supreme Court were present on the panel when this ruling was made. Acting Chief Justice Moon and Justice Levinson were the only permanent members. Justices Lum and Klein recused themselves and were replaced by Chief Judge Burns and Judge Heen of the Hawaii Intermediate Court of Appeals. The fifth seat was vacant at the time the case was argued. Retired Associate Justice Hayashi was temporarily assigned to fill the vacancy. However, by the time the court issued its opinion, the temporary vacancy had expired and therefore Judge Hayashi was not part of the final decision. Thus, Justice Hayashi's vote was not counted. The official case report noted that he would have joined in the dissent with Judge Heen. See *Baehr*, 852 P.2d, 48. The vote was therefore 3 to 1. If Justice Hayashi's vote were counted it would be 3 to 2. Only Justice Moon and Justice Levinson voted in the majority with Judge Burns writing a concurring opinion. He concurred only in the result. He filed a much narrower, separate opinion. The Equal Protection Clause in the Hawaii constitution provides as follows: "No person shall be deprived of life, liberty or property without due process of law, nor be denied the equal protection of the laws, nor be denied the enjoyment of the person's civil rights or be discriminated against in the exercise throughout because of race, religion, sex or ancestry." Haw. Const. art. I §5. Unlike the Fourteenth Amendment of the U.S. Constitution, the Hawaii state constitution expressly prohibits discrimination on the basis of sex. See *Baehr*, 852 P.2d, n. 26, 63.

7. 560 S.E.2d 47 (Ga. App. 2002).

8. See *Brady v. Dean*, 790 A.2d 428 (Vt. 2001). The law was unsuccessfully challenged after its enactment because a number of legislators participated in a betting pool on the house floor during the final vote to determine the margin by which the bill was to pass. The suit claimed that those participating legislators should have been disqualified and, thus, the bill defeated because the legislators had a financial interest in the outcome of the vote.

9. *Burns*, 560 S.E.2d, 49.

10. Ibid.

11. Lynn Wardle, "A Critical Analysis of Constitutional Claims for Same-Sex Marriage," *Brigham Young University Law Review*, 23 (1996).

12. *Harper & Row Publishers, Inc. v. National Enter.*, 471 U.S. 539, 582 (1985), (Brennan, J., dissenting) (quoting *Garrison v. Louisiana*, 379 U.S. 64, 74–75 (1964),); see also *New York Times Company v. Sullivan*, 376 U.S. 254, 270 (1964).

13. *Pickering v. Bd. of Education*, 391 U.S. 563, 571–72 (1968).

14. *Dunn & Bradstreet, Inc. v. Greenmoss Builders, Inc.*, 472 U.S. n.4 749, 757 (1985) (Brennan, J., dissenting).

15. Ibid., n.1, 775 (Brennan, J., dissenting).

16. *Police Department of Chicago v. Mosley*, 408 U.S. 92, 95–96 (1972).

17. See *Carey v. Brown*, 447 U.S. 455, 467 (1980).

18. *Stromberg v. California*, 283 U.S. 359, 369 (1931).

19. *Romer v. Evans*, 517 U.S. 620, 652 (1996) (Scalia, J., dissenting).

20. See Ruth Bader Ginsburg, "Speaking in a Judicial Voice," *New York University Law Review,* 67 (1992), 1185, 1205–08 (expressing the opinion that the U.S. Supreme Court's *Roe v. Wade* decision prolonged divisiveness on the abortion issue by halting a political process that was in a state of change).

21. Ibid., 1198; see also *Bowers v. Hardwick*, 478 U.S. 186, 194 (1986) ("The Court is most vulnerable and comes nearest to illegitimacy when it deals with judge-made constitutional law having little or no cognizable roots in the language or design of the Constitution.").

22. See *Ferguson v. Skrupa*, 372 U.S. 726, 731–32 (1963) ("We refuse to sit as a 'superlegislature to weigh the wisdom of legislation' and we emphatically refuse to go back to the time when courts used the Due Process Clause 'to strike down state laws . . . because they may be unwise, improvident or out of harmony with a particular school of thought.'"); see also *F.C.C. v. Beach Communications, Inc.*, 508 U.S. 307 (1993); *Vermont Yankee Nuclear Power Corporation v. National Resources Def. Council, Inc.*, 435 U.S. 519 (1978); *Panama City Medical Diagnostic Ltd. v. Williams*, 13 F.3d 1541, 1545 (11th Cir. 1994); see also *City of Erie v. Pap's A.M.*, 529 U.S. 277, 279 (2000) ("This Court will not strike down an otherwise constitutional statute on the basis of an alleged illicit motive.").

23. See *Romer*, 517 U.S. 620, 651 (Scalia, J., dissenting).

24. See *Lofton*, 358 F.3d, 804 (upholding Florida's law banning same-sex adoption).

25. *Utah Code Ann.*, § 78–30–1. ("(3)(a) A child may be adopted by: (i) adults who are legally married to each other in accordance with the laws of this state, including adoption by a stepparent; or (ii) any single adult, except as provided in Subsection (3)(b). (b) A child may not be adopted by a person who is cohabiting in a relationship that is not a legally valid and binding marriage under the laws of this state. For purposes of this Subsection (3)(b), 'cohabiting' means residing with another person and being involved in a sexual relationship with that person."

26. *Mississippi Code Ann.*, § 19–17–3. "Adoption by couples of the same gender is prohibited."

27. See *Arizona Review Stat. Ann.* § 8–103; "Appeal in Pima County Juvenile Action B-10489," 727 P.2d 830 (Ariz. Ct. App. 1986).

28. See *Colorado Review Stat.*, § 19–5–211; *Adoption of T.J.K.*, 931 P.2d (Col. App. 1996), 1332.

29. "In re Adoption of Luke," 640 N.W.2d 374 (Neb. 2002).

30. "In re H.H.," 830 So. 2d 21 (Ala. 2002).

31. Ibid., 4 (Moore, C.J., concurring) (emphasis added). On June 4, 2002, Judge Archie Brown of Washtenaw County issued a juvenile court order banning second-parent adoption. In essence, this banned homosexual adoption throughout the state of Michigan as Washtenaw County was the only one of Michigan's eighty-three counties to allow second-parent homosexual adoption and adoption by single homosexuals is not condoned in the state.

32. California's policy banning same-sex adoptions was reversed by Gov. Gray Davis in November 1999. See Robert Salladay, "Davis Ends De Facto Ban on Gay Adoptions," *San Francisco Examiner*, 18, November 1999, A–1. Connecticut permitted homosexual adoption in the case of "In re Baby Z," 699 A.2d (Conn. Sup. Ct. 1996), 1065. In 1995, a Washington, D.C. court allowed for same-sex adoption. See "In re M.N.D.," 662 A.2d 837 (D.C. 1995). Until 1999, New Hampshire barred same-sex adoption, but the law was then repealed. See "1999 N.H.H.B.," 90. The House of Representatives approved the bill by vote of 226 to 130 and the Senate passed the bill by a vote of 18 to 6. The bill was signed into law by Gov. Jeanne Shaheen on May 4, 1999. See also "N.H. Law Repeals Ban on Gay Adoptions," *Boston Globe*, 4 May 1999, B–5. New York allows for same-sex adoption. See *N.Y. Comp. Codes R. & Regs.* tit. 18, §421.16. Ohio appears to permit a homosexual to adopt. See "In re Adoption of Charles B," 552 N.E.2d 884 (Ohio 1990). A Tennessee appeals court also appears to allow same-sex adoption. See "Adoption of M.J.S.," 44 S.W.3d 41 (Tenn. Ct. App. 2000).

33. *Reynolds v. United States*, 98 U.S. 145, 165 (1878).

34. *Murphy v. Ramsey*, 114 U.S. 15, 45 (1885) (rejecting constitutional challenge to a federal statute denying franchise in federal territories to those engaged in polygamous cohabitation); George

W. Dent, Jr., "The Defense of Traditional Marriage," *Journal of Laity and Policy,* 15 (1999), 581, 598. ("Traditional marriage is a public good.")

35. See, e.g., *Ala. Code* § 30–1–19; *Alaska Stat.* § 25.05.013; *Ariz. Rev. Stat.* § 25–101; *Ark. Code* § 9–11–107, 109 and 208; *Cal. Fam. Code* § 308.5; *Colo. Rev. Stat.* § 14–2–104; *Del. Code* tit. 13 § 101; *Fla. Stat.* § 741.212; *Ga. Code* § 19–3–3.1; *Haw. Rev. Stat.* § 572–1, 1–3 and 1.6; *Idaho Code* § 32–209; 750 *Ill. Comp. Stat.* § 5/212 and 5/213.1; *Ind. Code* § 31–11–1–1; *Iowa Code* § 595.2; *Kan. Stat.* § 23–101; *Ky. Rev. Stat.* § 402.020, 040 and 045; *La. Civ. Code* art. 89 and 3520; *La. Rev. Stat.* § 9:272, 273 and 275; *Me. Rev. Stat.* tit. 19–A § 701; *Md. Code Fam.* § 2–201; *Mich. Comp. Laws* § 555.1 and 271; *Minn. Stat.* § 517.01 and .03; *Miss. Code* § 93–1.1; *Mo. Rev. Stat.* § 451.022; *Mont. Code* § 40–1–401; *Nev. Rev. Stat.* § 122.020; *N.H. Rev. Stat.* § 25–1–1 and 1–38; *Ohio Rev. Code Ann.* § 3101.01 and 3105.12; *Tenn. Code* § 36–3–113; *Tex. Fam. Code* § 2.001; *Utah Code* § 30–1–2; *Va. Code* § 20–45.2; *Wash. Rev. Code* § 26.04.010 and 020; *W. Va. Code* § 48–2–104 and 603. 1–38. To remain current on the legislative activity among the states and in Congress regarding the defense of marriage, visit Liberty Counsel's Web site at www.lc.org.

36. See, e.g., *Ala. Code* § 30–1–6; *Ark. Code Ann.* § 9–11–106; *Colo. Rev. Stat.* § 18–6–301; *Con. Gen. Stat. Ann.* §§ 46b–21 & 53a–191 (West 2001); *D.C. Code Ann.* § 30–101; *Ga. Code Ann.* § 19–3–3 (2003); *Kan. Stat. Ann.* § 21–3603; *Md. Code Ann. Family Law* § 2–202; *Mass. Gen. Laws Ann.* ch. 207, §§ 1–2; *Mich. Comp. Laws Ann.* § 551.4; *Miss. Code Ann.* §§ 93–1–1 & 97–29–5; *Mo. Rev. Stat.* § 568.020; *Mont. Code Ann.* § 45–5–507; *N.H. Rev. Stat. Ann.* § 639:2; *Okla. Stat. Ann.* tit. 43, § 2; *Okla. Stat. Ann.* tit. 21, § 885; *Oreg. Rev. Stat.* § 163.525; *R.I. Gen. Laws* §§ 15–1–1 to 2; *S.C. Code Ann.* §20–1–10; *S.D. Codified Laws Ann.* § 25–1–7; *Tenn. Code Ann.* § 36–3–101.

37. See *Zablocki v. Red Hail,* 434 U.S. 374 (1978); *Loving v. Virginia,* 388 U.S. 1 (1967); see also *Turner v. Safley,* 482 U.S. 78 (1987). Professor Wardle points out that the Supreme Court has not classified marriage as a "fundamental right" but instead has referred to marriage as a "fundamental interest" and described marriage as one of the "basic rights." Wardle, supra note 70, 29 n.111.

38. *Griswold v. Connecticut,* 381 U.S. 479, 486 (Goldberg, J., concurring).

39. Wardle, "Critical Analysis," 28.

40. *Skinner v. Oklahoma,* 316 U.S. 535, 541 (1942).

41. *Maynard v. Hill,* 125 U.S. 190, 205 (1888).

42. *Loving,* 388 U.S., 1.

43. *Boddie v. Connecticut,* 401 U.S. 371, 376 (1971). In 1977 the Supreme Court found unconstitutional a law that restricted the right of indigent fathers of children receiving public assistance. See *Zablocki,* 434 U.S. 374 (1978). See also *Califano v. Jobst,* 434 U.S. 447 (1997).

44. Robert P. George, *Making Men Moral: Civil Liberties and Public Morality* (Oxford University Press, 1993), 102; see also Dent, "The Defense of Traditional Marriage," *Journal of Laity and Policy,* 15, 586. Government may promote or discourage conduct because it believes that the conduct benefits or harms the individual, even if the individual does not agree. See also Richard F. Duncan, "Wigstock and the Kultur Kampf: Supreme Court Storytelling, the Culture War, and Romer v. Evans," *Notre Dame Law Review,* 72 (1997), 345.

45. Ibid., 51–52, 73; see also *Barnes v. Glen Theatre, Inc.,* 501 U.S. 560, 575 (1991). "All human societies have prohibited certain activities not because they harm others but because they are considered immoral."

46. See Daniels, "Intolerant Tolerance: The Weapon of Moral Relativism," 4 (available at www.ncfamily.org/PolicyPapers/Findings%200212-Tolerance.pdf); see also George, *Making Men Moral* (Oxford University Press, 1993), 36–37. "Perhaps every generation must learn for itself that 'private' immoralities have public consequences. . . . It is plain that moral decay has profoundly damaged the morally valuable institutions of marriage and the family, and has, indeed, largely undercut the understandings of the human person, marriage, and the family."

47. *State v. Smith,* 766 So.2d 501, 509 (La. 2000). See also Seth F. Kreimer, "Lines in the Sand: The Importance of Borders in American Federalism," *University of Pennsylvania Law Review,* 150 (2002), 973–74.

48. Wardle, "Critical Analysis," 58.

49. Ibid., see also Richard Duncan, "Homosexual Marriage and the Myth of Tolerance," *Notre Dame Journal of Legal Ethics and Public Policy,* 10 (1996), 593.

50. *Bowers v. Hardwick,* 478 U.S. 186, 192–94 (1986). The holding in *Bowers* was later overruled in *Lawrence v. Texas,* 539 U.S. 558 (2003), which struck down a Texas homosexual sodomy law.

51. Wardle, "Critical Analysis," 61.

52. *Loving v. Virginia,* 388 U.S. 1, 12 (1967).

53. Andrew Sullivan, *Virtually Normal: An Argument about Homosexuality* (New York: Alfred A. Knopf, 1995), 196.

54. Ibid.

55. See Peter Sprigg and Timothy Dailey, *Getting It Straight: What the Research Shows about Homosexuality* (Washington, D.C.: Family Research Council, 2004), 69–94.

56. See Alan P. Bell and Marin S. Weinberg, *Homosexualities: A Study of Diversity among Men and Women* (New York: Simon and Schuster, 1978), 308, Table 7.

57. See Van de Ven et al., "A Comparative Demographic and Sexual Profile of Older Homosexually Active Men," *Journal of Sexual Resources,* 34 (1997), 354.

58. John R. Diggs Jr., M.D., "The Health Risks of Gay Sex" (available at www.corporateresourcecouncil.org/white_papers/Health_Risks.pdf), 1 (citing "Increases in Unsafe Sex and Rectal Gonorrhea among Men Who Have Sex with Men—San Francisco, California, 1994–1997," *Mortality and Morbidity Weekly Report,* CDC, 48(3) (29 January 1999), 45–48; see also Erica Goode, "With Fears Fading, More Gays Spurn Old Preventive Message," *New York Times,* 19 August 2001. In the previous seven years, while the practice of anal sex had increased, with multi-partner sex doubling, condom use declined 20 percent.

59. See "In Their Own Words: The Homosexual Agenda" (available at www.forthechildren inc.com/issues/homosexuality/TheAgenda/index.html. (citing "Homosexuality in America: Exposing the Myths," *The Advocate,* 23 August 1994, 23).

60. Camille Paglia, "I'll Take Religion over Gay Culture," Salon.com online magazine, June 1998 (available at http://archive.salon.com/col/pagl/1998/06/nc_23pagl.html).

61. Richard D. Mohr, "The Case for Gay Marriage," *Notre Dame Journal of Legal Ethics and Public Policy,* 9 (1995), 215, 233.

62. Gordon Mansergh, Grant Colfax, et al., "The Circuit Party Men's Health Survey Findings and Implications for Gay and Bisexual Men," *American Journal of Public Heath,* 91 (2001), 953–58.

63. "Basic Statistics," *CDC Division of HIV/AIDS Prevention,* June 2001 (available at www.cdc.gov/hiv/stats.htm).

64. Bill Roundy, "STD Rates on the Rise," *New York Blade News,* 15 December, 2000, 1. "The increased number of sexually transmitted diseases (STD) cases is the result of an increase in risky sexual practices by a growing number of gay men who believe HIV is no longer a life-threatening illness." See also Jon Garbo, "Gay & Bi Men Less Likely to Disclose They Have HIV," *GayHealth News,* 18 July 2000. Researchers from the University of California, San Francisco found that 36 percent of homosexuals engaging in unprotected oral, anal, or vaginal sex failed to disclose that they were HIV positive to casual sex partners (available at www.gayhealth.com/templates/0/news?record=136).

65. See Diggs, "The Health Risks of Gay Sex," 3.

66. Ibid., 3 (emphasis added).

67. "Sexually Transmitted Disease Guidelines: Proctitis, Procto-colitis, and Enteritis" (Atlanta: Centers for Disease Control and Prevention, 2002) (available at http://www.guideline.gov/summary/summary.aspx?doc_id=3244); see also Jack Morin, *Anal Pleasure and Health: A Guide for Men and Women* (San Francisco: Down There Press, 1998), 220 (explaining that homosexual sexual activities "provide many opportunities for tiny amounts of contaminated feces to find their way into the mouth of the sexual partner . . . the most direct route is oral-anal contact").

68. Diggs, "The Health Risks of Gay Sex," 3–4.

69. Ibid.

70. Ibid., 3.

71. See Bob Roehr, "Anal Cancer and You," *Between the Lines,* 16 November 2000 (available at http://www.pridesource.com/oldarticle.shtml?article=3835560) (click on www.pride source.com and search for "Anal Cancer and You").

72. Katherine Fethers et al., "Sexually Transmitted Infections and Risk Behaviors in Women Who Have Sex with Women," *Sexually Transmitted Infections,* 76 (2000), 345–47.

73. See "Sex Toys Likely Caused Rare Case of HIV" (available at www.advocate.com/new_news.asp?ID=7628&sd=01/31/03).

74. See Ralph U. Whitten, "The Original Understanding of the Full Faith and Credit Clause and the Defense of Marriage Act," *Creighton Law Review,* 32 (1998), 255.

75. 28 U.S.C. § 1738C.

76. See *Burns,* 560 S.E.2d, 49 ("Georgia is not required to give full faith and credit to same-sex marriages of other states.") (citing 28 U.S.C. § 1738C).

77. *U.S. Constitution* art. IV, § 1. Congress passed federal legislation providing that "Such Act, Records and Judicial Proceedings or copies thereof . . . shall have the same full faith and credit in every court within the United States [that they have in the states] from which they are taken." 28 U.S.C. § 1738 (1988).

78. See Haviv A. Balian, "Till Death Do Us Part: Granting Full Faith and Credit to Marital Status," *Southern California Law Review,* 68 (1995), 397, 401, 406.

79. See e.g., *Osoinach v. Watkins,* 180 So. 577 (Ala. 1938); *People v. Kay,* 252 N.Y.S. 518 (1931); *Pennegar v. State,* 10 S.W. 305 (Tenn. 1889).

80. *Kay,* 252 N.Y.S., 518.

81. *Osoinach,* 180 So., 577.

82. *Toler v. Oakwood,* 4 S.E.2d 364, 366 (Va. 1939).

83. *Restatement (second) of Conflict of Laws* § 283(2) (1971).

84. Whitten, "Original Understanding," 392.

85. See "Statement of William Samuel Johnson" (3 September 1787), in *The Records of the Federal Convention of 1787,* 2 (Max Farrand ed., 1911), 488.

86. Joseph Story, *Commentaries on the Constitution of the United States* § 661 (1833) (Ronald D. Rotunda and John E. Nowak, eds. 1987).

87. Act of May 26, 1790, ch. 11, 1 Stat. 122.

88. Ibid.

89. 28 U.S.C. § 1738 ("Such Acts, Records and judicial Proceedings or copies thereof, so authenticated, shall have the same full faith and credit in every court within the United States and its Territories and Possessions as they have by law or usage in the courts of such State, Territory or Possession from which they are taken.").

90. *Alaska Packers Ass'n. v. Industrial Accident Comm'n of Cal.,* 294 U.S. 323, 547–48. See also *Sun Oil Co. v. Wortman,* 486 U.S. 717, 722 (1988) (Full Faith and Credit Clause does not compel one state to substitute statutes of other states for its own statutes dealing with subject matter within which it is competent to legislate.); Herman, "The Fusion of Gay Rights and Feminism: Gender Identity and Marriage after Baehr v. Lewin," *Ohio State Law Review,* 56, 985, 991 n.25 (1995) (observing that in family law questions the United States Supreme Court seems to balance the forum state's public policy interests against the interests of comity).

91. Whitten, "Original Understanding," 392 (The "United States Supreme Court affirmed the constitutionality as well as the continuing vitality of the public policy doctrine and choice of law."). L. Lynn Hogue, "State Common-Law Choice-of-Law Doctrine and Same-Sex "Marriage": How Will States Enforce the Public Policy Exception?," *Creighton Law Review,* 32 (1998), 29–30 (citing *Baker v. General Motors Corp.,* 522 U.S. 222 (1998).

92. *Baker,* 522 U.S. 232.

93. Hogue, "State Common-Law Choice-of-Law Doctrine and Same-Sex 'Marriage,'" *Creighton Law Review,* 32, 30.

94. Ibid., 36–37.

95. Ibid., 37.

96. *Williams v. North Carolina,* 325 U.S. 226, 232 (1945) ("Williams II").

97. Hogue, "State Common-Law Choice-of-Law Doctrine and Same-Sex 'Marriage,'" *Creighton Law Review*, 32, 42–43.

98. Lynn D. Wardle, "Williams v. North Carolina, Divorce Recognition, and Same-Sex Marriage Recognition," *Creighton Law Review*, 32, (1998), 187, 223.

99. See *United States v. Edgebroad Company*, 509 U.S. 418 (1993).

100. Mark Strasser, "DOMA and the Two Faces of Federalism," *Creighton Law Review*, 32 (1998), 457, 464.

101. *Loughran v. Loughran*, 292 U.S. 216, 223 (1934).

102. This sample legislation is similar to the Nebraska state constitution. See *Nebraska Constution*, art. I, § 29. See also Mathew D. Staver, "Same Sex Marriages," *The Liberator*, June–July 1996, 1–4. Some versions may also include a ban on civil unions and domestic partnership benefits.

103. *Burns*, 560 S.E.2d 49 (quoting *Ga. Code Ann.* § 19-3-3.1(a) (West 2002).

104. *Baker v. State of Vermont*, 744 A.2d 864 (Vermont 1999).

105. *Vt. Stat. Ann.* tit. 15 § 1201 (2004) *et seq.*

106. See *Baker*, 744 A.2d, 897–912 (Johnson, J., concurring in part and dissenting in part).

107. *Baker*, 744 A.2d, 886.

108. Ibid., 887.

109. Ibid.

110. Vt. H.B. § 1(1) (2000).

111. Ibid., § 1(10).

112. *Vt. Stat. Ann.* tit. 15 § 1201(4) (2004).

113. See *Burns*, 5690 S.E.2d 47. See also *Rosengarten v. Downes*, 802 A.2d 170, 175 (Connecticut Appeal, 2002), appeal dismissed as moot, 806 A.2d 1066 (2002) (petitioner died on appeal) (stating that a civil union is not recognized as marriage within the state of Connecticut or in the issuing state of Vermont). While the case was on appeal to the Connecticut Supreme Court, petitioner Glen Rosengarten died. Liberty Counsel sought to intervene to defend the matter in order to uphold the decision of the state in appellate courts which found that Connecticut was not required to recognize an out-of-state Vermont civil union as the equivalent of marriage. Peter Downs had moved out of state and was not a party to the case. Thus, the case was postured with only Glen Rosengarten poised to present arguments before the Connecticut Supreme Court to require the state to recognize same-sex marriage. However, pending our petition to intervene in the case, Mr. Rosengarten died.

114. Greg Johnson, "Vermont Civil Unions: The New Language of Marriage," *Vermont Law Review*, 25 (2000), 15, 55.

115. See Barbara Cox, "But Why Not Marriage: An Essay on Vermont's Civil Unions Law, Same-Sex Marriage, and Separate But (Un)Equal," *Vermont Law Review*, 25 (2000), 113, 118, 137.

116. Ibid., 136–37.

117. Ibid., 137.

118. Ibid., 140.

119. Ibid., 142.

120. See *Vt. Stat. Ann.* tit. 15 § 1201 (2004) *et seq.*

121. See *Vt. Stat. Ann.* tit. 15 § 1206 (2004); *Vt. Stat. Ann.* tit. 15 § 592 (2004).

122. 802 A.2d, 170.

123. Ibid., 184.

124. "How to Achieve Domestic Partnership Benefits in Your Workplace," 2 (available at www.HRC.org/worknet/dp/dp_achievethem.asp).

125. See Maggie Gallagher, "What Is Marriage For," *Weekly Standard*, 4–11 August 2003, 25.

126. Kohn, *The Domestic Partnership Organizing Manual for Employee Benefits*, 1.

127. *Irizarry v. Board of Education of the City of Chicago*, 251 F.3d 604, 609 (2d Cir. 2001).

Chapter 8

1. See http://www.chernobyl.info.

2. See *The American Heritage Dictionary of the English Language*, William Morris, ed. (Maynard, Mass.: Boston: Houghton Mifflin Co., 1976), 657.

Chapter 9

1. *Readings in Christian Thought,* Hugh T. Karr, ed. (Nashville: Abingdon, 1966), 200–3.

2. Ibid., 202.

3. Ibid., 203.

4. It appears that blasphemy against the Holy Spirit in Mark 3:29 is explained in Mark 3:30, where the Gospel says, "He said this because they were saying, 'He has an evil spirit.'" The teachers of the law approached Jesus and stated that he was actually operating by the power of Satan or Beelzebub, the prince of demons. Thus, the hearts of the religious leaders were so hardened and their eyes so blinded that they literally called God's Holy Spirit Satan.

5. Deuteronomy 28:27 states: "The LORD will afflict you with the boils of Egypt and with tumors, festering sores and the itch, from which you cannot be cured." The Hebrew word translated as "tumors" is *ophel,* which refers to a tumor in the vulva or anus. See William Gesenius, *A Hebrew and English Lexicon of the Old Testament* (New York: Oxford Press, 1978), 779; C. F. Keil and F. Delitszch, *Commentary on the Old Testament,* vol. 1 (Grand Rapids, Mich.: Wm. B. Eerdmans Pub. Co., 1980), 439.

6. Deuteronomy 28:30 states: "You will be pledged to be married to a woman, but another will take her and ravish her."

7. Deuteronomy 28:56–57 states: "The most gentle and sensitive woman among you—so sensitive and gentle that she would not venture to touch the ground with the sole of her foot—will begrudge the husband she loves and her own son or daughter, the afterbirth from her womb and the children she bears. For she intends to eat them secretly during the siege and in the distress that your enemy will inflict on you in your cities." In this context, the passage is stating in the surrounding stress of siege by an external force, mothers, who normally would have great affection toward their children, will kill them.

8. http://www.exodusinternational.org/testamonials_left_homosexuality_chambers.hstml.

9. Ibid.

10. Ibid.

11. Ibid.

12. Ibid.

13. Ibid.

14. Dietrich Bonhoeffer, "After Ten Years," in *Letters and Papers from Prison,* Enlarged ed., Eberhard Bethge, ed. (New York: Macmillan Co., 1971), 16–17.

15. Patricia Neil Warren, "Future Shock," *The Advocate,* October 1995, 80.

Chapter 10

1. See *Lawrence v. Texas,* 539 U.S. 558 (2003).

2. Mathew D. Staver, "Supreme Court's Decision Will Awaken the Sleeping Giant," 26 June 2003 (available at http://www.lc.org/pressrelease/2003/nr062603a.htm).

3. Exodus 3:8, 17; 13:5; 23:19; 33:3; Leviticus 20:24; Numbers 13:27; 14:8; 16:13–14; Deuteronomy 6:3; 11:9; 26:9, 15; 27:3; 31:20; Joshua 5:6.

4. See also Hebrews 4:1–11.

5. See the book of Judges. To read about the effects of cultural assimilation followed by subsequent revival at a later period in the Jewish history, see the books of Ezra and Nehemiah.

6. 478 U.S. 186 (1986).

7. *Planned Parenthood v. Casey,* 505 U.S. 833, 864-65 (1992). See also Michael Stokes Paulsen, "The Worst Constitutional Decision of All Time," *Notre Dame Law Review,* 78 (2003), 995, 1029–31.

8. *Casey,* 505 U.S. 865.

9. Ibid.

10. See Mathew D. Staver, *Judicial Tyranny* (Orlando, Fla.: Liberty Counsel, 1998); Michael Stokes Paulsen, "The Most Dangerous Branch: Executive Power to Say What the Law Is," *Georgia Law Journal,* 83 (1994), 217; Michael Stokes Paulsen, "The Merryman Power and the Dilemma of Autonomous Executive Branch Interpretation," *Cardozo Law Review,* 15 (1993), 81; Michael Stokes

Paulsen, "Nixon Now: The Courts and the Presidency after Twenty-Five Years," *Minnesota Law Review,* 83 (1999), 1337, 1349–59.

11. Haw. Const. art. 1, § 23. The referendum was in response to *Baehr v. Miike,* 994 P.2d 566 (Haw. 1999); see also *Baehr v. Lewin,* 852 P.2d 44, *reconsideration granted in part,* 875 P.2d 225 (Haw. 1993). The legislature then declared that marriage is "only between a man and a woman." Haw. Rev. Stat. § 572–1

12. 28 U.S.C. § 1738C.

13. See *Ala. Code* § 30–1–19; *Alaska Stat.* § 25.05.013; *Ariz. Rev. Stat.* § 25–101; *Ark. Code* § 9–11–107, 109 and 208; *Cal. Fam. Code* § 308.5; *Colo. Rev. Stat.* § 14–2–104; *Del. Code* tit. 13 § 101; *Fla. Stat.* § 741.212; *Ga. Code* § 19–3–3.1; *Haw. Rev. Stat.* § 572–1, 1–3 and 1.6; *Idaho Code* § 32–209; 750 *Ill. Comp. Stat.* § 5/212 and 5/213.1; *Ind. Code* § 31–11–1–1; *Iowa Code* § 595.2; *Kan. Stat.* § 23–101; *Ky. Rev. Stat.* § 402.020, 040 and 045; *La. Civ. Code* art. 89 and 3520; *La. Rev. Stat.* § 9:272, 273 and 275; *Me. Rev. Stat.* tit. 19–A § 701; *Md. Code Fam.* § 2–201; *Mich. Comp. Laws* § 555.1 and 271; *Minn. Stat.* § 517.01 and .03; *Miss. Code* § 93–1.1; *Mo. Rev. Stat.* § 451.022; *Mont. Code* § 40–1–401; *Nev. Rev. Stat.* § 122.020; *N.H. Rev. Stat.* § 25–1–1and 1-38; *Ohio Rev. Code Ann.* § 3101.01 and 3105.12; *Tenn. Code* § 36–3–113; *Tex. Fam. Code* § 2.001; *Utah Code* § 30–1–2; *Va. Code* § 20–45.2; *Wash. Rev. Code* § 26.04.010 and 020; *W. Va. Code* § 48–2–104 and 603. 1–38. To remain current on the legislative activity among the states and in Congress regarding the defense of marriage, visit Liberty Counsel's Web site at www.lc.org.

14. See Alaska Const. art. 1 § 25; Neb. Const. art. I, § 29; Cal. Fam. Code § 308.5. The Alaska referendum was in response to *Brause v. Bureau of Vital Statistics,* No. 3AN–95–6562 CI, 1998 WL 88743 (Superior Ct. Ala. Feb. 27, 1998), which held a restriction on marriage must survive strict scrutiny under the Alaska constitution. The amendment overruled *Brause.*

15. See *Goodridge v. Dept. of Public Health,* 798 N.E.2d 941 (Mass. 2003).

16. For a complete list of cases, visit Liberty Counsel's Web site at www.lc.org.

About the Author

*M*athew Staver is an attorney specializing in appellate practice, free speech, and religious liberty constitutional law. He serves as president and general counsel of Liberty Counsel; vice president of Law and Policy and member of the Board of Trustees for Liberty University, and Chairman of the Steering Committee of Liberty University School of Law.

Liberty Counsel is a nonprofit litigation, education, and policy organization dedicated to advancing religious freedom, the sanctity of human life, and the traditional family. Established in 1989, Liberty Counsel is a national organization headquartered in Orlando, Florida, with branch offices in Virginia and hundreds of affiliate attorneys in all fifty states. The Center for Constitutional Litigation and Policy ("Center") operates as one component of Liberty Counsel's training, education, and public policy program. The Center is headquartered on the campus of Liberty University School of Law in Lynchburg, Virginia. The Center trains attorneys, law students, policy makers, legislators, clergy, and world leaders in constitutional principles and government policies.

Staver graduated summa cum laude with a master's degree in religion. He was an honorary guest lecturer at the American Society of Oriental Research. He has authored hundreds of articles and written nine books, including *Quest for the Historical Jesus: An Inquiry into the Historicity of the Passion Predictions*. He reads Hebrew, Greek, Aramaic, and Syriac. Staver became a pastor and later graduated from the University of Kentucky law school where he was captain of the National Moot Court team.

Staver has argued in numerous state and federal courts across the country, including the United States Supreme Court. Mr. Staver is considered one of the premier constitutional litigators in the country and conducts hundreds of media interviews each year.

If you are interested in becoming involved in the ministry of Liberty Counsel, please contact:

> Liberty Counsel
> PO Box 540774
> Orlando, FL 32854
> 800-671-1776
> www.lc.org
> liberty@lc.org